MOBILITY PATTERNS AND URBAN STRUCTURE

Transport and Mobility Series

Series Editors: Richard Knowles, University of Salford, UK and Markus Hesse, Université du Luxembourg and on behalf of the Royal Geographical Society (with the Institute of British Geographers) Transport Geography Research Group (TGRG).

The inception of this series marks a major resurgence of geographical research into transport and mobility. Reflecting the dynamic relationships between socio-spatial behaviour and change, it acts as a forum for cutting-edge research into transport and mobility, and for innovative and decisive debates on the formulation and repercussions of transport policy making.

Also in the series

Sustainable Railway Futures
Issues and Challenges
Edited by Becky P.Y. Loo and Claude Comtois
ISBN 978 1 4094 5243 0

Institutional Challenges to Intermodal Transport and Logistics
Governance in Port Regionalisation and Hinterland Integration
Jason Monios
ISBN 978 1 4724 2321 4

Port-City Interplays in China
James Jixian Wang
ISBN 978 1 4724 2689 5

The Geographies of Air Transport
Edited by Andrew R. Goetz and Lucy Budd
ISBN 978 1 4094 5331 4

Innovation in Public Transport Finance
Property Value Capture
Shishir Mathur
ISBN 978 1 4094 6260 6

For further information about this series, please visit www.ashgate.com

Mobility Patterns and Urban Structure

Edited by

PAULO PINHO
CECÍLIA SILVA
Oporto University, Portugal

ASHGATE

Published by
Ashgate Publishing Limited
Wey Court East
Union Road
Farnham
Surrey, GU9 7PT
England

Ashgate Publishing Company
110 Cherry Street
Suite 3-1
Burlington, VT 05401-3818
USA

www.ashgate.com

British Library Cataloguing in Publication Data
A catalogue record for this book is available from the British Library

The Library of Congress has cataloged the printed edition as follows:
Mobility patterns and urban structure / [edited] by Paulo Pinho and Cecília Silva.
     pages cm. – (Transport and mobility)
  Includes bibliographical references and index.
  ISBN 978-1-4724-1297-3 (hardback) – ISBN 978-1-4724-1298-0 (ebook) –
ISBN 978-1-4724-1299-7 (epub) 1. Route choice. 2. Traffic patterns. 3. Traffic flow.
4. Urban transportation–Planning. 5. Central business districts. 6. Land use, Urban.
7. City planning. I. Pinho, Paulo (Paulo Manuel Neto da Costa)
  HE336.R68M63 2015
   711'.7–dc23

2014039913

ISBN: 9781472412973 (hbk)
ISBN: 9781472412980 (ebk – PDF)
ISBN: 9781472412997 (ebk – ePUB)

Printed in the United Kingdom by Henry Ling Limited,
at the Dorset Press, Dorchester, DT1 1HD

Contents

List of Figures

Permissions

Elsevier
Figures 4.20, 5.2, 5.3, 5.4 (adapted), 5.5, 5.7, 7.7 (adapted), 7.8 (adapted), 7.9
(adapted) and 7.10 (adapted) were reprinted from *Progress in Planning*, 81, Silva
C., 'Structural Accessibility for Mobility Management', pp. 1–49, 2013, with
permission from Elsevier.

Pion Ltd, London (www.pion.co.uk; www.envplan.com)
Figures 5.2, 5.3, 5.4 (adapted), 7.7 (adapted), 7.8 (adapted), 7.9 (adapted) and
7.10 (adapted) were reprinted from *Environment and Planning A*, 42 (11), Silva
C., Pinho P., 'The Structural Accessibility Layer (SAL): revealing how urban
structure constraints travel choice', pp. 2735–52, 2010.

Pion Ltd, London (www.pion.co.uk; www.envplan.com)
Figures 7.11 (adapted), 7.12 (adapted) and 7.13 (adapted) were reprinted from
Environment and Planning B, 41 (2), Silva C, Pinho P, Reis J, 'How Urban
Structure constrains sustainable mobility choices: comparison of Copenhagen and
Oporto', pp. 211–28, 2010.

Cecília Silva
Figures 4.20, 5.1, 5.2, 5.3, 5.4 (adapted), 5.5, 5.6, 5.7, 7.7 (adapted), 7.8 (adapted)
and 7.9 (adapted) were reprinted from Silva C., *Comparative Accessibility for
Mobility Management: The Structural Accessibility Layer*, 2008, University of
Porto, Porto.

Meryn Martens
Figures 2.2 and 2.3 were reprinted from Martens M., *Adaptive cities in Europe:
interrelationships between urban structure, mobility and regional planning
strategies*, 2006, University of Amsterdam, Amsterdam.

List of Tables

Permissions

Elsevier
Tables 5.2, 5.5, 5.6 and 7.5 (adapted) were reprinted from *Progress in Planning*, 81, Silva C., 'Structural Accessibility for Mobility Management', pp. 1–49, 2013, with permission from Elsevier.

Pion Ltd, London (www.pion.co.uk; www.envplan.com)
Table 7.5 was reprinted from *Environment and Planning A*, 42 (11), Silva C., Pinho P., 'The Structural Accessibility Layer (SAL): revealing how urban structure constrains travel choice', pp. 2735–52, 2010.

Pion Ltd, London (www.pion.co.uk; www.envplan.com)
Tables 7.9 and 9.2 were reprinted from *Environment and Planning B*, 41 (2), Silva C, Pinho P, Reis J, 'How Urban Structure constrains sustainable mobility choices: comparison of Copenhagen and Oporto', pp. 211–28, 2010.

Cecília Silva
Tables 5.1, 5.2, 5.3, 5.5, 5.6 and 7.5 (adapted) were reprinted from Silva C., *Comparative Accessibility for Mobility Management: The Structural Accessibility Layer*, 2008, University of Porto, Porto.

Notes on Contributors

Fabrizio Giulietti has a PhD in Spatial Planning Evaluation and Environmental Policy Analysis, an MSc in Mobility Planning and Management, and a BA in Sociology of Economy. He is an M&E consultant in sustainable integrated (physical and socioeconomic) development of the urban environment, transport and accessibility planning, and climate protection initiatives. His fields of expertise interests include cities competitiveness and innovation, as well as land use and infrastructures regional planning.

Petter Næss is Full Professor in Planning in Urban Regions at the Norwegian University of Life Sciences, and member of the Executive Board of the World Society for Transport and Land Use Research (WSTLUR). Combining qualitative and quantitative research methods, for more than two decades he has carried out research into the influences of urban structures on travel behaviour.

Paulo Pinho LEng, Dipl U&RP, PhD, is Full Professor of Spatial and Environmental Planning at the Faculty of Engineering, University of Oporto (FEUP), founder and Director of CITTA, the Research Centre for Territory, Transports and Environment, and Secretary General of AESOP (2015–2019), the Association of European Schools of Planning. His recent research focuses on urban and metropolitan morphology, dynamics and transport systems, and on urban metabolism and low carbon cities.

José Pedro Reis is a PhD candidate at the Department of Land Economy, University of Cambridge. He has a Master's in Civil Engineering with specialization in Urban Planning from the Faculty of Engineering of the University of Porto. His main research interests are the study of urban form, the processes of urban growth and shrinkage, and urban planning policy.

Cecília Silva is Assistant Professor at the Faculty of Engineering, University of Porto (FEUP). Her main research fields are on mobility management, accessibility planning and planning support instruments. She chaired the COST Action on Accessibility Instruments for European Planning Practice involving 22 countries and more than 100 members (2010–2014).

Fernanda Sousa is Assistant Professor of Mathematics at the Faculty of Engineering, University of Porto (FEUP), member of CITTA (the Research Centre for Territory, Transports and Environment), President of CLAD (Portuguese Association of

Classification and Data Analysis) and member of the IFCS Council Committee (International Federation of Classification Societies).

Miguel Torres is a Geospatial Developer at UNEP-WCMC. He holds Master's in Civil Engineering from the Faculty of Engineering, University of Porto (FEUP), with specialization in urban planning. He worked on several research projects on land use and transport planning and supervised a local master plan in an African city.

Acknowledgements

Most of the research portrayed in this book was carried out at the CITTA Research Centre for Territory, Transports and Environment and funded by the FCT – Fundação para a Ciência e a Tecnologia (the Portuguese Foundation for Science and Technology) – through the research contract no. PTDC/ECM/81123/2006.

The authors are thankful to the FCT for the necessary funding, and to their CITTA colleagues for providing a friendly and stimulating working environment throughout the three-year period of the project, which made research a most pleasant and rewarding intellectual activity.

In particular, the editors would like to thank the dedication and excellent collaboration provided by the researchers and book contributors, José Pedro Reis, Miguel Torres, Fabrizio Giulietti, Fernanda Sousa and, with a most deserved reference, Petter Næss, for sharing with the rest of the 'southern based' research team his 'Nordic' experience that made all the comparative exercise of research methodologies and case studies applications most useful and enlightening. We would also like to thank all undergraduate and postgraduate students who participated in the extensive data collection and compilation, in particular Luisa Batista for collecting and exploring the qualitative insights on travel behaviour (through a number of interviews).

Finally, the authors would also like to express a word of thanks to the anonymous referees and to the series editors for the constructive and valuable criticisms on earlier versions of this book.

Chapter 1

Introduction

Paulo Pinho and Cecília Silva

Context

Over the last few years there has been a growing consensus in the scientific literature on the need for innovative policy measures to reduce the environmental impact and the greenhouse gas emissions of urban mobility patterns. To make these actions efficient, policy measures must act on the factors influencing travel patterns and not simply on their symptoms. Therefore, a thorough understanding of the reasons underlying trip making is most required.

In both developed and emerging countries, travel has been rising, presenting more complex patterns and becoming more difficult to predict. The research areas concerned with the study of the factors and motivations underlying travel behaviour have also become increasingly complex, taking into consideration an ever-growing number of investigated aspects and disciplinary perspectives. The research field is vast but somehow disarticulated, lacking a systematic methodological approach, as well as, in most cases, a genuine concern on its applicability to policy making. Land use, transports and individual characteristics are generally considered part of the most important factors influencing travel behaviour.

Most publications reflecting on the factors influencing travel behaviour are individual case studies evaluating the influence of land use. Many of these case studies have arrived at different results and conclusions (for broad literature reviews on this topic see, for instance, Handy, 1996; Ewing and Cervero, 2010; van Wee, 2002). The volume of literature on how land-use patterns and the built environment influence urban travel demand has virtually exploded over the past decade. It is fair to say that most authors believe that land use does have an influence on travel behaviour (e.g., Handy, 1996; Cervero and Kochelman, 1997; Ewing and Cervero, 2010; van Wee, 2002) although, so far, many are sceptical about the composition and decisive nature of the influencing factors, because research methodologies do not seem solid enough, and the case study comparison of results is often difficult if not misleading. Indeed, many case studies have not produced conclusive findings reinforcing the scepticism on the real influence of land use on travel choice. Besides case studies and literature reviews, considerably less research is found on land use policy implications and recommendations. Furthermore, in spite of the extensive research carried out so far on the land use factors influencing travel behaviour, no general consensus has been reached.

This is also the case for research on the influence of transports or of individual characteristics on travel behaviour.

In the bibliography relating travel behaviour to individual characteristics a wide range of study themes can be found. The research in this field can be broadly categorized as focussing on demographic and socioeconomic characteristics of the populations in addition to motivational factors of a psychological nature. Examples of motivational factors, which can be found in this field of research, are, for instance, preferences (Scheiner and Kasper, 2002), value orientation (Scheiner and Kasper, 2002), needs, desires and symbolic affective motives (Steg et al., 2001), habits (Fujii and Kitamura, 2003), and beliefs and attitudes (Fujii and Kitamura, 2003). Case studies evaluating the influence of transport factors on travel behaviour are difficult to find. Research in this field seems to consider this influence as a matter of fact since it tends to concentrate on the formulation of policy measures. Within this research field, most studies evaluate attitudes towards and/or the effect of Transport Demand Management measures (or simply presented TDM measures), and their categorization (see, for example, Marshal and Banister, 1997; and Viegas, 2001). Although the influence of transport systems on travel behaviour is clear and therefore might be exempted from further considerations, the lack of research on the main factors responsible for that influence is one of the main flaws within this research area, especially bearing in mind the corresponding void in policy making this lack of understanding represents.

In spite of the amount of research centred on the factors influencing travel behaviour no consensus can be found in the literature on common orientations for further research. In this context, we intend to build a broader consensus on the factors influencing travel behaviour, being concerned, in particular, with both the influence of urban structure factors (namely, land use and transport system factors) and of motivational factors related to the social, economic and cultural characteristics of the individual traveller.

In recent years, in both developed and emerging countries, mobility patterns have undergone significant changes. The escalating use of the private car for the satisfaction of ever-growing travel needs has contributed, among other factors, to undermine the quality of life in many urban areas, as well as the economic competitiveness and the overall sustainability of larger metropolitan regions. It is, therefore, important to focus our attention on the reasons behind increasing travel needs within the framework of a post carbon society. The choice of urban mobility policies can no longer be solely directed towards fighting the effects of current travel patterns. A broader understanding of the aspects influencing travel behaviour is crucial for the definition of effective low carbon mobility policies.

The 'predict and provide' paradigm of traditional transport planning is clearly inadequate for the management of current mobility needs. Within the new 'predict and prevent' paradigm, urban mobility management policies are facing new challenges. In this respect, the European Commission standpoint can be summarized in the following two main objectives: reduction of travel needs, and making remaining travel more sustainable. However, these simple and straightforward objectives go well beyond the normal scope of transport planning. Several authors argue that the effective reduction of the environmental impact and carbon footprint of urban mobility requires the adoption of a truly holistic attitude. Indeed, the need to integrate land use and transport policies has been widely recognized as a more effective approach to meeting these new mobility requirements, than traditional transport planning policies. Nevertheless, these integrated policies have seldom been applied into practice. Furthermore, policies intended to address personal behaviours and choices, taking into consideration socioeconomic and demographic conditions are also being increasingly suggested, although, again, seldom implemented into practice.

Objectives

The principal objective of this book is to present an assessment of the influence of alternative urban structures of metropolitan areas on corresponding mobility patterns. This research also recognizes the influence of socioeconomic and demographic characteristics. Although these characteristics are taken into consideration in our analysis, we will pay particular attention to the influence of urban structures on mobility, as the book title clearly suggests. In particular, two European metropolitan areas of similar sizes and different urban structures, Copenhagen and Oporto, will be compared. In the north, Greater Copenhagen portrays an essentially monocentric urban area with long established growth corridors, whereas Greater Oporto, in the south, still exhibits a marked polycentric structure, grounded in a distinct historic settlement pattern.

At a more detailed level, the reader will find the following associated or more operational objectives:

- to provide a deeper understanding of the relationship between urban structure and travel behaviour;
- to assess the accessibility potential of urban structures;
- to typify the relationships between travel behaviour and potential accessibility;
- to develop social profile and area based targeted policies to enhance low carbon mobility patterns in the case study areas of Greater Oporto and Greater Copenhagen;
- to recommend integrated land use and transport strategies tailored to the specific physical and functional characteristics of these two metropolitan areas; and
- to foster the combined application of structural and behavioural methodologies in mobility studies.

Methodological Approach

This book presents the results of the MOPUS project (MObility Patterns and Urban Structure), funded by the Fundação para a Ciência e a Tecnologia (FCT, the Portuguese Research funding agency) and was carried out between 2008 and 2010. The MOPUS project was based on two previous research projects concerned with complementary factors and motivations underlying urban passenger mobility patterns (Figure 1.1). One of these research projects, carried out in Portugal at the Research Centre for Territory, Transports and Environment (CITTA), was focused on the development of an innovative concept to be applied to urban and metropolitan areas, the so-called structural accessibility. This approach considers only structural factors, i.e., factors related to land use and transport systems, and was initially applied to Greater Oporto. The corresponding methodology, the *Structural Accessibility Layer* (SAL), was designed to reveal the potential of land use and transport systems to provide the necessary conditions (although not necessarily sufficient in themselves) for more energy efficient mobility. In parallel, this innovative methodology is also able to provide a design-support tool for low carbon mobility policies.

The other research project, carried out at Aalborg University (Denmark), developed a complementary methodology; the *Explanatory Qualitative-*

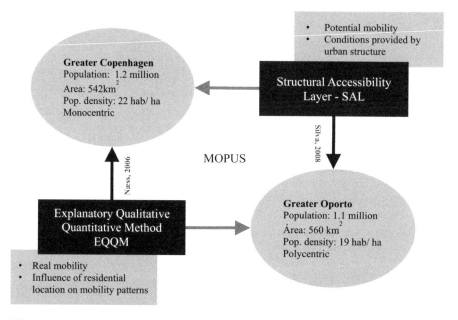

Figure 1.1   Research methodology: combined application of SAL and EQQM

Quantitative Method (EQQM), and was initially applied to the Copenhagen Metropolitan Area. The aim of this methodology, focusing on behavioural aspects, is to identify the overall relationships as well as the more detailed mechanisms through which the location of residence is able to influence travel behaviour. In a number of important aspects the Copenhagen metropolitan study goes beyond the scope of previous investigations into the complex relationships between urban land use and travel patterns, including a comprehensive analysis of the socioeconomic and the attitudinal characteristics of travellers.

The possibility to combine these two complementary research methodologies is the distinctive and innovative contribution of this book. In addition to the first two experiments, referred to above, this combination will involve the application of the SAL to Greater Copenhagen and the application of the EQQM to Greater Oporto. In this way, the structural and behavioural aspects of mobility patterns will be analyzed and compared in both case studies, taking advantage of the previous work already carried out in both research centres. Despite the significant differences between the social and economic characteristics of the metropolitan areas of Oporto and Copenhagen (although fairly similar in area and population size) this book will provide clear evidence of the real importance of different metropolitan structures on mobility patterns.

Indeed, MOPUS was able to compare the mobility patterns of two important European metropolitan areas with contrasting internal structures – one predominantly monocentric (Greater Copenhagen) and the other historically polycentric (Greater Oporto). The exercise was also able to reveal the potentials of these methodologies to support the formulation of planning and transport policies for low carbon metropolitan areas, coming at a time of profound restructuring of public transport systems in many European countries.

Book Structure

This book starts by presenting the research theme's background and motivation, as well as the principal and associated research objectives. This introductory chapter also includes a brief description of the general methodological approach adopted and the book's general outline.

The second chapter, on recent changes in urban areas, presents a brief overview of the cultural, social and demographic changes of contemporary societies and discusses their profound implications in people's travel behaviour and on the cities' mobility patterns. The chapter also addresses the relationships between the spatial and the functional structure of cities and related transport factors and motivations. The chapter concludes with a section on monocentric and polycentric models of urban development and associated implications for the emergence of distinctive urban travel patterns.

Chapter 3 presents a review of empirical evidences on the complex relationships between personal characteristics, urban structure and travel behaviour. The review looks for motivations behind travel choices revealed by previous research, in particular research on the influence of personal characteristics and urban structure, namely land use and transport systems. With regard to the latter, particular attention was given to the influence of monocentric and polycentric urban structures on travel behaviour.

Chapter 4 presents the main case study areas – Greater Copenhagen and Greater Oporto – regarding geographical distribution of population and employment, the existing transport network and service level, as well as the main travel patterns identified.

The results of the literature review developed in Chapter 2 and Chapter 3 frames the research methods presented in Chapter 5 and Chapter 6, consisting of the combination of two previously developed, applied and tested methods: the *Structural Accessibility Layer* (SAL) and the *Explanatory Qualitative-Quantitative Method* (EQQM). Each method is presented in detail at the conceptual level, providing also insights for the practical applications on the two case study areas, briefly characterized in the previous chapter.

This is followed by two chapters (7 and 8) which present the results of the application of these two complementary methods in both case studies.

Chapter 7 summarizes the main results of the application of SAL to Greater Copenhagen and to Greater Oporto. This chapter discusses potential mobility choices made available (or disabled) by urban structure in each study area. The individual discussions are followed by the comparison of the potential mobility choices enabled by the two different urban structures in analysis. Results are compared to real modal choices in both areas in order to discuss connections between potential and real mobility patterns.

Chapter 8 summarizes the main results of the application of EQQM to both case studies. After a brief review of typical mobility patterns, this chapter presents the results of the analysis of the relationships between residential location and travel behaviour. Residential location is analyzed based on local density (combined population and job density), on the distance of residence to main and second order centres, to main railway stations and to main regional retail centres. Travel behaviour is analyzed based on travel distance (total and by mode) and mode share (based on values of mode travel distance). This chapter includes some remarks on the influence of residential location, such as distance to facilities and location of activities, on particular travel options. In addition, a discussion of the influence of residential location on travel across different population groups is also developed. In this discussion, especial attention is given to gender differences.

The book ends with Chapter 9 which summarizes the main lessons learned throughout the entire MOPUS research project, and the conclusions and recommendations, which are twofold: of a general nature for spatial and transport planning theory and practice, and of a specific nature, relevant to each metropolitan area under analysis.

Chapter 2

Recent Changes in Urban Areas

José Pedro Reis and Fabrizio Giulietti

People and Travel Patterns

The last decades have been marked by important cultural changes in European and North American cities. The so-called industrial society, very much structured and segmented, offering a limited spectrum of life patterns, has left space to a complex era labelled as Information Age (Negroponte, 1995). This section will make a brief overview of the cultural, social and demographic changes in contemporary societies and discusses their implications in people's travel behaviour and, subsequently, on cities' mobility patterns.

The recent social and demographic changes, particularly in the most developed economies, have been interpreted and labelled as the *Second Demographic Transition* (Lesthaeghe, 1995; Haase et al., 2010). This theory argues that in the post–Second World War period societies underwent a series of profound changes, namely:

- decreasing birth rates, rising life expectancy and an increasingly ageing population;
- structural changes in households, with a higher number of smaller households and an increasing number of single-person households and families without children;
- changes to the traditional pattern of marriage, with new more informal family arrangements; and
- more diversified lifestyles and professional careers, including changes in the women's role in society and more urban-oriented lifestyles, particularly of couples with no children.

These social and demographic changes have, of course, implications in the spatial and functional organization of urban areas, but also on the behavioural patterns of its residents, including their travel behaviour.

Population ageing in industrialized countries is one of the most studied demographic trends. According to Eurostat projections, the number of elderly people as a share of the working population in Europe will double between 2010 and 2050 (Lanzieri, 2011). In Denmark, for instance, the share of people aged 65 or older is increasing steadily and is expected to be 24 per cent of the total population by 2040 (Siren and Haustein, 2013). The share of population over

80 years old in Europe (EU-27) is projected to grow from 4.1 per cent in 2006 to 11.2 per cent in 2050, and life expectancy at birth is now 81 on average for women and 75 for men, against the substantial lower values of, respectively, 73 and 65 in the 1960s (Eurostat, 2008).

The increase in the number of elderly people with better quality of life is fostering the development of new markets and activities oriented to the needs and interests of these individuals (normally retired people over 60 years old). Private investors and public institutions quickly adapt to this new reality diversifying their products and services, offering, for instance, senior universities and a new range of cultural events. Because elderly people are healthier, they will tend to have more active lifestyles with different consumption patterns, attending various leisure activities and travelling more often and over longer distances (Siren and Haustein, 2013). This will alter urban travel patterns in European and North American cities, providing a new potential market for public transport companies, that now have to deal with a different service scheduling, different destinations and adjusted means of transports to their specific needs (more comfort, easiness in accessing busses and trains, toilets in stations and in urban trains, etc.).

The changing role of women in the labour market is also affecting mobility patterns in cities of developed countries. According to Pacione (2009), there are considerable gender differences regarding urban travel behaviour. It is more common for women to combine journeys to work with other travel purposes such as shopping or taking children to school. The need for many women to deal simultaneously with responsibilities of home and work means that in a no-car or single-car household women tend to make more journeys by public transport.

Women are also increasing their participation in tertiary education in Europe, where there are 122 female students for every 100 males. These figures already indicate an increase of people mobility for the purposes of attending classes and courses, but the disaggregated data provide further information, allowing us to speculate about the future role of women in the labour market. According to Eurostat (2008), 75 per cent of students in education, health and welfare related studies and 66 per cent in humanities and arts are female. This means that, in the future, jobs such as teachers, doctors, nurses and other roles in the public sector, which require non-standard working times, will increasingly be undertaken by women. On the contrary, women are considerably under-represented in engineering and manufacturing studies (24 per cent) as well as in science, mathematics and computer sciences (37 per cent), disciplines that offer more chances of jobs in the private sector and with more traditional working hours. Therefore, women's daily trips could potentially become more flexible than men (Balbo, 1991), and the increase in the importance of women in the labour market strongly affects traditional travel predictions.

Despite these changing patterns, women still spend, on average, more time on domestic tasks than in work/study related tasks compared to men. Moreover, men enjoy more free time than women. These reasons justify the fact that nowadays men spend, on average, slightly more time on daily travel than women.

Regarding working times, data shows that European full-time employees continue to work on average around 40 hours per week. However, working hours are becoming more flexible, with 36 per cent of EU employees having jobs that require working during evenings/nights, and 44 per cent working on Saturdays or Sundays. More flexible working hours have contributed to more diversified leisure times, which together with the tendency to increase out-of-home leisure (in line with the second demographic transition), are likely to generate more complex travel patterns.

Working hours are not necessarily spent in an office. Thanks to new communication technologies, the places of work are now more diverse, with more and more people working from home or even in public spaces, as long as they have access to a computer or smartphone. For instance, bars and parks can be used as working locations as long as they offer a Wi-Fi Internet connection (Augé, 2000).

If it is true that new technologies have had a strong impact on travelling, sometimes making traditional 'commuting' (mainly work related) journeys unnecessary, they have not considerably reduced urban mobility. They have rather contributed to a higher diversification of travel behaviours: in some large cities non-work trips are already more frequent than work-related journeys (Ingram, 1998) and leisure trips sometimes hold the highest travel distances (Schlich et.al, 2004; Lazendorf, 2000). It should still be noted that journeys to work probably make up a higher proportion of actual travel time and distance than reported in many trip-based travel surveys, since these often tend to underestimate the role of daily commuting fixed and basic trips when compared with other trip purposes (Næss, 2010a).

People living and working in cities are now less collectively organized and structured as mass consumption, and traditional travel patterns are being replaced by more varied and segmented patterns (Harvey, 1990). People tend to organize themselves individually and to move in a more intelligent way (Banister, 2002), using flexible strategies to adapt their journeys taking more into account mobility opportunities and the various modifications of the local traffic, rather than simply the shortest distance (Cerasoli, 2005). The visual consumption of the territory has its role in travel choices, because 'to look on landscape with interest and curiosity ... has become a right of citizenship' (Urry, 1995: 176).

Places and Travel Patterns

This section concerns the relationship between the spatial and functional structure of cities and transport factors. A brief overview of the development trajectories of cities in the developed World will be carried out, highlighting the importance of transport developments in shaping the structure of cities (from medieval towns based on pedestrian mobility, to the car-oriented extensive metropolitan areas of the post-war period). This is however a reciprocal relationship, as different urban spatial structures also generate different mobility patterns. In the second part of this section we will discuss this influence. Later on, a particular focus will be set on monocentric and polycentric urban structures, discussing the origins and patterns of these two models of development as well as their implications on travel behaviour.

Before the industrial revolution only a limited number of places were actual cities: most people lived in small towns and rural villages (Antrop, 2004). Cities functioned as administrative, commercial, cultural and defensive centres (Cheshire, 1995) and their location and structure were still based on the medieval and colonization patterns of, respectively, Europe and North America (Antrop, 2004; Filion, 2010; Wilczyński and Wilczyński, 2011). Because most people had to walk to engage in essential daily activities, cities were generally compact (Pacione, 2009).

By the end of the nineteenth century, however, European and North American cities were undergoing huge transformations following the advent of industrialization and technological development. Transport played an important part in this process, notably with the development of railways. The Industrial Revolution converted an agrarian society into one increasingly dominated by cities, which also became centres of goods production and distribution (Cheshire, 1995; Nechyba and Walsh, 2004; Rieniets, 2005). During the first half of the twentieth century, most large European and North American cities experienced an unprecedented process of intense and enduring growth, where strong urbanization caused by long term rural-urban migration was clearly the dominant tendency (Antrop, 2004; Beauregard, 2009; Cheshire, 1995; Rieniets, 2005).

The post–Second World War period brought about, once again, considerable changes. Cities in Europe experienced high population centralization into metropolitan cores (urbanization) during the 1950s – mainly driven by migration from rural peripheries – followed by a process of decentralization during the 1960s, in which metropolitan areas as a whole were still growing but the population was decentralizing from urban cores to suburban rings. This decentralization process accelerated during the 1970s to a point where metropolitan areas only grew on the account of their suburbs, with urban cores ceasing to grow or even starting to decline (Hall and Hay, 1980; Cheshire and Hay, 1989; van den Berg et al., 1982).

The urban change trajectories of European cities during the twentieth century inspired van den Berg et al. (1982) to develop the largely cited 'theory of consecutive stages of urban development'. According to this theory, cities evolve through a set of sequential stages characterized by specific urban developments that will occur everywhere unless policy actions drive urban development in a different direction. These consecutive stages of urban development are 'urbanization', 'suburbanization' and 'desurbanization'.

If the process of 'urbanization' was triggered by industrialization and the subsequent creation of a massive number of new industrial jobs in cities, developments in transport had a critical role in the two subsequent stages.

Together with a generalized increase in household incomes, the evolution of motorized transport allowed families to pursue better quality of living locations beyond city centres, starting the process of 'suburbanization'. New residential areas grew fast in suburban locations, leaving the city centre mostly reserved for office buildings. People start to live in the suburbs while working in the city centre, and the daily commuting trips between centre and periphery become more and more frequent.

The third stage – desurbanization – occurs when agglomerations grow beyond their road infrastructure capacity and central workplaces and facilities become less and less accessible due to congestion. Old residential neighbourhoods in the city cores are often knocked down to give place to wider streets, new access roads and extensive parking facilities, further fostering the on-going movement of residents to suburban locations and later to peripheral towns. These are soon followed by shops, service facilities and other public provisions, leading to population decline not only in the centre but also in the urban fringes. If the suburbanization stage is characterized by intense urban expansion which turned cities into sprawling suburban areas, the desurbanization stage may result in more complex urban patterns, such as regional urban systems or polycentric metropolises, as will be further discussed later in this section.

Van den Berg et al. (1982) also foresaw a fourth stage of urban development – reurbanization – in which people would eventually return to the city centres mainly due to government policies aiming at restoring the city's image, such as old housing stock rehabilitation, traffic improvements or social structure upgrades.

Although this theory was formulated following an extensive analysis of European cities, the trajectories of major cities in North America were quite similar, though the changes there occurred earlier in time and often to a larger extent. According to Parr (1993), the first trends towards decentralization in America were observed in the 1920s, and 1950 census data revealed that 35 per cent of the population of the largest US urban areas already lived in the suburbs. This decentralization tendency continued through the subsequent three decades, and was also driven by increasing incomes and transport factors. Amongst the latter, improvements in transport infrastructures (mainly radial motorways) and increasing car ownership must be highlighted (Linneman and Summers, 1993; Parr, 1993).

More recent literature emphasizes the significant differences in urbanization trajectories of cities in different regions, different countries and even within countries, as well as the complexity of processes behind urbanization at the turn of the century. There is not a single path of development for European and American cities, but a set of forces working simultaneously producing different spatial patterns and structures (Beauregard, 2009; Champion, 1995). Turok and Mykhnenko (2007) and Kabish and Haase (2011) also concluded that no single evolutionary trajectory for European cities could be found during the 1990s and the early 2000s, but there were a variety of experiences and great differences depending on factors such as city size or regional location, stressing the difference between Western and Eastern Europe.

Another conceptualization of urbanization trajectories can be found in urban economics, with the so-called theory of the 'tree waves' of urbanization (Scott, 2011). The author identifies three broad phases of capitalist development corresponding to three waves of urbanization: the first refers to the nineteenth-century manufacturing towns of the Industrial Revolution and the second to the large metropolitan areas which grew intensely during the mid-twentieth century based on the Fordist mass production system. Scott then argues that a third wave of urbanization has been emerging since the 1980s, based on what he calls 'cognitive-cultural capitalism'.

This led to considerable changes in the structure of urban areas, from different divisions of labour – with the emergency of jobs demanding diverse cognitive and cultural capacities of workers and the progressive elimination of routine work – to more complex city geographies in which multiple industrial districts occur within the same urban area – for example the location of high-level financial activities in the core central areas, cultural industries in both the centre and surrounding inner city areas and high-technology industry concentrated in dense 'technopoles' in more suburban areas of city-regions (Scott, 2011, 2013). Other outcomes of this process are the major economic resurgence of large cities all over the world accompanied by land use intensification and high-value architecture, or the increasing gentrification of former working-class inner-city neighbourhoods (Scott, 2011, 2013).

Other authors emphasize the idea that the economic base of cities is shifting towards the service sector and more knowledge-based and creative activities that require a higher skilled, higher educated and generally wealthier labour force which Florida (2002) calls the 'creative class'. According to these principles, urbanization and urban growth is related to the city's capacity to develop human capital and to attract people who tend to value urban amenities that are normally found in the cores of older cities, such as museums, cafes, restaurants, concerts, or just a more interesting architectural landscape or a more bohemian and tolerant atmosphere (Glaeser and Gottlieb, 2006; Storper and Manville, 2006).[1]

All these changes in the structure of cities have a considerable influence on their travel patterns. Urban areas are becoming more complex regarding the variety of their functions (e.g., political and financial institutions, administrative and cultural services, etc.), not only increasing in the number and diversity of activities and

---

1   This section regards patterns of urbanization and urban change mainly from a socio-demographic perspective. Important contributions on these issues can also be found from an Urban Economics and Economic Geography perspective (see, for instance, Scott, 2011; Storper and Scott, 2006; Storper et al., 2012; Kloosterman and Lambregts, 2007; or Glaeser et al., 2001).

services they offer, but also diversifying the places where these activities take place. This affects the patterns of mobility of their residents, leading to an increase in local mobility but also to changes in travel patterns at a larger scale, attracting commuters from other cities and regional areas (Banister, 2005; Ascher, 2003; Urry, 1995).

Many cities in Europe and North America suffered a process of extensive outward expansion triggered by suburbanization, acquiring a sprawled urban structure characterized by low-density and single-use peripheries, and thus higher distances between dwellings, services and offices. The debate about the most desirable urban development pattern – 'urban sprawl' or the 'compact city' – has been lively in the planning literature, and mobility issues are in the core of that debate.

While some authors consider that low-density peripheral development can have positive effects in mitigating congestion (Gordon et al., 1989; Kim, 2008), the growing concerns about sustainable development are fostering an increasing belief that urban sprawl brings about an array of negative environmental, economic and social implications (Clifton et al., 2008; Newman and Kenworthy, 1991; Ewing, 1997; Torrens, 2008; Frenkel and Ashkenazi, 2008). Low-density and single-use development fosters longer travel distances and times for daily commuting trips. The dispersion of activities and households reduces the efficiency of public transport provision and of soft transport modes (such as walking and cycling).

These factors together lead to higher car dependency and car use resulting in increased traffic congestion, energy consumption, greenhouse gases emissions and air pollution. The 'compact city' model, inspired by characteristics of the traditional European cities such as high-density settlements with mixed functions and offering diverse urban amenities, is often seen as the ideal alternative to sprawling cities and has been the base of movements like the 'compact city strategy' in Europe or 'smart growth' in America.

Peripheral development may also lead to the marginalization of poor people in terms of access to jobs, urban amenities and social networks, forcing people to spend disproportionate amounts of time and money on transportation for commuting to fulfil their basic needs. This is likely to discourage further mobility, inhibiting these people from satisfying other non-primary needs and limiting their freedom (Biermann et al., 2003).

City growth did not always mean sprawl. There are other types of urban growth based on densification or coalescence, i.e., through 'infill development' and increasing built up density, or in a process of 'decentralized concentration', with the formation of new 'centralities' that concentrate a wide diversity of economic activities and services in the peripheries. The latter process is related to the polycentric model of urban development.

The Monocentric and Polycentric Models

Amongst the numerous models that have been suggested by researchers from different disciplinary backgrounds to allow for the analyses of the internal structure of cities, it is possible to distinguish between two general categories: models that conceptualize cities as a monocentric spatial structure and models that attempt to explain the polycentric pattern of urban change (Davoudi, 2003).

As was referred to above, car ownership and the development of the road network made it possible for workers to disconnect, to some extent, their place of work from their place of residence. This freedom allowed for a large number of households to move away from the crowded cities to other settlements – the 'suburbs' – which were too small and not dense enough to be considered urban centralities but neither large or well-structured enough to be called rural (Martens, 2006). This process of outward urban expansion gave origin to the monocentric model of urban development, which assumes that regional functions – like jobs, services, etc. – are concentrated in the inner-city, while residential areas are further out and clustered around this centre (Martens, 2006).

The monocentric city model remained the most widespread representation of urban structure until at least two decades after the Second World War, as it enabled a good understanding of the broad population decentralization that had occurred in numerous cities around the world (Davoudi, 2003). Nevertheless, during the 1970s, it started to become clear that some cities would develop towards a more polynucleus structure due to a number of factors such as the decentralization of economic activities; increased mobility due to new transport technologies; changes in household structure and lifestyle; and the existence of complex cross-commuting (Davoudi, 2003). Kloosterman (2001) argues that the monocentric model – even with adaptations – is no longer suitable to describe the spatial patterns of current European and North American urban areas.

According to Anas et al. (1998), the process of decentralization has taken a more polycentric form, with a number of concentrated employment centres making their mark on both employment and population distributions. They state that these sub-centres can be older towns that progressively became integrated into an expanded but coherent urban area; or new urban centres built up next to nodes of a transportation network often distant from the urban core, the so called 'edge cities'. The 'edge cities' (see Garreau, 1991) or 'suburban downtowns' (see Hartshorn and Muller, 1989) are characterized by large concentrations of office and retail activities often in conjunction with residential and other types of development.

Whilst the literature is fairly consensual in recognizing the growing importance of the polycentric development structure, several methodological variations can be found when trying to determine the extent to which a metropolitan area is more or less polycentric or monocentric. When trying to determine the degree of monocentricity/polycentricity of an urban area, most authors use indicators like population density, proportion of population in the inner areas, number of jobs or proportion of employment in the centre (Gordon et al., 1989; Newman and Kenworthy, 1989; Schwanen, 2002) or employment size and density in the centre and in the sub-centres (Cervero and Wu, 1998). References to mobility – for instance whether the sub-centres constitute privileged spaces of attraction for commuters – are scarcer, but often appropriate (Aguilera and Mignot, 2004).

Notably, van der Laan (1998), in a study of Dutch cities, suggested a method to classify urban structure based on the direction of commuter trips inside the urban area and reflecting the degree to which suburban commuters travel to the central city. This classification considers four types of urban structures: one monocentric – 'centralized' – and three different types of polycentric urban areas – 'decentralized', 'cross-commuting' and 'exchange commuting'.

Therefore, in the 'centralized' pattern most of commuter traffic is directed to the city centre, and the suburbs barely attract commuters. This is the traditional monocentric form where workers living in suburban areas commute to the centre in the morning and return to their dormitory towns in the evening, while employees who live in the central city usually work there too. In the 'decentralized' pattern, suburbs attract a significant number of commuters both from other suburbs and from the city centre. In this case the suburbs are complementary to the centre and are important in job supply (van der Laan, 1998).

The 'exchange commuting' pattern is the case in which a large number of inner city residents work in the suburbs, while many inhabitants of suburban areas have their jobs in the city centre. Finally, van der Laan (1998) also presents the concept of a cross-commuting pattern, in which many suburban residents work in the suburbs and, at the same time, many inner city dwellers are locally employed. There is a dual spatial labour market without a strong relationship between the core city and the suburbs (van der Laan, 1998). This archetypal polycentric area emerges when workers seek to minimize travel expenditure (Schwanen et al., 2004b). These four types of urban structures are schematically represented in Figure 2.1.

Notwithstanding the importance and innovation of this methodology in including mobility patterns on the characterization of urban spatial structures, it does not consider several important factors. Authors like Gordon and Richardson (1996) or Aguilera and Mignot (2004) argue that sub-centres should not be defined only according to their number of jobs, but it is also important to take into account the nature of these jobs, since different activity centres may generate clearly different levels of traffic, even if they have the same number of jobs. They also argue that the same methodology does not distinguish in any concrete way the sub-centres located in the periphery from the ones located in the vicinity of the city centre.

In a study developed in France, Aguilera and Mignot (2004) define the sub-centres based on the attraction of intra-urban commutes: first, they identify the municipalities most attractive to non-local workers and then they define the sub-centres maximizing internal commutes. These authors also consider two types of sub-centres: 'suburban sub-centres', larger and located near the city centre, and

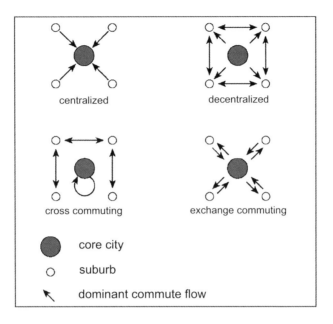

Figure 2.1   Types of urban systems
Source: Adapted from Schwanen et al., 2004b.

'outlying sub-centres', smaller and located further from the centre, but still well-connected by main transport axes.

This distinction between sub-centres located inside the central city and the ones to be found in the urban periphery is also highlighted by Martens (2006). After studying several West European cities, the author found that in the European context there are roughly three relevant types of polycentric urban structures, besides the traditional monocentric structure: peripheral polycentric, urban-polycentric and regional-polycentric structures (Figure 2.2).

The peripheral polycentric structure is the classical polycentric urban model where Edge cities emerge outside the central city, usually competing with the inner city. According to the author, this model is common in American cities but has only limited relevance in Europe. A second model more common in Europe is the urban-polycentric structure, where sub-centres develop inside the central city, instead of at the urban periphery. The author states that the urban-polycentric structure emerges when there is a lack of space for development in an inner city that still is attractive for that development or as a result of urban planning policies. The last model is the regional-polycentric structure. According to Martens (2006), this model combines peripheral sub-centre formation with central city sub-centre formation and it is also commonly seen in Europe.

Even if nowadays it is widely recognized that contemporary urban systems present a complex and multi-nodal structure, the exact nature of this polycentric

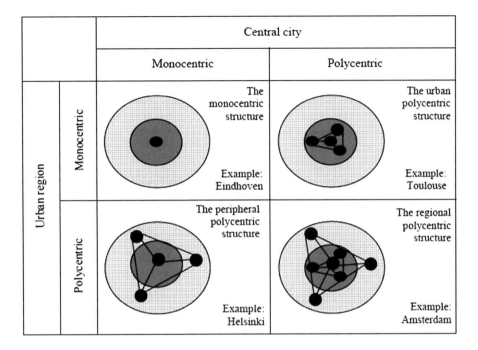

Figure 2.2   Types of urban structures in Europe
Source: Martens, M., 2006, 'Adaptive cities in Europe: interrelationships between urban structure, mobility and regional planning strategies', University of Amsterdam, Amsterdam.

structure has been subject to multiple interpretations (Davoudi, 2003) and misleading concepts – such as 'concentration/deconcentration' – are often found in the literature. In this context, a clear distinction must be made between an organized system of sub-centres – *polycentrism* – and a dispersed and apparently unorganized urban pattern – urban *sprawl* – depending on factors like the definition of sub-centres (as job locations only or as activity centres) and the level of interaction between the centres and sub-centres.

Moreover, scholars like Ewing (1997) see polycentrism as a type of compact development rather than sprawl, arguing that it requires some concentration of employment, some clustering of housing and some mixing of land uses. The author seeks to clarify the concept of urban sprawl, suggesting a definition of sprawl based on two quantifiable indicators: poor accessibility and lack of functional open space. Martens (2006) also highlights the distinction between a polycentric structure and a dispersed one, conceptualizing the dispersed urban structure as a complete different model for urban development, to be considered together with the monocentric and the polycentric models. Furthermore, Martens argues that these three urban models can be distinguished by the analysis of two dimensions: the number of urban centres and the level of concentration (Figure 2.3).

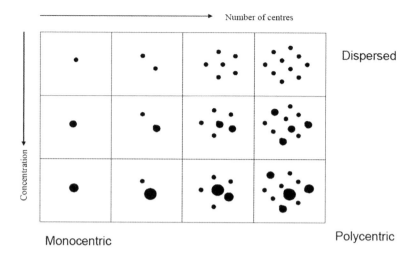

Figure 2.3   Classification of urban structures
Source: Martens, M., 2006, 'Adaptive cities in Europe: interrelationships between urban structure, mobility and regional planning strategies', University of Amsterdam, Amsterdam.

The spatial distribution of activities forces people to modify their travel behaviour (Maat et al., 2005) and people can either decide to move closer to the new centralities (where they might work) or commute from their houses. In the latter case diverse traffic flows are generated, quite often out of the traditional radial centripetal pattern.

Therefore, when studying the relationship between urban structure and travel behaviour, the particular urban structural model of a city assumes special relevance, since the distinction between polycentrism and urban sprawl has accessibility and mobility implications. For instance, a system of medium density and relatively autonomous sub-centres may be suitable for non-motorized modes (such as walking and cycling) and may allow for an efficient public transport system, while a sprawling or dispersed pattern will probably foster an increase in car use.

Chapter 3

Empirical Evidences
on Motivations for Travel

Cecília Silva, Petter Næss and José Pedro Reis

Household Characteristics (People) and Travel Behaviour (Patterns)

The issues of transport cost, time and system connectivity are central to the analysis of travel behaviour, but not on their own or in isolation from other social processes and structures (Pratt, 1996). According to Lazendorf (2000) mobility is not just travelling, because it is possible to find at least three dimensions within it: spatial (trips from A to B), socioeconomic (i.e., the purpose), and a symbolic/expressive dimension where attitudes and lifestyle elements are expressed in transport modes, car types, etc. Most of these latter aspects tend to get neglected in quantitative research and modelling not because they are not important, but because they are difficult to quantify satisfactorily (Dargay and Goodwin, 2000). Nonetheless there is some interesting literature that shows the importance of psychological, sociocultural and economic matters, alone or combined in different ways, in influencing travel behaviour.

The spatial dimension will be explored in the next section while this section focuses on the socioeconomic and demographic dimensions (including lifecycle and lifestyle characteristics).

Although research in this field seems to have gained strength in the last decades, it is still rather under-investigated in comparison to the influence of urban structure characteristics on travel behaviour (Stead, 2001). In fact, much of the causality research findings on the influence of socioeconomic and demographic characteristics on travel behaviour have resulted from research focussed on urban structure variables. There is still limited research fully considering the effect of such variables (although good examples are becoming more frequent in the literature) and even less focussed on these characteristics. As research on travel behaviour is strongly oriented towards land use and transport planning purposes (considering the limited potential of policy action on socioeconomic and demographic characteristics), this situation comes as no surprise. Nevertheless, there is a rising awareness within travel behaviour research, of the influence and importance of socioeconomic and demographic characteristics in travel behaviour and of the importance of understanding such influence even for land use and transport planning purposes.

Taking a closer look at the research findings concerning the influence of socioeconomic characteristics on travel behaviour, it is fair to say that the main variables considered in this research field are: gender, age, employment, income, education, driver's licence/car ownership, household size and composition (see, for instance, Boarnet and Crane, 2001b; Boarnet and Sarmiento, 1998; Dieleman et al., 2002; Handy, 1996; Lee and McDonald, 2003; Næss, 2005; Næss et al., 1995; Schwanen et al., 2001; Stead, 2001; Steg et al., 2001; Zegras, 2010. For an earlier review see, for instance, Stead et al., 2000). Some case studies have presented more complex variables with different disaggregation of variables like employment, education and household size and composition.

With regard to the influence of **gender** on travel behaviour it is reasonable to expect shorter travel distances in total and by car among women than among men, and higher proportions of public transport and walking/bike use among women than among men, due to (amongst other factors) prevailing gender imbalances with regard to job access and income. Stead (2001) found congruent results showing higher travel distance for men. Similar results have been found by, amongst others, Giuliano (1979), Hanson and Johnston (1985), Hanson and Pratt (1995), Hjorthol (2000), Hjorthol (2008), Lee and McDonald (2003), Srinivasan (2008) and Wachs (1992).

The expected influence of **age** on travel behaviour is that of shorter travel distances in total and by car, and a lower proportion of car travel among young and old people when compared to adults of working age (Næss, 2005), closely connected to the availability of access to a car and a driver's license, as well as to income and workforce participation.

According to Næss (2005), the expected influence of **employment** on travel behaviour is that of longer travel distances in total, by car and by public transport among workforce participants. Similar results have been found by, among others, Ryley (2006) and Blumenberg et al. (2012).

With regard to **income**, longer travel distances in total and by car, and a higher proportion traveled by car (and lower by public and non-motorized transport) are expected from higher income households in comparison to low income counterparts. A high income enables people to pay the price of high mobility, including the purchase of vehicles, expenses for maintenance and taxes, the purchase of fuel, as well as public transport fares. Therefore, it is no surprise that a number of studies have found that a high income contributes to increasing car use and energy use for transportation (Boarnet and Crane, 2001b; Handy et al., 2005; Kockelman, 1997; Næss, 2005; Schipper, et al., 1994; Zegras and Shrinivasan, 2006). Higher household income has been found to increase both trip frequency and travel distance for commuting. At the same time, high income may contribute to reducing daily traveling distances by enabling people to get a house of a preferred standard closer to their workplace (Cervero, 1989, Næss and Sandberg, 1996).

Relatively few studies have investigated the influence of people's **education** level on their local transportation. Those few investigations do not indicate that the education level has much direct influence on either the extent of intra-urban transportation or the choice between car and public transport (see, among others, Næss and Sandberg, 1998). By influencing the income level, and possibly also the chance of a company car arrangement, the education level may still have indirect effects leading to longer travel distances and higher shares of car usage. However, some studies have shown an influence of the disciplinary field of higher education on travel (specifically regarding technical or economical education) (Hartoft-Nielsen, 1997; Næss, 2006a[1]). On the other hand, within the segment of short or medium education, 'blue-collar' workers tended to have longer travel distances in total and lower proportions of public transport and non-motorized modes than 'white-collar' workers with short or medium education. Apart from cultural differences between these groups, different typical job locations might also play a role, since 'blue-collar' jobs more often than 'white-collar' jobs are located in suburban districts poorly accessible by public transport (Næss, 2006a).

Several studies have found the possession of a **driver's license**, together with **car ownership**, to exert substantial influence on travel behaviour (e.g., Bagley and Mokhtarian, 2002; Dieleman et al., 2002; Krizek, 2003; Næss et al., 1995; Schwanen et al., 2002). These characteristics are generally associated with longer travel distances in total and by car, and a higher proportion travelled by car, shorter distance travelled by public transport and walk/bike, and lower proportions of these modes. This should come as no surprise, as car ownership implies increased mobility, increasing both the 'cruising range' of a household and the ability to take frequent trips. A review developed by Stead et al. (2000) revealed that car ownership may increase trip frequency, travel distance, car use and travel time.

However, in recent years several authors have called attention to the fact that car ownership is in itself influenced by urban structural conditions (Fosli and Lian, 1999; Giuliano and Narayan, 2003). Among other things, it may be argued from a time-geographical perspective (Hägerstrand, 1970) that the location of the dwelling influences the residents' need for having private motor vehicles at their disposition. Households living far away (or at long travel times) from desired destinations may be encouraged to buy a car (or a second car) to save time from travel for other activities. On the other hand, households living in areas where parking is expensive and limited may be discouraged from buying a car (or a second car). In fact, authors such as Næss (2009a)[2] and Acker and Witlox (2010) argue that the impact of urban structure on travel behaviour tends to be underestimated if car ownership is included as a control variable.

Finally, some studies, most of which are from Scandinavia, suggest that **household size/composition** also holds a significant influence on travel behaviour

---

1   This study compared a technical or economical education with a social sciences and humanities education.

2   This study found that higher car ownership rates among outer-area residents persisted among a sample of residents of Copenhagen Metropolitan Area when controlling for a number of socio-demographic variables as well as attitudes to car driving.

of the adult household members. Namely, households with children tend to have shorter travel distances in total and a lower proportion by public transport (Næss et al., 1995; Næss, 2005). Some other studies have, however, not found any such effects (e.g., Nielsen, 2002; Næss, 2010c). In the former studies, the weekly travel distance was instead found to increase if there were schoolchildren in the household. In the latter study, based on data from a Chinese city, the share of non-motorized travel was found to decrease if there were more than one adult household member.

Most research shows the influence of socioeconomic/demographic variables in many aspects of travel behaviour. Several authors in this field of research argue that, in certain circumstances, socioeconomic/demographic descriptors explain more variations in travel behaviour than land use variables do (Stead et al., 2000; Stead, 2001; Schwanen et al., 2002). The relative importance of individual respondent characteristics and urban structural variables may depend, however, on the level of spatial aggregation. For example, in a study of residential location and travel in Greater Oslo, Næss et al. (1995) found that 58 per cent of the explained variance in households' travel distance by motorized modes of travel could be attributed to urban structural variables, whereas urban structural variables accounted for as much as 93 per cent of the explained variance when comparing the mean values of the 30 residential areas investigated. Similarly, the explained variance (measured as adjusted R^2) is usually lower in studies where the units of analysis are individuals than in studies with households as the unit of analysis. Regardless of their relative importance on travel behaviour, it is clear that both socioeconomic and urban structure characteristics have a significant influence on travel.

Discussion on the influence of socioeconomic/demographic characteristics on travel behaviour would not be complete without a reference to research on transport psychology. In parallel to causality research exploring the influence of these type of characteristics on travel behaviour, transport psychology has provided a separate research track mainly focussed on motivational factors, i.e., of a psychological nature. The importance of motivational factors on travel choice has been argued by several authors, e.g., Schlich et al., 2004 and Steg et al., 2001. Examples of motivational factors found in the literature are, for instance, preferences (Scheiner and Kasper, 2002; Schlich et al., 2004), value orientation (Scheiner and Kasper, 2002), need and desires, and symbolic affective motives (Garvill, 1999; Steg et al., 2001), habits (Fujii and Gärling, 2003; Fujii and Kitamura, 2003; Gärling and Axhausen, 2003), beliefs and attitudes (Fujii and Kitamura, 2003).

Transport users are not just making their modal choices on the basis of what is currently available to them, but also refer to (selective) memories, images in their decision-making processes (Guivert, 2007). Eagly and Chaiken (1993) and Gärling et al. (1998) along with other attitudinal researchers in social psychology identify past behaviour, intention, and the situation (opportunities and/or constraints) as potential determinants of behaviour. Pendyala et al. (2000) claim that travel patterns tend to repeat themselves day by day with inertia. This is supported by other behavioural scientists like Verplanken et al. (1994 and 1997) and Aarts and

Dijksterhuis (2000), hence affirming the automaticity of behaviour (Bargh, 1997; Oelette and Wood, 1998). The relationship between how strongly past behaviour or habit and intention determine behaviour is assumed to be reciprocal (Triandis, 1977) 'the stronger determinant habit is, the weaker determinant intention is, and vice versa' (Gärling and Axhausen, 2003: 3). When behaviour becomes habitual, no intention is formed, resulting in less conscious, more automatic processing of information (Ouelette and Wood, 1998; Verplanken et al., 1994). Therefore, a choice that is non-deliberate cannot be influenced with rational arguments (Gärling and Axhausen, 2003). However, the fact that choices are repeated does not make it a habit if there is a deliberation, the result of which is always the same choice. Nevertheless, Fujii and Gärling (2003: 118) argue that 'the more frequent a choice with positive outcome is made, the more likely this is to result in a script-based choice'.

On the contrary, in the theories of reasoned action (Ajzen and Fishbein, 1980; Fishbein and Ajzen, 1975) and planned behaviour (Ajzen, 1991), intention is defined as the probability the actor consciously assigns to engagement in a particular behaviour. In the theory of planned behaviour a choice is made on the basis of the strength of several competing intentions.

Other authors like Garvill (1999) and Steg et al. (2001), focussing more on specific travel modes, found that affective motives like feelings of freedom, independence, power, status, or privacy may be important determinants of car use. Steg et al. (2001) refers symbolic-affective motives (such as feelings or sensations, power, superiority, privacy, status, independence) in opposition to instrumental-reasoned motives (such as travel cost, time, safety).

Research by Scheiner and Kasper (2002) refers to another important connection – that between lifestyle and housing location – which in return will again influence travel behaviour. According to these authors, lifestyle is beginning to be identified as having a potential effect on house location choice (according to local facilities, personal needs and even house types, to name just a few), although this connection seems to be harder to identify and understand. With household location choice being increasingly recognized as an important factor in travel behaviour, lifestyle does not only directly influence travel choices, but also indirectly through house location choice.

On the other hand, for transport-attitude-based residential location preferences to make sense at all, urban structural characteristics must influence the actual possibilities for pursuing different travel behavioural lifestyles. If there were no such influence, people who, for example, prefer to travel by non-motorized modes might as well settle in the peripheral part of the metropolitan area, far away from public transport stops and the concentration of workplaces and service facilities found in the central and inner city (Næss, 2009a).

It should also be noticed that the literature on lifestyle and travel has focused mainly on how attitudinal factors influence the choices of travel *modes*. The extent to which lifestyle factors influence travelling *distances* in quotidian travel, and the importance of such lifestyle factors compared to urban structural and 'traditional' socioeconomic and demographic characteristics, has been far less investigated. In addition, according to Costanzo et al. (1986), the psychological approach by itself underestimates the complexity of human behaviour, and other elements (cultural, social and economic) need to be considered. Thus, awareness of psychological motivations, regardless of their relative importance when compared to other socioeconomic/demographic characteristics, provides additional knowledge contributing to a more comprehensive understanding of travel choice. In accordance, regardless of the importance of socioeconomic characteristics on travel choice, it is also essential to recognize and understand the role of land use and transport systems on travel behaviour. While urban structure defines the exogenous baseline conditions provided for travel choice, socioeconomic and demographic characteristics provide the individual/household setting in which travel choices are finally made (choosing from the range of choices made available by the urban structure). Figure 3.1 presents a summary of the main socioeconomic and demographic characteristics found to influence travel behaviour. Debate on the influence of land use and transport systems on travel behaviour is presented in the next section.

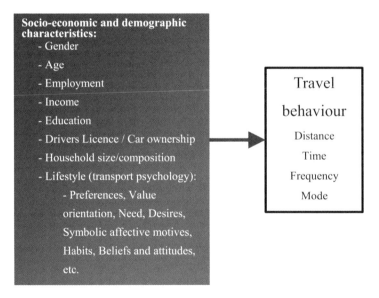

**Figure 3.1   Summary of the main household characteristics influencing
                travel patterns**

Urban Structure (Places) and Travel Behaviour (Patterns)[3]

There is an extensive discussion in the literature on the influence of urban structure on mobility patterns; in other words, the influence of land use and transport systems on travel behaviour. According to Erwing and Cervero (2010) the volume of literature on how urban structure influences travel demand has exploded over the last decades, becoming more sophisticated and considering a growing range of environmental variables and potentially confounding influences. In the literature reviewed on the influence of urban structure on mobility, most publications present the results of case studies searching for the main land use factors influencing travel choice. These case studies have developed mainly aggregate analyses. Other publications present broad literature reviews, complementing the results found in the reviewed case studies (Ewing and Cervero, 2001; Handy, 1996; Stead et al., 2000; van Wee, 2002). Considerably less research has addressed urban structure policy implications and recommendations.

It is fair to say that in this research field most authors believe that the built environment has an influence on travel behaviour (e.g., Cervero and Kochelman, 1997; Ewing and Cervero, 2001; Handy, 1996; van Wee, 2002). Nevertheless, some are sceptical about the wide range of identified influence factors mainly because research methodologies have been quite diverse or strictly focused on case-specific conditions and constraints. Indeed, some case studies have produced inconclusive results (e.g., Boarnet and Crane, 2001a; Cervero, 1995; Handy and Clifton, 2001). However, many studies evaluate a limited set of variables, which may not be necessarily the most adequate for the intended research purposes. Also, specific local planning traditions or local and national contexts may have led to different results. Indeed some empirical studies, concluding that urban structure has little influence on travel behaviour, focused on other urban structural conditions (e.g., detailed neighbourhood design) than those which, from theoretical considerations, could be expected to exert the strongest influences on travelling distances and modal split. Notably, research in the United States on land use and transport relationships has to a large extent been directed towards the influence of local-scale urban structural conditions on travel behaviour, without taking into consideration the location of the neighbourhoods investigated (e.g., Cervero, 1995; Handy and Clifton, 2001). According to Boarnet and Crane (2001a), a limited geographical scale has been typical of virtually all recent American empirical research into relationships between built environment characteristics and travel. Other studies are based on model simulations where the models simply assume that any such influences are weak (see, for example, Williams et al. (2000), where some of these studies are referred).

Among the vast number of case studies on the influence of land use on urban mobility, density has been the most frequently evaluated land use factor

---

3   This section brings a new arrangement and update to an earlier review published in Silva (2013).

Mobility Patterns and Urban Structure

(see for instance, Næss, 1993; Næss et al., 1996; Kenworthy and Laube, 1999; Simmonds and Coombe, 2000; Boarnet and Crane, 2001a; Giuliano and Narayan, 2003; Coevering and Schwanen, 2006; Giuliano and Dargay, 2006; Næss, 2005; Chatman, 2008; Chen et al., 2008; Milakis et al., 2008). While some authors found inconclusive results or low levels of the influence of density on particular travel choices, Kenworthy and Laube (1999), Chen et al. (2008) and Milakis et al. (2008) revealed a considerable influence of land use density on mode choice and Giuliano and Narayan (2003) and Giuliano and Dargay (2006) revealed a considerable influence of density on travel frequency and on travel distance. Coevering and Schwanen (2006) and Chen and McKnight (2007) found that urban form features, such as density, still appear relevant when considering other non-structural factors (such as, housing, urban development history and socio-demographic data). The geographic scale at which density has been measured also matters. While neighbourhood density has been found in some studies to exert little influence on travel behaviour, the studies that have investigated the influence of the density of the city as a whole, measured within the demarcation of the continuous urbanized area, have found considerable influences of density at this level on energy use for transport (Newman and Kenworthy, 1999; Lefèvre , 2010; Næss, 1993; Næss et al., 1996).

Studies of the influence of land use diversity on travel behaviour have found little evidence (Van and Senior, 2000; Handy and Clifton, 2001; Milakis et al., 2008) reinforcing the sceptical tone of recent American research on this topic. Nevertheless, when considering simultaneously density, diversity and design (in what has been named as the *3Ds of the built environment* by Cervero and Kockelman, 1997), research has found far more promising results on the influence of built environment on travel behaviour (for instance, Cervero and Kockelman, 1997; Boarnet and Sarmiento, 1998; Stead, 2001). Stead (2001) found an influence of the 3Ds on travel distance when also considering individual/household characteristics (e.g., age, gender, household composition and size). This author found that the influence of household characteristics is even stronger than that of land use characteristics. Similar results on the relative importance of individual/ household characteristics and urban structure characteristics have been found by other authors (Chen and McKnight, 2007; Acker et al., 2007; Ewing and Cervero, 2010) when considering individual/household characteristics together with other urban structure characteristics.

Ewing and Cervero (2010) have further extended the concept of the 3Ds of the built environment, adding to the list, destination accessibility, distance to transit and demand management (including parking supply and costs), building up the 6Ds (based on previous results by these and other authors). They even suggest a seventh D, although not part of the environment, as influencing travel – demographics. A broad literature review conducted by these authors found that the relationship between travel variables and some built environment variables is inelastic. Nevertheless, these authors believe that 'the combined effect of several built environment variables on travel could be quite large' (Ewing and Cervero, 2010: 275).

Among the D variables researched this study found destination accessibility to exert the strongest influence on travel.

More complex studies, considering several built environment characteristics (including transport characteristics) as well as socioeconomic characteristics (as, for instance, the ones reviewed by Erwing and Cervero, 2010) have found statistically significant results for different features, providing evidence on the relationship between urban structure and travel, and showing the complexity of this relationship. Studies carried out by Næss (2005, 2010c) found an influence of urban structures, namely of residential location within an urban structure, on the amount of travel and modal split. Næss (2005) found that the main urban structure factors influencing travel from residence are: distance to the central city; distance to the closest second order urban centre; distance to the closest urban railway station; and residential and employment density in the surrounding area. Also the influence of the distance from the dwelling to the city centre was found to be strong by Næss et al. (1995), Nielsen (2002), Næss and Jensen (2004) and Næss (2010c) in studies of cities and metropolitan areas ranging in population size from 30,000 to around four million. A literature review carried out by Stead et al. (2000) found the following main land use characteristics affecting travel behaviour: proximity of households to an urban centre; settlement size; mixed land use; provision of local facilities and services; population density; proximity to main transport networks; and availability of residential parking.

Based on a literature review, van Wee (2002) believes that there is enough evidence to conclude that the built environment can influence travel behaviour. He believes in the existence of a relatively strong consensus on the most important factors that may affect travel behaviour. According to this author, these are density, level of mixed land use, neighbourhood design and distance to railway connections. Nevertheless, this author suggests that these aspects are not sufficient to grant their potential effects on travel behaviour and that many other conditions need to be taken into consideration. The importance of distance to major transport infrastructure has been referred to by several other authors such as Newman and Kenworthy (2000), Cullinane (2003), Cameron et al. (2004), Næss (2005, 2006a). In particular, public transport oriented nodal development and densification around rail stations, in combination to other land use and transport policies, is believed to have a significant influence on mode choice, particularly car ridership.

In comparison to land use factors, the research on the influence of transport factors on travel behaviour is far less developed. One argument for this is that the relationship between transport systems and travel has always been assumed to exist. Traditional transport planning was expected to develop transport policies and infrastructures in order to satisfy travel needs, therefore, transport systems, and travel patterns have been considered somewhat similar. Only recently has it been recognized that the transport system can actively be used to influence travel behaviour (rather than simply satisfy travel needs). This recognition has led to the development of a significant number of transport-based Travel Demand Management (TDM) measures. Although some research has been developed on the effects of some of these measures (Parkhurst, 2000; Thorpe et al., 2000; Root, 2001; Rye, 2002; Kenyon and Lyons, 2003; Vuk, 2005; Davison and Knowles, 2006; Dziekan and Kottenhoff, 2007; Rose and Marfurt, 2007; Thøgersen and Møller, 2008), this research field is also still underdeveloped and not specifically focussed on revealing the main transport factors influencing travel behaviour. In this context, Gärling et al. (2002) suggest that the classification of TDM measures is a promising means for understanding potential reasons for behavioural change or lack thereof. This suggests that categories of TDM measures provide clues of which transport factors (and also other factors, such as land use and socioeconomic factors also included in TDM approaches) are believed by the authors to have the capacity to influence travel behaviour. Several categorizations of TDM measures have been proposed over time. In addition to new evidences from the emergent research field on the effects of TDM measures, this information can be used for the identification of the main transport factors underlying travel behaviour.

Traditionally, TDM measures are divided into *push* measures, enhancing the attractiveness of alternative modes, and *pull* measures, designed to fight the attractiveness of the car. Several categorizations can be found in the literature. For instance, the European project DANTE identified 10 main categories of travel reduction measures: capacity management; pricing and taxation; land use planning; communications and technology; policy measures; physical measures; subsidies and spending; location, time and user restrictions; public awareness; and other measures (DANTE Consortium, 1998). Another example is provided by Meyer (1999) who identified the following broad categories: offer alternative transport modes and services (intended to increase vehicle occupancy); provide incentives and disincentives to reduce travel; accomplish trip purpose without making the trip (e.g., telecommuting).

Service level or quality, availability, and price of each transport system seem to be the main transport system factors underlying the different TDM categories (and the remaining TDM measures found in the literature) as well as evidence from research on the effects of TDM measures. These factors are also in line with the traditional utility-based theories underlying the idea of derived demand of traditional transport planning, suggesting that travel will only be engaged when positive utility of the participation in the pursued activity exceeds the disutility of travelling (generally expressed in time and money spent). From the perspective of transport economics, price and service level are baseline features of travel choice, assuming that the desired transport system is always available. The recognition that transport services are not homogeneously available, or even that the withdrawal of certain transport systems can be used in travel demand management actions, draws attention to the importance of adding availability to traditional transport economy factors.

Service level or quality refers to, for instance, the capacity of every transport mode (road capacity or passenger capacity of the public transport system) and the quality of that service including, for instance, speed, reliability and flexibility, road construction quality and available services or public transport quality associated, for instance, to ticket technology, information systems, comfort and security. The importance of this factor is supported by Everett and Watson, who claim that: 'A long number of TDM measures are based on the assumption that the use of travel mode can be influenced by improving the service level of public transport and/ or reducing the service level of automotive transportation' (Everett and Watson, 1987, cited in Fujii and Kitamura, 2003: 81–2). Availability includes, for instance, the existence of a viable transport option for the required travel pattern, within a viable access distance. Stead et al. (2000) also identified availability (referred to as proximity to the main transport network and availability of residential parking) as one of the main factors influencing travel behaviour. The price refers, naturally, to the monetary cost of the transport service purchase and is one of the main transport system aspects changed by TDM measures, such as, congestion charging and public transport subsidy.

The available literature provides several case studies on the influence of a number of aspects of urban structure on travel behaviour, as well as reviews of these case studies. Nevertheless, few publications can be found studying urban structure policy effects on travel behaviour and even fewer take the step further towards policy recommendations. There seems to be some disregard for supporting decision-making in this research field. Even within the group of authors believing that urban structure influences travel behaviour there is some scepticism on the effect of policies and their contributions to sustainable urban mobility. The lack of research on policy effects does not help to dissipate these doubts. Several authors (e.g., Handy, 1996; Van and Senior, 2000; van Wee, 2002) have argued that besides studying the potential factors influencing travel behaviour there is also a need for research on how this knowledge can be used in policy design. It is important to evaluate potential travel behaviour changes due to urban structure modifications (Van and Senior, 2000). 'Finding a strong relationship between urban form and travel patterns is not the same as showing that a change in urban form will lead to change in travel behaviour, and finding a strong relationship is not the same as understanding that relationship' (Handy, 1996: 162). Furthermore, van Wee (2002) believes that 'even if land use has an impact on transportation, it does not mean that it is easy to use land-use policy as an instrument to influence travel behaviour' (van Wee, 2002: 265). Even though less research has been developed on the combined effect of land use and transport on mobility patterns, several authors are convinced that combined policy actions will contribute to enhance the sustainability of urban mobility (such as Kitamura et al., 1997; Kenworthy and Laube, 1999; Marshall and Banister, 2000; Cameron et al., 2004).

Figure 3.2 presents a summary of the main land use and transport characteristics found to influence travel behaviour in the literature, grouped into three main categories: location-based influence, relation-based influence and cost-based influence.

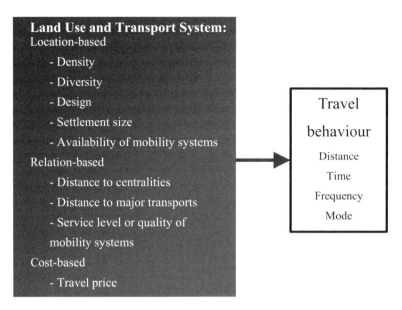

Figure 3.2   Summary of the urban structure characteristics influencing travel patterns

The Particular Case of Monocentric vs Polycentric Urban Systems

The literature on how monocentric and polycentric metropolitan structures affect travel behaviour is far from being consensual. On this subject, and according to Schwanen et al. (2001), there are two positions: on one side are the *liberals*, who believe in the efficiency of market mechanisms and advocate that housing and jobs mutually co-locate allowing for shorter commuting times and distances; on the other are the *regulators*, who recognize in urban planning the answer for environmental and congestion problems caused by travel behaviour, essentially by the extensive use of the car. The latter state that a higher urban density and a strong city centre leads to shorter trip lengths and higher use of public transport and non-motorized modes. Both these theories are supported by several empirical studies.

Some authors consider that households periodically change their place of residence or work as a way of avoiding the increased travel times caused by the extensive congestion in monocentric urban areas (Gordon et al., 1989; Kim, 2008). This theory, normally referred to as the 'co-location hypothesis', sees suburbanization as a successful mechanism to mitigate congestion, as jobs and housing mutually co-locate allowing for different travel modes and high travel speeds that maintain a fairly constant average commuting time.

Firms also try to avoid some of the disadvantages of high density locations (such as traffic congestion, poor accessibility to the suburban labour force, higher land prices and limited potential for spatial extensions) choosing new locations in less congested places of the metropolitan area or locations where potential employees reside (Cervero and Wu, 1998; Schwanen et al., 2004b). These trends foster the development of polycentric urban areas with a higher dispersal of activities across urban space and lower average commuting times and distances. As workers are assumed to minimize travel distances and times, the advocates of the so-called co-location hypothesis expect these factors to be lower in polycentric than in monocentric urban structures.

Several empirical studies, mostly in American literature, support the co-location theory based on positive correlations between density and travel times and on the assumption that travel times decrease with decentralization independently of the distance travelled (Gordon et al., 1989; Levinson and Kumar, 1994). Other authors refute this positive view of the effect of polycentrism and decentralization on travel behaviour. They argue that travel minimization may be challenged by constraints on the choice of residential location since there might be several workers in a household, lags in housing development near employment centres, policy measures creating restrictions to development, or reluctance to change job or place of residence due to social and economic costs (Cervero and Wu, 1998; Schwanen et al., 2001; Schwanen et al., 2004b). In America, Cervero and Wu (1998) found that commute distances and times as well as car use tend to increase with the decentralization of employment, while the share of carpooling and public transport use tend to drop.

Most of the European literature on this matter also contradicts the point of view argued by the co-location hypotheses. It is also important to note that the concept of polycentrism used by the advocates of this theory is often more related to decentralization or suburbanization rather than to the concept of polycentrism more common in the European literature (discussed in Chapter 2).

Schwanen (2002) argues that the relocation of employment and residences may not occur to the same extent in European countries as in the US, which might be due to the more comprehensive regulation on housing and land markets in Europe. The analysis developed in this study shows that concentration of employment in the city centre results in shorter travel distances, and that travel times are shorter in the inner-city area, though with a less significant impact, probably as a result of congestion.

Although the above-mentioned study did not find significant effects of employment concentration on modal split, there are several other studies reaching significant findings in this respect in a number of other cities, including Oslo (Næss and Sandberg, 1996); Copenhagen and Århus (Hartoft-Nielsen, 1997, 2001); Helsinki (Lahti, 1995) and Trondheim (Strømmen, 2001). In these cities, the proportion of commuting by car was considerably lower among employees of inner-city workplaces than among their suburban counterparts. Correspondingly, the proportions of non-motorized as well as public transport were higher among inner-city than outer-area employees in these cities.

Moreover, there was little difference between inner-city and suburban workplaces in terms of commuting distances, albeit with an average tendency of slightly longer commutes to outer-area office workplaces.

The above-mentioned study in Oslo (Næss and Sandberg, 1996) also investigated long-term consequences of workplace relocations within the urban area, following up on an earlier study of short-term effects (Monsen, 1983). The immediate increase in average commuting distance resulting from workplace decentralization was not reversed by subsequent turnover and residential changes among the employees, as postulated by the co-location hypothesis. On the contrary, among the companies investigated the mean commuting distance increased at a considerably higher rate for the company that had moved to the urban fringe than for the remaining relocating companies, which had moved to less peripheral suburbs.

Another study developed by Schwanen et al. (2004b) in the Netherlands also reached important conclusions regarding the influence of urban structure on modal choice and travel distances and times as a car driver. The types of urban structure used for this study were based on the classification developed by van der Laan (1998) that distinguishes four types of urban systems: one monocentric – 'centralized' – and three different types of polycentric urban areas – 'decentralized', 'cross-commuting' and 'exchange commuting' (see Figure 2.1, Chapter 2).

This study found that, despite the influence of a monocentric or polycentric urban structure on mode choice is rather limited, the probability of driving a car to work seems to be lower in high-density environments. Concerning commute distance and time for car drivers, evidence shows that both are significantly longer in the majority of polycentric areas than in monocentric centralized urban structures (Schwanen et al., 2004b). Only in one type of polycentric area – the 'cross-commuting' region consisting of relatively independent nodes – are commuting distances and times equivalent to the values found in monocentric systems.

Another study developed in France by Aguilera and Mignot (2004) suggests that the effects of polycentrism on travel behaviour depend on the nature of the employment sub-centre, its location (distance to the city centre or positioning in terms of the transport axes), its size and its density (Aguilera and Mignot, 2004). The study consisted in comparing data from the 1990 and the 1999 census in several French urban areas with different sizes and also different structures in terms of level of employment suburbanization (Aguilera and Mignot, 2004).

The analysis considered four types of places in the urban area: centre, suburban sub-centres, outlying sub-centres and rest of the urban area (see previous chapter). The study results show that average commuting distances are shorter in the sub-centres than in the rest of the urban area. Furthermore, the city centre and the suburban sub-centres form a greater centre where commuting distances are reduced (Aguilera and Mignot, 2004). The analysis of the data from 1990 and 1999 reveals that while most jobs continue to concentrate in the centre and suburban sub-centres, people live more and more in outlying sub-centres and in the rest of the urban area. This phenomenon led to an average lengthening of commuting distances between

1990 and 1999, since the number of locally employed people has fallen and the distance between work and residence amongst non-locally employed workers has increased (Aguilera and Mignot, 2004).

In summary, the empirical literature on the influence of urban structure on travel behaviour – particularly the case of monocentric vs polycentric structures – is quite contradictory and sometimes inconclusive. While several authors state that a higher urban density and a strong city centre lead to shorter trip lengths and higher use of public transport and non-motorized modes, others argue for lower densities advocating that housing and jobs mutually co-locate allowing for shorter commuting times and distances.

In addition, several methodological differences can be found in the numerous studies analysed, such as the level of aggregation of the data used, the variables choice, whether or not leisure trips are also considered and, mainly, whether or not socioeconomic factors are taken into consideration.

Synthesis

One of the objectives set out by this research project was to provide a deeper understanding of the relationship between urban structure and travel behaviour. With this aim in mind, this chapter set out to review previous research exploring motivations behind current travel behaviour. This review aimed to identify the main factor influencing travel as a baseline input for research on the influence of urban structure on mobility. Recognizing the importance of a comprehensive assessment of travel behaviour motivations, in accordance with previous research (showing how research disregarding the influence of, for instance, socioeconomic variables, may result in misleading results) we have collected evidence of urban structure factors, as well as socioeconomic and demographic factors, influencing travel choices. With regard to urban structure, in addition to causality research findings of specific land use and transport characteristics, this chapter also presents a review of the debate of the influence of monocentric versus polycentric urban structures on travel choices, following another of the main objectives of this research.

Aiming to inform policy making, we developed a *tentative* identification of some of the main factors found to influence travel behaviour in the literature, in the absence of a consensus in current research.

With regard to urban structure factors, density, diversity (or mixed use), design, settlement size, availability of mobility systems, distance to centralities, distance to major transports, service level and quality of mobility systems, and travel price were recognized by several authors as having an important role in travel choice. Within otherwise constant conditions, increased density is believed to reduce travel distance and time and to enable the economic viability of public and non-motorized transport and therefore its use (due to higher service level). Increased diversity is believed to reduce the need to travel long distances and enable the use of non-motorized and slower travel modes. An adequate design is believed to encourage the use of slower modes. Smaller settlements are believed to facilitate soft modes, while larger settlements make public transport viable. Availability of a certain mobility system enables its use while its absence (for instance of a public transport system) disables people from having that particular mode choice. Households located farther away from centralities are expected to have longer travel distances, to be more car dependent and to have low propensity for soft modes. Similarly to availability of mobility systems, short distance to major transport infrastructure, such as highways or major rail lines, is expected to increase competitiveness of that particular transport mode and thus encourage its use, enabling longer travel distance by that same mode. Increased service level/ quality of a strategically preferred transport mode will increase the demand of that transport mode in relation to other alternative modes. Finally, increasing the price of a transport mode will reduce its demand (and the reverse is also valid).

With regard to household and individual characteristics, gender, age, employment, income, education, availability of drivers licence and car, and household size and composition were recognized by several authors as socioeconomic and demographic factors having an important role in travel choice. For instance, it is reasonable to expect shorter travel distances in total and by car, and higher proportions of public transport and walk/bike among women than among men. Young and old people are expected to have shorter travel distances in total and by car, and lower proportion of car travel than adults. Workforce participants are expected to have longer travel distances in total, by car and by public transport than non-participants. Higher income households are expected to have longer travel distances in total and by car, and a higher proportion travelled by car (and lower by public and non-motorized transport) than lower income households. Availability of driver license and car ownership is generally associated with longer travel distances in total and by car, and a higher proportion travelled by car, shorter distance travelled by public transport and walk/bike, and lower proportions of these modes.

In addition, research has revealed the increasing influence of other lifestyle-based factors on travel choice, such as preferences, value orientation, needs, desires, symbolic affective motives, habits, beliefs and attitudes. While research suggests that the first group holds a stronger influence on travel behaviour (even stronger than urban structure factors), most of these factors are not influenced by public policy. On the other hand, the ability to influence travel behaviour through public policy aimed at lifestyle factors has shown promising effects (though is still an underdeveloped research field). For instance, habit and policies aimed at breaking habits have shown interesting results in changing travel patterns.

With regard to the debate on the influence of monocentric versus polycentric urban structures, American and European research has resulted in contradicting findings, to a high extent connected to different understandings of polycentrism (frequently associated to decentralization and suburbanization phenomena in American research). Nevertheless, there is a reasonable degree of consensus in

European literature around the idea that a high density, centralized city with a strong transport system may contribute to lower car use and shorter commuting and leisure trips. However, some results indicate that more polycentric regions with several high-density centres and an efficient public transport service can also show lower car use and high shares of public transport and non-motorized modes.

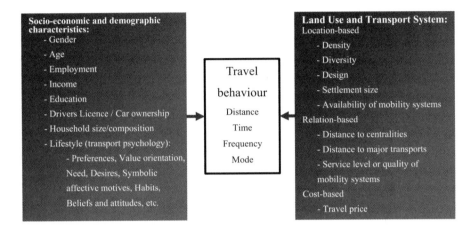

Figure 3.3   Main household and urban structure factors influencing travel behaviour

This review provides the necessary background for the development of this research, by identifying the state of the art knowledge on travel behaviour motivations. The review has also acknowledged the importance of a comprehensive assessment of travel behaviour motivations to avoid misleading results, by providing a comprehensive starting point for our research, which will build on this conceptual framework aiming to provide a deeper understanding of the relationship between urban structure and travel behaviour and, in turn, contribute to building a broader consensus on the factors influencing travel behaviour.

Chapter 4

People, Places and Travel Patterns in Copenhagen and Oporto

Miguel Torres, Petter Næss, José Pedro Reis,
Fernanda Sousa and Paulo Pinho

Greater Copenhagen

Copenhagen is the largest city in Denmark. It is located in the northeast of the island of Zealand in the centre of the transnational region of Øresund, which includes several Danish islands and the Swedish region of Skåne (Figure 4.1).

The area chosen for this research – Greater Copenhagen (GC) – has no formal administrative boundary, but refers instead to the municipalities encompassing the more or less continuous urban area of Copenhagen. It corresponds to the municipalities comprising the Capital Area ('Hovedstadsområdet') as defined by Statistics Denmark. Greater Copenhagen is 541.7 km² and encompasses 17 municipalities according to the new local government reform. This area also corresponds to the central part of the Copenhagen Metropolitan Area.

Whereas Hovedstadsområdet covers the continuous urbanized area of Copenhagen and surrounding municipalities, Greater Copenhagen as referred to in this report also covers some rural areas and other settlements within these municipalities. Greater Copenhagen is thus in this book defined as the municipalities of Copenhagen, Frederiksberg, Albertslund, Brøndby, Gentofte, Gladsaxe, Glostrup, Herlev, Hvidovre, Lyngby-Taarbæk, Rødovre, Tårnby, Vallensbæk, Ishøj, Greve, Ballerup, Rudersdal and Furesø.

The process of spatial development of the Copenhagen Metropolitan Area is strongly connected to the history of land use planning in Denmark, notably the 'Finger Plan'. This plan, of which the first version dates back to 1947, suggests an urban pattern with a form of a hand: the 'palm of the hand' – central Copenhagen – should remain the principal regional centre, concentrating most of the jobs and services, while new urban development should be concentrated in the five 'fingers', along the existing radial commuter railway (S-train) and main motorways leading out towards the closest cities some 40 km away. Between these fingers (along the southwest, west, northwest, north-northwest and north directions), the land would remain undeveloped in favour of farmland and forest.

More recently, the construction of the Øresund Bridge introduced new dynamics of growth in the south finger that received a new railway and motorway, as well as a new metro line to the Airport. From being a backyard of the

Figure 4.1   Europe, Denmark and the Copenhagen Metropolitan Area

Copenhagen Metropolitan Area, the southern finger has attracted new business centres reinforcing its role in the overall urban structure of the metropolis that, nonetheless, remains largely unchanged overall.

Population

The study area – Greater Copenhagen – has around 1.3 million inhabitants, which is roughly two thirds of the metropolitan population (around 1.9 million). The central area of the city of Copenhagen – where density is the highest – is also the centre of five radial corridors with higher densities.

Greater Copenhagen had for several decades a very moderate population growth, with a population in 2006 only two per cent higher than in 1981. In the period from the early 1950s to around 1980 there was a considerable exodus of the population from the municipalities of Copenhagen and Frederiksberg to suburban municipalities. As can be seen in Figure 4.2, the population of Greater Copenhagen as a whole dropped by nearly 130,000 over the nine-year period from 1971 to 1980, after which it remained almost constant for nearly three decades. In recent years this stagnation has been replaced with considerable population growth, with an increase in the number of inhabitants by nearly 100,000 over the five-year period 2008–2013, reaching 1.34 million at the beginning of 2013.

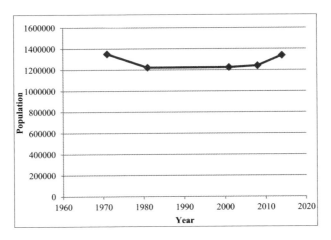

Figure 4.2   Changes in the population size of Greater Copenhagen since 1971

Data Source: Statistics Denmark, 2014.

Figure 4.3 shows in more detail how the size of the population has developed in different parts of Greater Copenhagen. Between 1971 and 1980, the two central municipalities (Copenhagen and Frederiksberg) lost more than 145,000 inhabitants. There was also some population decrease in the inner northern and western suburban municipalities. The only part of Greater Copenhagen experiencing growth in these years was the outer southern municipalities. There was also considerable population growth in the outer parts of the metropolitan area (i.e., outside Greater Copenhagen, but within the metropolitan area).

The population growth of Greater Copenhagen since 2008 has mainly taken place in the two central municipalities. These municipalities also experienced a certain population growth since the 1980s, but it was not until 2006 that the growth began to increase towards its present high rate.

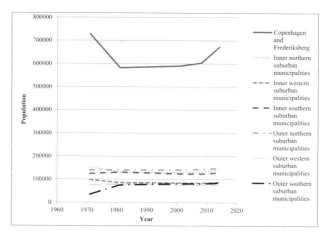

**Figure 4.3   Changes in the population size within different parts of
                 Greater Copenhagen since 1971**
Data Source: Statistics Denmark, 2014.

The distribution of the population between age groups shows a 'Christmas tree-like'
pattern (Figure 4.4), where the largest five-year interval group is those between 25
and 29 years old, relatively few children and teenagers aged 10–19, and an almost
linear reduction in the number of inhabitants per five-year band among those over
30 years of age. The low number of schoolchildren and the correspondingly modest
number of inhabitants belonging to their parent's generation reflects the fact that
single-family houses in the outer parts of the metropolitan area (outside Greater
Copenhagen) are attractive places of residence for families with children, offering
cheaper houses with gardens than those available in the inner suburbs.

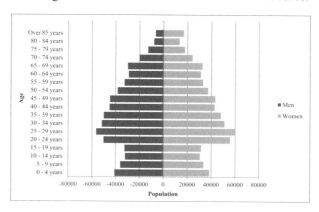

**Figure 4.4   Distribution of the population of Greater Copenhagen between
                 age groups**
Data Source: Statistics Denmark, 2014.

Socioeconomic Conditions

Greater Copenhagen is not a formal unit in the Danish statistics on socioeconomic matters such as Gross Domestic Product (GDP). Instead, we have used statistics comprising the Capital Region, which encompasses all of Greater Copenhagen as defined in this book but also several other municipalities. Greater Copenhagen has, however, more than three fourths of the population of the Capital Region. We therefore think the GDP figures of the Capital Region make up a fairly good approximation of the GDP development within Greater Copenhagen. As can be seen in Figure 4.5, the GDP of the Capital Region has been increasing steadily in the 1990s and in the first years of the present century, but with some stagnation between 1999 and 2002 and a certain drop in 2007 and 2008 due to the financial crisis. Since 2009 there has again been a slight increase.

GDP per capita (Figure 4.6) has followed a similar trajectory of the total regional GDP, yet with a more stagnant tendency over the latest years. This difference between total and per capita GDP growth reflects the considerable population growth since 2008.

Distinct from the statistics on GDP development, statistics for gross value added are available for a geographic area corresponding quite well with Greater Copenhagen as defined in this book. The data on which Figure 4.7 is based refer to the combined statistical units ('landsdele') of 'the city of Copenhagen' and 'the surroundings of Copenhagen', which include 87 per cent of the population of Greater Copenhagen. The trades contributing the most to the gross value added are 'trade, transport, etc.', and 'public administration, education and health'. Each of these trades contributes nearly twice as much as the third and fourth contributors, which are 'finance and insurance' and 'business services'. 'Industry' is only number six, after 'information and communication' but before 'culture, leisure and other services' and 'residential'.

Compared to other EU countries, Denmark has a relatively moderate unemployment rate (6 per cent for the country as a whole). As can be seen in Figure 4.8, the unemployment rate in Greater Copenhagen is a bit above the national average, and with somewhat higher rates in the municipality of Copenhagen and its closest neighbour municipalities (7.2 per cent) than in the inner suburban municipalities (5.8 per cent). The island of Zealand as a whole (including the outer parts of the metropolitan area) has a similar unemployment rate as the inner suburban municipalities.

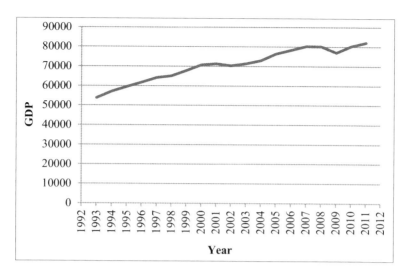

Figure 4.5   Changes in the regional GDP of the Capital Region of Denmark since 1993. Current values have been adjusted to fixed 2005 values

Data Source: Statistics Denmark, 2014.

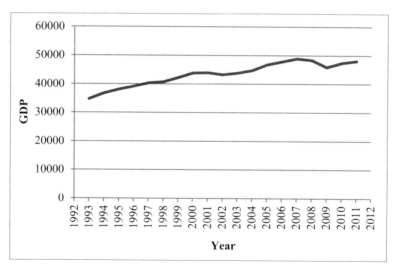

Figure 4.6   Changes in the regional GDP per capita of the Capital Region of Denmark since 1993. Current values have been adjusted to fixed 2005 values

Data Source: Statistics Denmark, 2014.

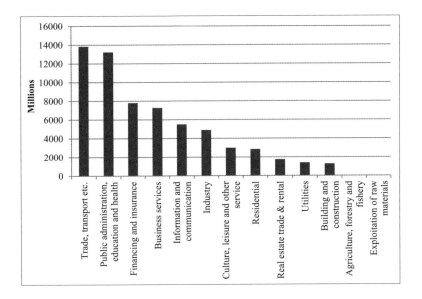

Figure 4.7   Gross value added by different trades within the combined statistical units ('landsdele') of 'the city of Copenhagen' and 'the surroundings of Copenhagen'

Data Source: Statistics Denmark, 2014.

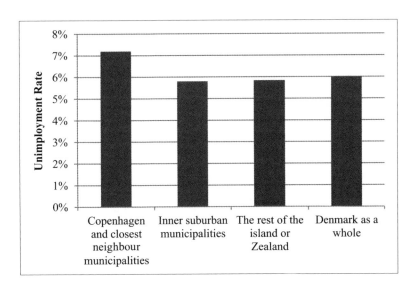

Figure 4.8   Unemployment rates within different geographical parts of Denmark

Data Source: Statistics Denmark, 2014.

Figure 4.9 shows how the purchasing power of the inhabitants of the same two statistical units as in Figure 4.7 has developed since 2000. As can be seen, there was a considerable increase up to 2007, followed by a slight drop and then a small increase in 2009/2010 with stabilization since then at a level slightly above the level before the outburst of the financial crisis in 2007. Over the years 2000–2011, the purchasing power increased by 21 per cent, which is twice as much as the corresponding growth in GDP per capita. It should, however, be noted here that the GDP per capita figures are based on the entire Capital Region, the outer parts of which may have experienced weaker economic development than the more central areas to which the purchasing power figures apply.

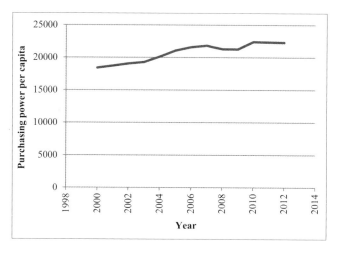

Figure 4.9   Changes in purchasing power per capita since 2000 within the combined statistical units ('landsdele') of 'the city of Copenhagen' and 'the surroundings of Copenhagen'

Data Source: Statistics Denmark, 2014.

The purchasing power is unevenly distributed between different parts of Greater Copenhagen, as can be seen in Figure 4.10. The northern suburban municipalities have all through the period considerably higher purchasing power than the other municipalities, with around 45 per cent higher per capita figures than those of the southern suburban municipalities. The difference between the rich northern and the less affluent southern and western municipalities has increased over the period 2000–2012. Whereas the average purchasing power among inhabitants of the inner northern municipalities increased by nearly 9 per cent, the poorer outer western suburban municipalities experienced growth in purchasing power per capita of only 1.5 per cent. The two central municipalities, Copenhagen and Frederiksberg, have experienced growth nearly as strong as the inner northern municipalities, but

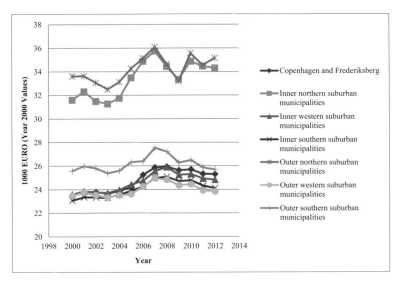

Figure 4.10   Changes in purchasing power per capita since 2000 within different parts of Greater Copenhagen
Data Source: Statistics Denmark, 2014.

their mean purchasing power was at the outset similar to the less affluent southern and western suburban municipalities. The outer southern suburban municipalities, which were the most affluent ones apart from the northern suburban municipalities in 2000, have barely experienced any growth in purchasing power since 2000 and are now at a level similar to the four other non-northern groups of municipalities.

Figure 4.11 and Figure 4.12, respectively, show the geographical distribution of population and job densities across Copenhagen Metropolitan Area. In line with theories of how land values vary with the distance from the city centre (Alonso, 1964) as well as cultural conceptions of appropriate densities in inner-city and suburban contexts (e.g., Fishman, 1996), there is a clear centre-periphery gradient in the density of population as well as jobs, with higher densities in the inner than in the outer parts. As can be seen in Figure 4.13, there is a clear correlation between the distance to the city centre and the combined job and population density in the local neighbourhoods of the investigated residential areas in Greater Copenhagen (Pearson's $r = -0.724$). Densities are particularly high within some 5–6 km from the city centre, whereas the decline in density with increasing distance from the city centre is less pronounced when moving beyond 10 km from the city centre. Densities are also strongly correlated to the distance to the closest second-order centre, the closest urban rail (S-train) station and the closest main regional retail centre. However, local area densities are influenced to a higher extent by the distance to the main city centre than by distances to lower-order centre.

Observing the maps, the influence of the Finger Plan on Copenhagen's urban pattern becomes clear. In fact, there is a clear concentration of jobs and most of all,

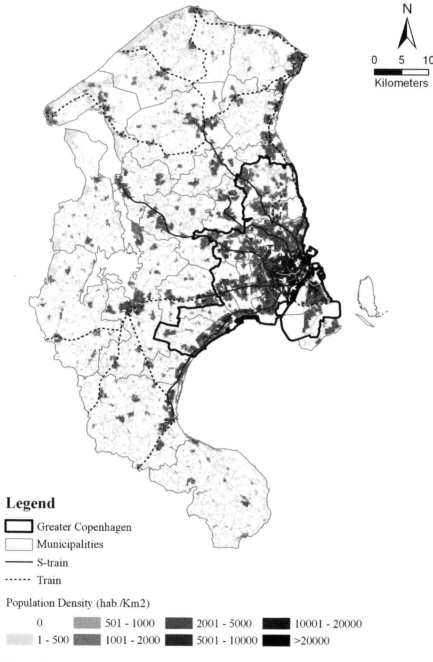

Figure 4.11   Population density in Copenhagen Metropolitan Area
Data Source: DST, 2009.

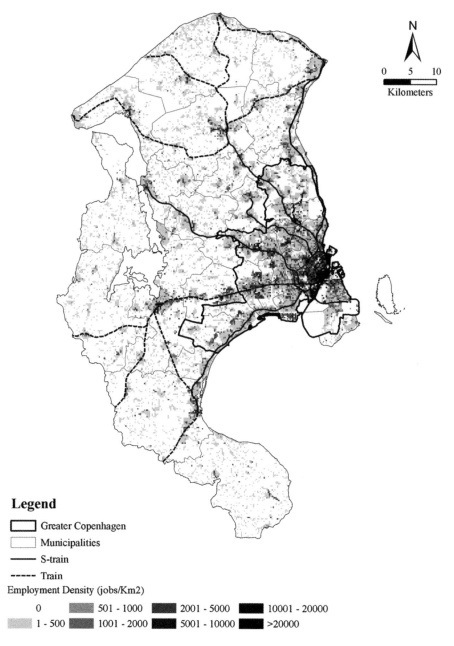

Figure 4.12   Employment density in Copenhagen Metropolitan Area
Data Source: DST, 2009.

of population along the five fingers defined by the Finger Plan. Moreover, the maps show a high concentration of population and jobs (especially the latter) in Copenhagen's city centre.

Contrarily to several other European cities, whose inner core has lost most of its dominance due to population and job decentralization during the last decades, Copenhagen's urban core is still the dominant centre of the metropolitan region. The Copenhagen Metropolitan Area shows not only a high concentration of population and jobs in the centre, but also different degrees of concentration of population and employment. In fact, while there are some clusters of relatively high population density along the fingers (some decentralization of housing in second-order centres), employment is still rather concentrated in the 'palm of the hand'.

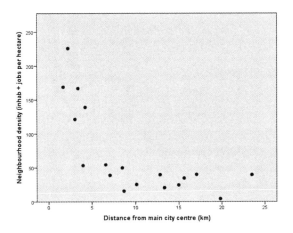

Figure 4.13   Neighbourhood densities (inhabitants and jobs per area unit) in investigated residential areas in different distances from the city centre of Copenhagen

Like many modern European cities, Greater Copenhagen has a trade and business structure dominated by service and knowledge industries, with a sharply declining number of jobs in manufacturing industries since the 1970s, most dramatically within the municipality of Copenhagen. Distinct from many cities in the USA, where mainly low-income groups populate the inner parts, there is no centre-periphery income gradient among the investigated residential areas of Greater Copenhagen (Pearson's r = 0.030). On the other hand, inner-city residents tend to have higher education than their outer-area counterparts, with a correlation coefficient of −0.356 between education level and the distance from the dwelling to the city centre. In contrast to some other European cities (including Oporto) where there is an over-representation of pensioners in the inner districts, inner-city dwellers in Copenhagen are on average younger than their suburban counterparts (Pearson's r = 0.285), and the proportion of pensioners is somewhat lower (Pearson's r = 0.154).

Compared to the previously published studies of residential location and travel behaviour in Copenhagen Metropolitan Area, the present study is, as mentioned earlier, delimited to the part of the metropolitan area consisting of the municipalities that include the continuous urban area of Copenhagen. In the parts of the metropolitan area located outside the continuous urban area, there is a large deficit of jobs compared to workforce participants, and a high proportion of the inhabitants therefore make inward commutes. The inhabitants of the continuous urban area of Copenhagen are to a higher extent located within the part of the metropolitan area where employment and service facilities are concentrated, and commuting and other trips in daily life are not to the same extent directed inward toward the city centre, but also to other employment and service concentrations in more local centres.

According to the 2000 CORINE Land Cover (European Environment Agency, 2010), almost a third of the study area is artificial land and the discontinuous urban fabric is dominant (40 per cent). These discontinuous areas are around the city centre and in the five radial fingers. Continuous urban fabric represents only 5 per cent of the whole study area while industrial areas are 6 per cent and other artificial surfaces represent 16 per cent.

The agriculture sites represent 19 per cent and are mainly located in the south between the 'fingers'. They are mainly non-irrigated arable lands. Forestland is the third most common land use (following artificial land and agriculture sites). These areas are more common in the north of the study area. Water bodies represent 2 per cent of Greater Copenhagen and wetlands are only 1 per cent. They are both more common in the north. Figure 4.14 and Figure 4.15 replicate this information graphically.

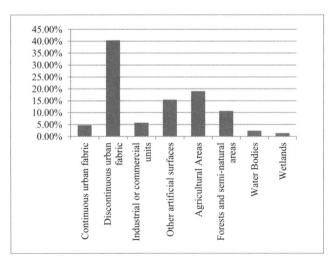

Figure 4.14 Percentages of different land use categories in Greater Copenhagen

Data Source: European Environment Agency, 2007.

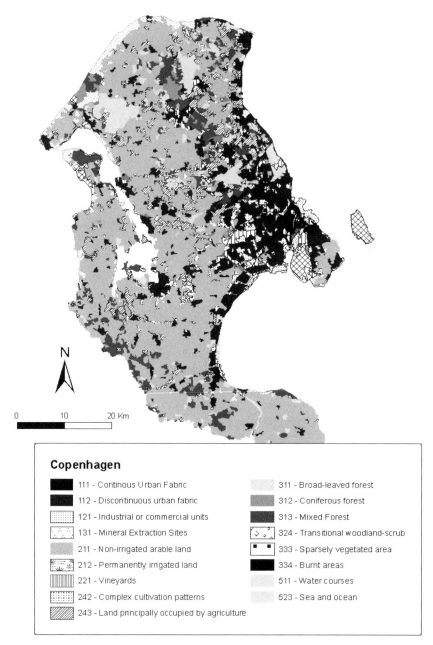

Figure 4.15   Greater Copenhagen land use in 2000
Source: European Environment Agency, 2007.

Characterization of Transport Infrastructure and Travel Behaviour

The 'Finger Plan' was, once more, a basic tool to shape the Copenhagen Metropolitan Area transport network, and the rail network was also an important element for land use planning, a perfect example of transit oriented development (Curtis et al., 2009). Copenhagen has a high railway capacity and an average highway capacity, when compared to other European cities. It has also a large bus network and a recently built underground system.

Figure 4.16 provides an overview of the Greater Copenhagen transport network for different modes of travel. The motorway network is denser in the borders of the 'palm of the hand' with one ring road and several radial motorways mainly near the fingers.

The rail network is divided into the S-train network (for suburban trains) and the train network with national and international links. The S-train network is in the basis of the 'Finger Plan' and its routes are in the centre of the fingers. The train network also uses the same corridors but it reaches more peripheral areas in Zealand. It also links Copenhagen to Malmö by the Øresund Bridge and to other regions in Denmark.

The underground network (Metro) has a common section which crosses the city centre from north to south and then it is divided in two different lines towards the southern suburbs and the airport. The bus network is very dense in the study area and encompasses several routes that stretch outside it, covering all the Copenhagen Metropolitan Area. Contrarily to the S-train network, these outer routes do not follow strictly the fingers pattern.

The construction of the Øresund Bridge (finished in 2000) had great impact on the transport system. The Copenhagen airport is now linked to southern Sweden, and new urban developments are expected in the southern suburbs of Copenhagen, including the placement of an extra finger to Orestad New Town according to the most recent version of the 'Finger Plan' (Knowles, 2012).

When we look at the Copenhagen's modal split we conclude that walking and cycling together have roughly the same share as the private car. Public transport has lower shares than other European cities (only 11.2 per cent) possibly due to the very high share of walking and, especially, cycling. These figures refer to proportions of the total number of trips. If instead proportions of the inhabitants' total travelling distance are measured, the shares accounted for by walking and cycling are smaller.

Despite the important use of both sustainable modes of transport, car is, by itself, the most common mode of transport used in daily trips (Figure 4.17). Concerning travel purpose (Figure 4.18), most of trip destinations are leisure related places (35.5 per cent), followed by workplaces (27.1 per cent), shops (25.9 per cent), places of education (6.8 per cent) and others (4.6 per cent) (DTU Transport, 2006).

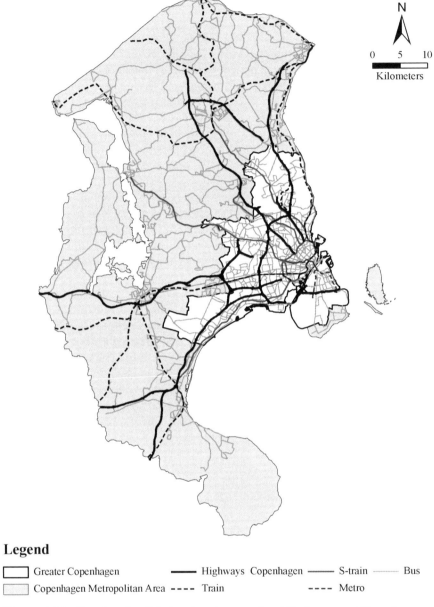

Legend

☐ Greater Copenhagen ▬▬ Highways Copenhagen ▬▬ S-train ⋯⋯ Bus

▨ Copenhagen Metropolitan Area ▬ ▬ ▬ Train   ▬ ▬ ▬ Metro

**Figure 4.16   Road and rail infrastructure and public transport lines in
            Copenhagen Metropolitan Area and in Greater Copenhagen**

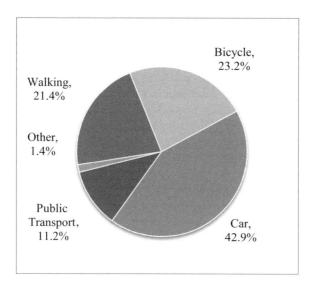

Figure 4.17   Modal share in Greater Copenhagen

Data Source: DTU Transport, 2006

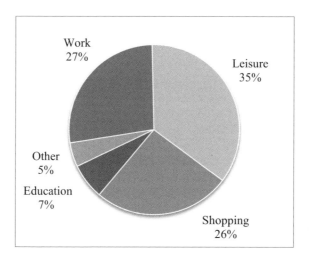

Figure 4.18   Purpose of trips in Greater Copenhagen

Data Source: DTU Transport, 2006.

Spatial and Traffic Development

Worldwide as well as in Europe, urban dispersal has been a dominant trend since the Second World War (see, for example, Bruegmann, 2005; Iamtrakul and Hokao, 2012). In many European city regions, spatial urban expansion has slowed somewhat down during recent decades compared to the 1950s and 1960s (Kasanko et al., 2006), but in the post-communist Eastern Europe urban sprawl has, on the other hand, been particularly prominent. Against this general backdrop of ongoing urban dispersal, Greater Copenhagen shows a more concentrated pattern of development.

Copenhagen Metropolitan Area has a long history of spatial urban expansion in the second half of the twentieth century, in spite of low, and for long periods even negative, population growth in the decades prior to 2000. Figure 4.19 shows how population densities have developed within the continuous urban area of Greater Copenhagen since the mid-1950s. Population densities were significantly reduced during the three first decades of this period. This coincides with high economic growth, with GDP in 1985 35 per cent higher than in 1970 (Statistics Denmark, 2010a). Since the mid-1980s, however, the drop in density has been halted.

During recent years, densification in the central parts of the region has accounted for an increasing part of the development taking place in Copenhagen Metropolitan Area. Residential development during the latest decade has taken

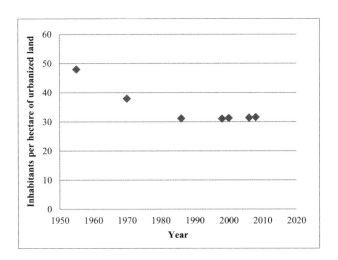

Figure 4.19   Changes in population density within the continuous urban area of Greater Copenhagen

Data Sources: Statistics Denmark, 2008; AaU Spatial Data Library, 2009; MOLAND project, 2010.

place closer to the city centre, compared to the preceding decades, and especially in the two core municipalities (Copenhagen and Frederiksberg) the population density has increased. The tendency of more central locations also applies to workplace development. Even though considerable development has taken place outside the continuous urban area of Greater Copenhagen, the tendency of re-urbanization and density increase – or at least reduced sprawl – is also evident when looking at the metropolitan area scale.

Table 4.1 and Table 4.2 summarize how a number of spatial, demographic, economic and transport variables have developed over the periods 1996–2008 and 2000–2008, respectively. The analysis of growth in urbanized land covers the period 2000–2008. This growth has been measured within the whole geographic demarcation of Copenhagen Metropolitan Area, thus including Greater Copenhagen as well as smaller urban settlements outside the main city (AaU Spatial Data Library, 2009). The analysis of traffic growth covers the period 1996–2008, divided into two equally long sub-periods. The indicator for growth in car traffic refers to average traffic volumes along 14 main roads within the geographical limits of Copenhagen Metropolitan Area (Statistics Denmark, 2010b).

Table 4.1   Development of key demographic, socioeconomic, political and other urban variables in Copenhagen Metropolitan Area from 1996 to 2008

Year	1996	2002	2008
Metropolitan population (millions)	1.722	1.807	1.857
Greater Copenhagen population (millions)	1.110	1.136	1.154
Population within core municipality (millions)	0.477	0.501	0.510
Share of population within core municipality	27.0%	27.4%	27.5%
Annual floor area constructed per capita during preceding six-year period (m²)		0.73	0.95

continued

Table 4.1   *(concluded)*

Year	1996	2002	2008
Length of motorway and motor traffic road lanes completed during preceding six-year period (km)		122	30
Length of railway and metro lines completed during preceding six-year period (km)		56	32
Percentage of car-owning households		44%	50%
Road traffic volume index (1996 = 1000)	1000	1208	1325
Index for NO$_2$ pollution in the inner city (1990 = 1000)	800	890	800
Regional GDP index (1996 = 1000)	1000	1127	1296
Regional GDP per capita index (1996 = 1000)	1000	1093	1234
National political regime during preceding six-year period		Social democrats	Conservative / liberalist
Political regime in core municipality during preceding six-year period		Social democrats / left	Social democrats / left

Table 4.2   Changes in the size of urbanized land, metropolitan population and urban population densities in Copenhagen Metropolitan Area from 2000 to 2008

Year	2000	2008
Size of urbanized land (km^2) within metropolitan area	630	645
Metropolitan population (millions)	1.807	1.857
Urban population density (persons per hectare of urbanized land)	27.43	27.66

According to the European Environmental Agency (2006: 12) the annual growth in built-up areas in Copenhagen Metropolitan Area was about 1.8 per cent in the period from the 1950s to the1960s, while the pace had been reduced to 0.8 per cent annually in the period from the 1980s to the 1990s. In spite of this reduced pace of spatial urban expansion, Copenhagen Metropolitan Area had the ninth highest percentage of annual growth in built-up areas in the period from the mid-1980s to the late 1990s (1997/1998) among the 24 investigated metropolitan areas (ibid.: 12, 51). During the latest decade, this tendency has been reversed, at least within the continuous urban area of Copenhagen. For Copenhagen Metropolitan Area as a whole, the size of the urbanized land increased by only 0.31 per cent annually between 2000 and 2008, corresponding to a population density increase from 27.4 to 27.7 persons per hectare of urbanized land, i.e., by 0.9 per cent. Within the continuous urban area of Copenhagen, the population density increased by 1.1 per cent during the same period. In the parts of the metropolitan area located outside the continuous urban area of Copenhagen, development has predominantly taken place as spatial urban expansion. The considerable density increases that have taken place in Copenhagen and the surrounding municipalities nevertheless represent an important departure from the dominant trend within the metropolitan area until the 1990s.

Copenhagen has made considerable investments in a new Metro, but substantial road capacity increases have also taken place. Much of the construction of transport infrastructure (motorways as well as rail lines) has taken place as part of a large-scale transport infrastructure project, namely the Øresund connection between Copenhagen and Malmö. Together with the low-density development in the outer areas the motorway construction has contributed to a steady and rapid growth in car traffic. During the period 1996–2008, car traffic within Copenhagen Metropolitan Area increased on average by 33 per cent. Adjusted for population growth, the increase was 23 per cent, whereas public transport decreased by 7 per cent. It should be noted that the growth rate for car traffic has been reduced from 2.4 per cent per year in the period between 1996 and 2002 to 1.1 per cent annually in the period between 2002 and 2008.

Moreover, the amount of bike travel has increased considerably, facilitated by a continual improvement of a bike network that was probably Europe's best already in the 1980s. According to the Municipality of Copenhagen (2011), 55 per cent of commuting trips (to job or education) carried out by inhabitants in the Municipality of Copenhagen are nowadays carried out by bike (including commuting trips to other municipalities).

Planning Strategies

Denmark had until 2007 a hierarchical land use planning system where national plans were binding for regional plans adopted by the counties, while municipal plans (master plans as well as local development plans) had to be in accordance with the regional plans. If a lower-order plan deviated from a higher-order plan, this could only be approved if an adjustment was simultaneously adopted to the higher-order plan. Since 2007 this hierarchical system has been abolished. The 14 counties were then replaced with five regions, and so were the regional land use plans. Instead, the new regions are obliged to adopt so-called regional growth and development plans. These plans include no land use control but instead focus on how each region can be made more competitive in the globalized economy.

Since 2007, the Danish municipalities have thus had a much more autonomous position in land use planning than they used to have earlier, opening up for a stronger focus in the plans than earlier on local concerns of business development and the attraction of 'good taxpayers' than on the protection of regional or national environmental interests. In some parts of Denmark this has led to increased competition between municipalities and resulted in a sprawling pattern of development along the main transport arteries, such as in the 140 km-long functional urban region of East Jutland (of which Aarhus is a part). There is, however, one important exception from this decentralization of land use planning authority: Copenhagen Metropolitan Area. Here, key aspects of land use are regulated through a national planning directive entitled Finger Plan 2007.

National land use policies in Denmark since the 1990s have aimed at counteracting urban sprawl but have not focused very explicitly on compact city development. Rather, the focus has been on decentralized concentration, with guidelines by the Ministry of the Environment recommending urban development in the Copenhagen region to be located close to urban rail stations as the clearest example. This policy is in line with long-standing ideals in Danish urban planning, where the Finger Plan of Copenhagen Metropolitan Area has through six decades had an almost iconic status. However, market agents have sometimes pushed for 'greenfield' development at locations poorly served by public transport in the outer parts of the region. Inter-municipal competition for inward investments has often implied that such demands have been accommodated. This competition, combined with the availability of large vacant areas released for urban expansion long ago, has made it difficult for higher-level authorities to maintain the national objectives of decentralized concentration of office and residential development close to urban rail stations. Land-consuming urban development in the outer parts of the metropolitan area has also been encouraged by the fact that outward urban expansion in the Copenhagen region usually requires low infrastructure costs. In addition, the designation in the original Finger Plan of the open land between the 'urban fingers' as areas for non-development has not been backed by strong recreational interests, at least not in the outer areas. Farmland is ample in Denmark, and converting some of it into building sites has not been considered a serious loss (Næss et al., 2009, 2011).

Building on a continuation of the urban developmental principles of the famous Finger Plan prepared for the Copenhagen Region in 1947, the Finger Plan 2007 sets limits to urban sprawl and requires residential development and new office workplaces to be located in proximity of urban rail stations. Similar regulations also existed in the regional plans issued by the counties (four of which belonging fully or partly to Copenhagen Metropolitan Area) until 2006, but the Finger Plan 2007 has sharpened those regulations and given them the status of a national directive. Among other things, requirements have been set concerning the scheduling of development within the urban zone areas, with first priority given to areas close to stations, as a remedy to prevent scattered development all over the oversized developmental areas.

There has also increasingly been a market demand for more intensive land use within existing urban areas in the central parts of the region, reflecting, among other things, cultural trends and changes in the household structure. During the latest decade the amount of such development has outweighed low-density housing and low-rise commercial development. There is, however, a widespread opinion among planners and policy-makers that the regional coordination of spatial development in Copenhagen Metropolitan Area still needs to be improved.

Whereas public transport improvement has been backed by broad political consensus, road capacity increases have been contested. In particular, there has been scepticism against urban highway development among land use planners, environmental organizations and politicians to the left. Transport authorities and planners involved in transport infrastructure development in the Copenhagen region have generally considered road development as a measure to combat congestion. Following the recommendations of the government-initiated Infrastructure Commission (2008), considerable road capacity increases are currently being planned in Copenhagen Metropolitan Area, anticipating traffic growth of 70 per cent from 2005 to 2030.

During most of the investigated period, road pricing has not been on the political agenda, but the municipality of Copenhagen has during recent years been acting as the spearhead of a coalition of municipalities putting pressure on the national government in order to allow the introduction of this demand management instrument (Næss et al., 2009, 2011).

Greater Oporto

Oporto, located in the northwest of Portugal, is the country's second largest city. Our study area – Greater Oporto – has approximately the same area and population as Greater Copenhagen. It can be considered the labour market basin of Oporto.

Greater Oporto (GO) has not a specific administrative body. It encompasses six different municipalities (Gondomar, Maia, Matosinhos, Oporto, Valongo and Vila Nova de Gaia, represented in Figure 4.20) with politically independent local administrations; each one is responsible for its local policies, including land use planning. Vila Nova de Gaia is the one with the largest area and the highest population, and Oporto the one with the smallest area but with the highest population density. Greater Oporto covers a hilly territory with altitudes from the seaside level to 450m on the east. Its coastline is more than 31 km long, and it partially includes the downstream basins of the rivers Leça and Douro.

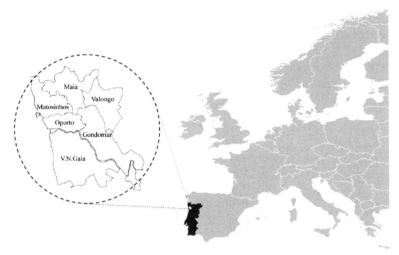

Figure 4.20   Europe, Portugal, Greater Oporto and its municipalities
Source: Silva, 2008.

Population

According to the National Statistics Institute (INE, 2014) the actual resident population of Greater Oporto is 1,113,950 inhabitants. Since 1960 the GO population has increased in a consistent way (Figure 4.21). However, this increase was higher in the first two decades (around 40 per cent) than in the period 1960–2008 (15 per cent).

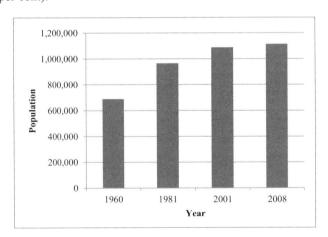

Figure 4.21   Evolution of the number of inhabitants in Greater Oporto
Data Source: INE, 2014.

The increase of population occurred mainly in the outer parts of Greater Oporto. Oporto municipality lost more than 80,000 inhabitants between 1981 and 2008 while all the other five municipalities saw their population increase in every period (Figure 4.22). This growth is slowing down in the last years.

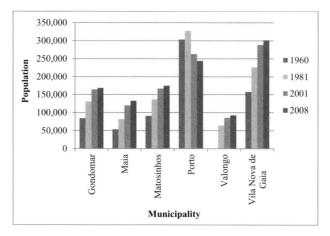

Figure 4.22   Evolution of the number of inhabitants in each Greater Oporto municipality

Data Source: INE, 2014.

The population pyramid of this area is quite constrictive (Figure 4.23). There is a low birth ratio and the great majority of the population is between 30 and 50 years old. The rate of natural increase is getting lower and the net migration rate is now negative. So, in the near future, the number of inhabitants may decrease.

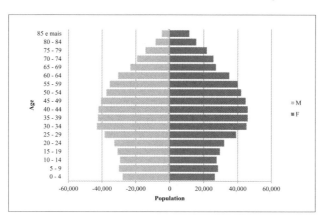

Figure 4.23   Distribution of the population of Greater Oporto between age groups

Data Source: INE, 2014.

Socioeconomic Conditions

As Greater Oporto does not constitute a formal statistics region, there is no data about its Gross Domestic Product (GDP). The available data is for the corresponding NUT III region which comprises five more municipalities but all of them with considerably less inhabitants than the six ones of our study area.

In this larger region, between 1995 and 2008, the GDP has risen from 11.708 million euros to 20.226 million euros, which is an increase of almost 73 per cent (Figure 4.24).

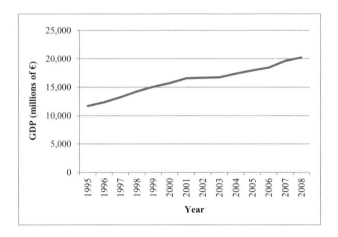

Figure 4.24   Evolution of the GDP (millions of euro) in Greater Oporto
Data Source: INE, 2014.

We can divide the evolution of the GDP in three distinct periods. The first one from 1995 to 2001 where it grew more than 4 per cent per year, including a maximum of 7.6 per cent between 1997 and 1998. The second period comprises 2001, 2002 and 2003 when the economy stalled. In the last period, GDP grew but to a less extent in the first period (below 4 per cent per year, except 2006–2007). These periods can be seen in Figure 4.25.

The GDP per capita has also grown during these years, and to a higher extent due to the population increase. In any case, this growth was lower than the national average. In 1995 Greater Oporto's GDP per capita was €9.800, well above the national average, but in 2003 the national average was already slightly above the study area average. After that, the Greater Oporto GDP per capita has remained near the national value (Figure 4.26).

In fact, between 2001 and 2003 the GDP per capita in Greater Oporto fell 0.8 per cent, mainly in the first year. This recession period was only felt in this area and did not happen at regional and national level (Figure 4.27).

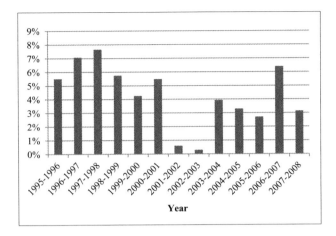

Figure 4.25   Yearly variation of the GDP growth
Data Source: INE, 2014.

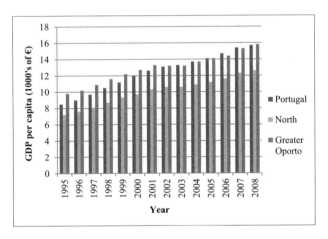

**Figure 4.26   Evolution of GDP per capita (1000s of euro) between 1995 and
2008 in Portugal, North Region and Greater Oporto**
Data Source: INE, 2014.

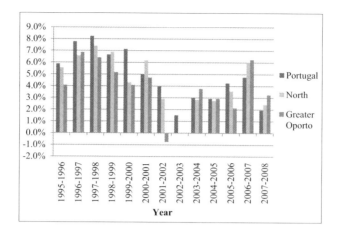

Figure 4.27   Yearly variation of the growth in GDP per capita in Portugal, North Region and Greater Oporto
Data Source: INE, 2014.

This weak economic performance had impacts on the labour market. The unemployment rate in Greater Oporto in 2008 exceeded 16 per cent, while the Portuguese rate was near 13 per cent, and the North of Portugal rate near 14 per cent (Figure 4.28).

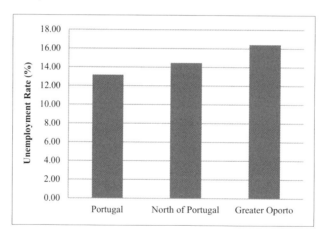

Figure 4.28   Unemployment rates in 2008 in Portugal, North Region and Greater Oporto
Data Source: INE, 2014.

The unemployment rate inside Greater Oporto varied between 14 per cent in Maia and 18 per cent in Vila Nova de Gaia. We can see that the two municipalities with the highest unemployment rates are the ones with the highest number of inhabitants – Oporto and Vila Nova de Gaia. It is also visible that the municipalities with lower unemployment are in the North of the study area and the ones with higher unemployment are in the South (Figure 4.29).

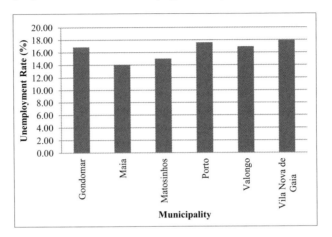

Figure 4.29   Unemployment rate in Greater Oporto municipalities
Data Source: INE, 2014.

Looking to the economic sectors, the areas with the highest gross value added are trade, and finance, consultancy and real estate. The service sector is undoubtedly the strongest sector of the Greater Oporto economy (Figure 4.30).

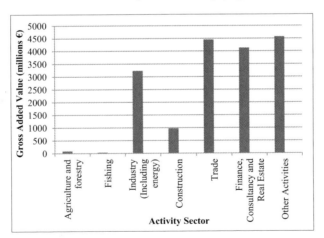

Figure 4.30   Gross value added (millions of euro) in Greater Oporto
Data Source: INE, 2014.

The average income figures for Greater Oporto are in line with national values. Oporto is the municipality with the highest average monthly income per inhabitant, followed by Matosinhos and Maia. The eastern municipalities have the lowest incomes (see INE, 2014). Indeed, the significant differences between municipalities reflect a prevalent socioeconomic divide between the western and the eastern part of the Oporto metropolis. Nevertheless, Greater Oporto is still one of the most important urban areas of Portugal. This small area includes more than 10 per cent of the population and of the GDP of the country.

The purchasing power in Greater Oporto is slightly higher than the Portuguese average (with a reference value of 100). In a similar way to what happened with the metropolitan economy, during the last decade the Greater Oporto purchasing power has been dropping down from 130 to 111 (Figure 4.31).

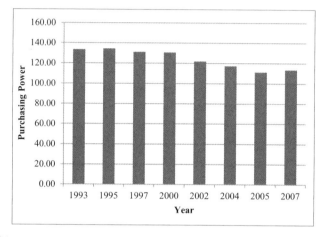

Figure 4.31   Purchasing power in Greater Oporto
Data Source: INE, 2014.

This loss occurred mainly in the core municipality of Oporto where in 1995 the purchasing power was above 250 and in 2009 it had dropped to 177. The population of all the other municipalities has maintained its purchasing power, which is above the national levels (100) with the exceptions of Valongo and Gondomar. Again, it is apparent that the population living in the eastern zones of Greater Oporto have a significantly lower purchasing power (Figure 4.32).

The inhabitants of the inner parts of Oporto have on average lower education levels than their suburban counterparts (Pearson's r = 0.104), and their income is also on average lower (Pearson's r = 0.098). In contrast with Greater Copenhagen, there is a certain over-representation of pensioners in the inner districts of Oporto (Pearson's r = −0.166), and the inner-city dwellers in Oporto are also on average older than their suburban counterparts (Pearson's r = −0.200).

Despite some demographic indicators are sowing an aging population the number of inhabitants has grown in the last decades but it is not clear that this trend will continue in the future.

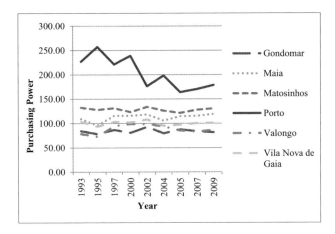

Figure 4.32   Evolution of purchasing power in Greater Oporto
**   municipalities**
Data Source: INE, 2014.

In the overall, the economic performance of Greater Oporto is, on average, higher than the country levels but in the last decade its relative importance came down. Currently, Greater Oporto is not a region that is pulling the country's economy anymore, but a region that is gradually being overtaken by other regions in the country.

As we have also seen there are several asymmetries inside this area. The socioeconomic wealth of the Northern and the Western areas is higher than in the rest of the metropolitan region. On the other hand, the core of Greater Oporto is clearly losing population and it is the part of the study area that contributes more to the metropolitan ageing.

Characterization of Land Use

With regard to land use Greater Oporto is a polycentric territory with a core area with higher density than the second order centres. According to the 2006 CORINE Land Cover (European Environment Agency, 2010), artificial surface makes up around 43 per cent of the area. The majority of this artificial surface is a discontinuous urban fabric mostly in the areas that surround Oporto city centre. The continuous urban fabric makes up only 6 per cent of the study area and it is situated mainly in the centre but also in some second order centres. The other artificial surfaces are more common in the west side of Greater Oporto.

Forestlands occupy 32 per cent of the area and are mainly located in the eastern parts of the study area, in the municipalities of Valongo and Gondomar. It is also possible to see smaller forest areas in the northern and southern peripheries of Greater Oporto.

Agricultural lands cover 23 per cent of the area with a strong presence in the northern municipalities and small and scattered pocket areas throughout the rest of the metropolitan area. Water bodies, in which the river Douro is included, make up only 2 per cent of this territory. Figure 4.33 summarizes this data and Figure 4.34 shows the geographical distribution of the various land use categories referred to in the text.

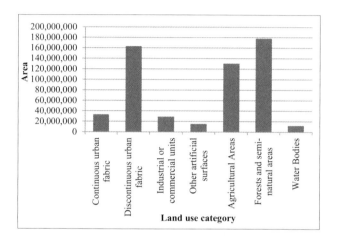

Figure 4.33   Areas of land use categories in Greater Oporto
Data Source: European Environment Agency, 2010.

The city of Oporto is clearly the municipality with the highest number of jobs, almost 200,000, for a city population of approximately 240,000 inhabitants (in 2011). In this context, and although significant circular movements between surrounding municipalities are becoming noticeable in recent years, radial commuting to work is still prevalent in the entire metropolitan area.

Population as well as employment densities (see Figure 4.35 and Figure 4.36[1]) are clearly higher in the central zones of the core municipality, an area framed by the internal ring-road motorway and the Douro River. Similar to Copenhagen Metropolitan Area, there is a clear centre-periphery gradient in the density of population as well as jobs in the Metropolitan Area of Oporto (see Figure 4.37).

Although, historically, Greater Oporto has a more polycentric urban structure than Greater Copenhagen, the correlation between the distance to the city centre and the combined job and population density in the local neighbourhoods of the investigated residential areas (see below) is in fact even higher in Greater Oporto (Pearson's $r = -0.801$) than in Greater Copenhagen (Pearson's $r = -0.724$). Densities are also strongly correlated to proximity to the main regional retail centres and to second-order centres. However, local area densities are influenced

---

1   All full-page maps are presented at the scale of 1:200,000.

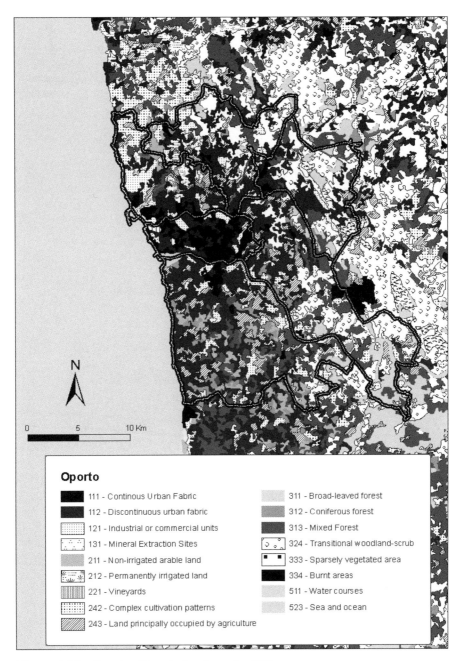

Oporto

111 - Continous Urban Fabric

112 - Discontinuous urban fabric

121 - Industrial or commercial units

131 - Mineral Extraction Sites

211 - Non-irrigated arable land

212 - Permanently irrigated land

221 - Vineyards

242 - Complex cultivation patterns

243 - Land principally occupied by agriculture

311 - Broad-leaved forest

312 - Coniferous forest

313 - Mixed Forest

324 - Transitional woodland-scrub

333 - Sparsely vegetated area

334 - Burnt areas

511 - Water courses

523 - Sea and ocean

Figure 4.34   Greater Oporto land use in 2006
Source: European Environment Agency, 2010.

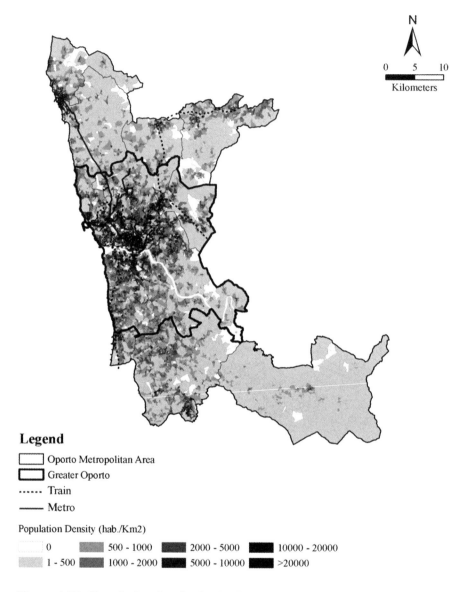

Figure 4.35   Population density in the Oporto Metropolitan Area
Data Source: INE, 2001.

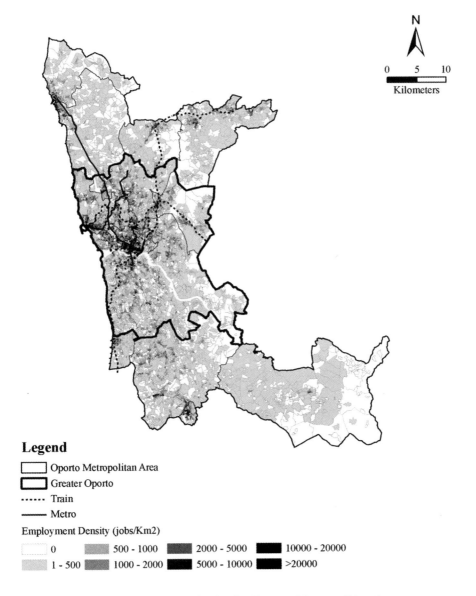

Legend

☐ Oporto Metropolitan Area
☐ Greater Oporto
······ Train
───── Metro

Employment Density (jobs/Km2)

☐ 0	▨ 500 - 1000	▨ 2000 - 5000	■ 10000 - 20000
▨ 1 - 500	▨ 1000 - 2000	■ 5000 - 10000	■ >20000

Figure 4.36   Employment density in the Oporto Metropolitan Area
Data Source: INE, 2001.

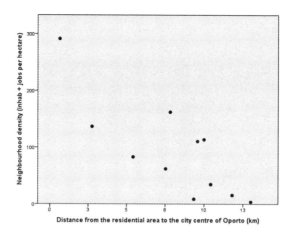

Distance from the residential area to the city centre of Oporto (km)

Figure 4.37   Neighbourhood densities (inhabitants and jobs per area unit) in investigated residential areas in different distances from the city centre of Oporto

to a higher extent by the distance to the main city centre than by the distances to the main regional retail centres and second-order centres.

As referred to before, in Greater Oporto, the employment location pattern is far more centralized than population, which, in the last decades, has steadily been spreading outwards to an external circle made of the adjacent municipalities – the typical *doughnut effect* – taking advantage of a denser and faster motorway network built in the last 20 years. These decentralization trends are also present in job location patterns however to a far lesser extent. As a result, the population of Greater Oporto is more densely concentrated in the municipality of Oporto and in a land strip surrounding this municipality and along the coastline. Other urban areas, somehow detached from this main population centre, can also be found.

Asymmetries in the employment geography are considerably greater. The central area of Oporto is clearly dominant, although several other areas with high employment densities can be found scattered across the study region. In Greater Oporto, it is possible to find some continuous urban development spreading from the central city. This continuum is no longer visible outside of these municipalities. The remaining metropolitan area includes other more autonomous urban centres scattered on periurban and rural lands. Some of these urban centres constitute the capital cities of these adjoining municipalities.

Characterization of Transport Infrastructure and Travel Behaviour

Figure 4.38 provides an overview of the Greater Oporto transport networks (road and rail). As compared to other regions in Portugal, Greater Oporto presents a very high road density. In the last decades several new motorways were built

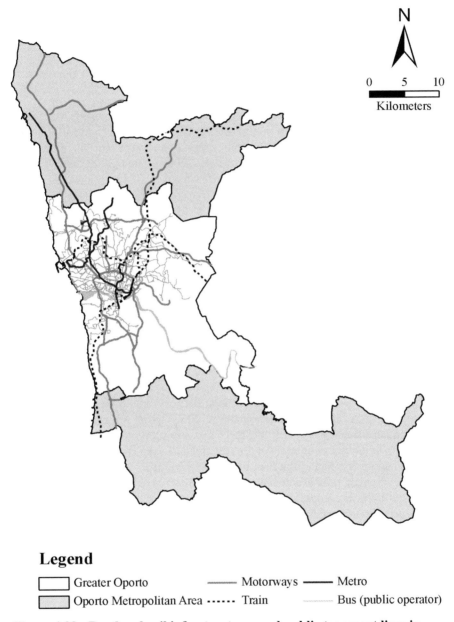

Legend

☐ Greater Oporto	—— Motorways	—— Metro
▨ Oporto Metropolitan Area	・・・・・ Train	—— Bus (public operator)

Figure 4.38   Road and rail infrastructures and public transport lines in Greater Oporto

linking the most important urban centres of the area to the national and the Iberian motorway network.

The Greater Oporto motorway network exhibits two ring roads and several radial motorways. The internal ring road, located in the municipalities of Oporto and Vila Nova de Gaia surrounds the centres of these two cities. The external ring road follows approximately the boundaries of Greater Oporto.

The rail network also underwent significant modifications in the last years. Besides the old railway system, a new and, in fact, successful light rail network was built between 2003 and 2009 with approximately 60 km (for an overall evaluation of this project see Pinho and Vilares, 2009). The light rail network has five main lines linking Oporto to Vila Nova de Gaia, Maia, Matosinhos, the airport and a municipality outside Greater Oporto, Póvoa de Varzim, in the North. Greater Oporto includes 44 km of the light rail system. In addition, the old suburban rail network crosses the study area in the north–south direction and it includes three main lines, connecting Greater Oporto to the cities of Braga and Guimarães (to the north), Marco de Canavezes (to the northeast), and Aveiro (to the south). There are also national railway connections to other important Portuguese cities like Coimbra, Lisbon and Faro.

Concerning (road) public transport, the main public operator has a 532 km long network. Oporto is the municipality best covered by bus lines. The great majority of the lines serving the outer municipalities of the study area have also their origins in the city of Oporto. The network is denser in the northern part of Greater Oporto and there are no publicly operated routes in the southern districts of Vila Nova de Gaia and Gondomar. This public network is complemented by 50 smaller private operators, which serve the areas not covered by the main public operator and some other outer municipalities of the Oporto Metropolitan Area.

Throughout the 1980s and 1990s there was a rapid increase in the use of the private car for daily trips in Greater Oporto and a corresponding fall in the use of public transport. By 2000 more than half of the main trips were made by car. The opening of the light rail system had a positive impact in curbing this upward trend of car use (Pinho and Vilares, 2009). In the last couple of years modal split figures have been relatively stable with private car representing approximately 50 per cent of the total number of trips, public transport 26 per cent and walking 20 per cent, with 4 per cent for all other transport means (Figure 4.39). Regarding travel purpose, trips to work are the most common (40.8 per cent), followed by trips to leisure destinations (21.7 per cent), education (11.6 per cent), other places (15.6 per cent) and shopping (10.4 per cent) (Figure 4.40).

According to the last mobility survey (INE, 2000) the large majority of the trips in Greater Oporto are internal trips (i.e., they have both origin and destination inside Greater Oporto), being the city of Oporto the most frequent destination. Despite the fact that radial commuting patterns are dominant, circular commuting between municipalities around Oporto is becoming more frequent.

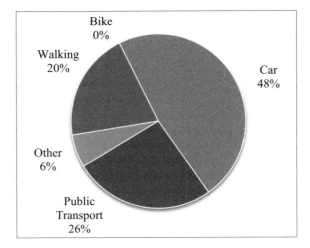

Figure 4.39 Modal split in Greater Oporto
Data Source: INE, 2000.

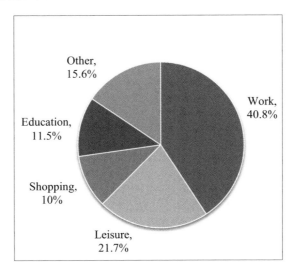

Figure 4.40 Trip purpose in Greater Oporto
Data Source: INE, 2000.

The Spatial Planning System

The Portuguese planning system is a typical plan-led system operating at three distinct levels: national, regional and municipal. On a regional perspective, Greater Oporto belongs to the Northern Region (including 86 municipalities), one of the five administrative regions (NUTS 2) in which Portugal mainland is divided. The corresponding regional body, the Northern Region Coordination and

Development Commission, is a decentralised body of the central administration with some responsibilities and competences in environmental policy, spatial planning and regional economic development. This Commission is responsible for the preparation and implementation of the Regional Spatial Plan, a strategic plan designed to act as a general framework for municipal plans and local planning policies. At the time of writing this plan, prepared some five years ago, is still waiting for the final approval by the central government. This is possible because the regional tier of the Portuguese planning system is not backed by a political regional authority elected by the population. Indeed, only the Islands of Madeira and Azores have autonomous regional administrations. This situation leads to a stronger influence of both the central and the local municipal governments on planning policies and, on comparative terms, a weaker regional intervention.

In this context, planning policies in Greater Oporto tend to be fragmented among its different municipalities. Coordination between these (municipal) policies and a common and overall metropolitan vision are clearly lacking. In practice, Greater Oporto consists of a continuous urban area that is divided by six different plans with different and, often times, competing objectives and spatial strategies.

Oporto is the only municipality in this area that has a long history of land use planning. Indeed, urban planning is a common practice since the nineteenth century. In the twentieth century, several important municipal master plans (1952, 1962, 1993) had been prepared and implemented, and the plan currently in force dates from 2005. In the other five municipalities, and apart from older urban development plans, the first municipal master plans were approved in the mid-90s and are still in force. At present the majority of these plans are under major reviews and updates. In the cases of Vila Nova de Gaia and Maia the new versions of these master plans have already been ratified by central government, others, such as Valongo, are in the final public participation stages before approval.

Due to the huge population growth in the municipalities surrounding Oporto, particularly in the 1980s and 1990s, the master plans approved in the last decade of the twentieth century were oriented towards the accommodation of urban growth. This fact along with the inexistence of a metropolitan or regional land use plan providing an overall view of this vast and dynamic territory, and the lack of the necessary coherence and articulation between and among the different municipal master plans, led, inevitably, to urban sprawl and to the steady depopulation and decline of the historic centre of Oporto.

In the absence of a proper metropolitan administration backed by an independent political authority, a Junta Metropolitana was created and has been operating for the last few decades; however, with very limited powers and scarce technical and financial resources. The Junta is basically an association of the municipalities (at present 14) that makes the so-called Greater Metropolitan Area of Oporto. Similarly to the Copenhagen case study, our study area – Greater Oporto – is the core of this greater metropolitan area, and is made of the six most central municipalities, which constitute, nonetheless, the second most important employment basin of the country, after Greater Lisbon.

Copenhagen and Oporto in Comparison

Greater Oporto and Greater Copenhagen show, as one would expect, both differences and similarities. From a geographical point of view, these two metropolises are very similar, both in area and population: Greater Copenhagen has about 1.2 million inhabitants living within an area of 542 km^2, while Greater Oporto has about 1.1 million people and a surface of 563 km^2. Therefore, population density is, on average, only slightly higher in Greater Copenhagen (Table 4.3).

Table 4.3   Surface and population in the two study areas and in each metropolitan area

Oporto Metro Area	Greater Oporto		Greater Copenhagen	Copenhagen Metro Area
1574	563	Area (km^2)	542	3132
1.6 million	1.1 million	Population	1.2 million	1.8 million
1016	1936	Mean population density (persons per km^2)	2218	593

However, the metropolitan regions spanning from these two study areas are quite different. Copenhagen Metropolitan Area is larger, both in area and in population. In fact, Copenhagen is a larger city than Oporto and it is the capital city with, consequently, a higher and wider range of services and functions.

In Oporto 94 per cent of trips are made within the study area whereas the proportion of internal trips in Greater Copenhagen is lower at 81 per cent. Figure 4.41 shows the two study areas – Greater Copenhagen and Greater Oporto – as well as the respective metropolitan areas, represented in the same spatial scale.

Greater Copenhagen inhabitants have higher incomes and more purchasing power than Greater Oporto inhabitants. This is true both in general terms and in comparison to their respective countries.

The age group composition shows similarities. Both areas follow the trend of many Western Metropolitan Areas with the population getting older.

Both study areas have new metro systems and fairly large and comprehensive bus networks. The Copenhagen rail network is much bigger and denser, covering almost the entire metropolitan area. The Oporto rail network only has three main lines (north, east and south) nonetheless complemented by a larger and fairly efficient light rail system.

In both areas the car is still, by far, the most used means of transport. In Oporto the share of this mode is slightly higher than in Copenhagen. The main differences in the travel behaviours are in the use of the other modes. In Copenhagen non-motorized transport has an important share (walking and cycling, together, are more used than the car) while the Oporto population uses public transport more frequently (mainly bus and metro). Train trips are more common in Copenhagen.

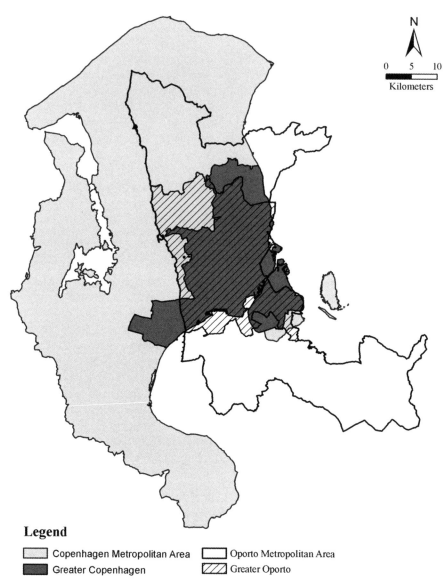

Legend

Copenhagen Metropolitan Area   Oporto Metropolitan Area

Greater Copenhagen   Greater Oporto

Figure 4.41   The overlay of the two study areas

Although the Greater Oporto is commonly recognized in the literature as an example of a polycentric metropolis and the Copenhagen Metropolitan Area is normally seen as monocentric, none of these study areas appear to suit entirely any of these theoretical models. In fact, we can argue that, nowadays, there are no completely or pure polycentric or monocentric cities but, as Martens (2006) suggests, all metropolitan regions have some levels of 'monocentrism', 'polycentrism' and 'dispersion' (see Figure 2.3 in Chapter 2), so they should be classified considering the relative importance of these three dimensions.

The polycentric roots of the Greater Oporto date back to the second half of the nineteenth century, with the relatively decentralized location of the industry in some peripheral areas. The concentration of employment in these areas, associated with the lower housing costs – due to the extensive provision of inexpensive land and the absence of land use regulation – fostered the household settlement in these areas (Breda-Vásquez, 1992). However, the development of a service-based economy during the second half of the twentieth century promoted the prominence of the Oporto urban core as the main employment and population centre, leading to a more monocentric form.

During the last decades, though, Oporto has been experiencing a decentralization process, characterized by the migration of population and tertiary employment towards the peripheral municipalities. This process of suburbanization, however, is leading to an expansion of the central area to its vicinities, assuming the shape of an 'urban ring', rather than creating a traditional polycentric pattern. The growing importance of the circular commuting patterns between the peripheral municipalities is a result of this process.

We could argue, then, that the Greater Oporto has a particular type of polycentricism in a smaller spatial scale, in which several centralities can be found within a metropolitan core of relatively high density. These centralities encompass the inner city centre (currently losing strength), the surrounding municipalities that have recently experienced a population and employment growth, creating a ring of developing areas surrounding Oporto's municipality, and a few more peripheral centres, such as Maia and Valongo, with still some relative importance within the entire metropolitan area.

Conversely, Copenhagen Metropolitan Area – traditionally seen as a highly centralized urban structure – has experienced a decentralization process which is more extensive in area (partially due to a faster and heavier transport system based on railways) and, simultaneously, more concentrated around secondary centres (as a consequence of restrictive land use polices), leading this monocentric metropolis towards a more polycentric urban shape.

In fact, clusters of relatively high population density can be found along the fingers, showing housing and activity decentralization into second-order centres. Yet, employment density is still higher in the 'palm of the hand'. Copenhagen Metropolitan Area can, then, be characterized as hierarchic, with the city centre of Copenhagen as the main centre; a number of 'second-order' centres – among others the towns of Roskilde, Køge, Hillerød and Helsingør – that concentrate some regional-oriented retail activities and services; and also some more local centres that have emerged in the vicinity of railway stations (Næss, 2006a).

Regarding the study area – Greater Copenhagen – this decentralisation phenomenon is not so clear because Greater Copenhagen corresponds just to the central part of the metropolitan region, encompassing the 'palm of the hand' and only the first part of the 'fingers'. However, the strongly hierarchic structure and the influence of the Finger Plan's principles are still visible in Greater Copenhagen, where the dense metropolitan centre along with some secondary centralities concentrating both population and jobs are evident (see Figure 4.11 and Figure 4.12).

We can say then that the main differences between the urban structure of these two urban regions is not only the dominant monocentric or polycentric form they exhibit but also the fact that Copenhagen has a much clearer structure of urban centralities than Oporto, with a strong city centre and several second order centres along five urban corridors. Population and activities are concentrated throughout these centralities and the public transport system is coherent with this structure it helped to build and to consolidate.

Oporto, on the other hand, has a more complex urban structure with a strong centre but a more sprawled urbanization pattern – frequently emerging along the road network and the main intersections – and strong second order centres mainly due to administrative functions. Indeed, the structure of centralities is not as evident as in Copenhagen when we look at the geographical distribution of population, employment and other activities.

These differences in urban structure reflect different planning traditions and different administrative structures. While the Greater Metropolitan Area of Oporto is divided into 14 different municipalities, which have their own plans and land use planning policies, Copenhagen Metropolitan Area consists of 34 municipalities, with a common and clear planning strategy in the 'Finger Plan'. The Portuguese metropolis still does not have a common strategy despite a few attempts in the past (e.g., the Plano Regional do Porto) to prepare a regional plan that was never officially approved, let alone implemented.

The differences are also reflected in socioeconomic terms. While in Copenhagen, young people and people with higher levels of education tend to live in the centre, in Oporto, the residents of central areas are predominantly old people with low incomes and a low level of education. The residents with the highest incomes live in Oporto municipality but also in areas outside the historical centre, namely in Antas and Boavista-Foz (on the coastline).

Chapter 5
The Structural Accessibility Layer[1]

Cecília Silva

The Structural Accessibility Layer (SAL) provides a geographical representation of comparative accessibility levels by types of transport modes to different types of travel generating opportunities (Silva, 2008). This tool is based on the concept of Structural Accessibility (Silva and Pinho, 2010) assessing how urban structure constrains travel choices. By urban structure we refer to the land use and transport system. This tool uses activity-based accessibility concepts (for a review see Geurs and Eck, 2001), analyzing the ability to reach the main travel generating activities from a given origin, i.e., analyzing how the urban structure enables or disables people to fulfil everyday travel needs and what choices they have to fulfil those needs. Thus structural accessibility reveals which travel choices are made available to inhabitants by the urban structure, in what could be referred to as potential travel behaviour.

The Structural Accessibility Layer uses two measures: the *diversity of activity index* and the *accessibility clusters*. The diversity of activity index (see pp. 81–4) is used to measure the accessibility level by different transport modes. Accessibility clusters (see pp. 84–7) use the results of the first measure to develop a comparative analysis of accessibilities by these transport modes and hence assess which travel choices are made available by urban structure. The application of these measures to any case study requires a number of choices (discussed in detail on pp. 87–90) to make the SAL operational for analysis of local accessibility conditions. A discussion of the theoretical potentials and limitations of the SAL as an analysis and decision support tool is developed (see pp. 90–92). This chapter ends with a presentation of the set of choices used to make SAL operational for the two case study applications developed in this research.

The Diversity of Activity Index

The diversity of activity index, based on the 'dissimilarity index' of Cervero and Kockelman (1997), counts the number of activity types that one can reach from a

---

1 The SAL has been thoroughly presented and discussed in earlier publications (such as Silva, 2008; Silva and Pinho, 2010; Silva, 2013). This chapter reproduced a part of previous descriptions published in the referred publications, namely chapter 4 of Silva (2008), section 4 of Silva (2013) and section 2 of Silva and Pinho (2010).

given origin, within the number of activity types most relevant for travel demand generation. The general form of the diversity of activity index is the following:

$$DivAct = \frac{\sum_{y}(Act_{y} * f_{y})}{\sum_{y} f_{y}} \qquad [1]$$

Where, y is the activity type, Act_{y} a value representing the existence or not of the activity type y inside accessibility boundaries[2] ($Act_{y} \in \{0;1\}$) and f_{y} the potential use frequency of the activity type.[3]

This index is measured at a high spatial disaggregation level, with the study area divided into several small sub-areas. The diversity of activity index is then measured for each central point of the sub-areas (theoretically representing all potential travel origins of the sub-area). The level of spatial disaggregation is a case-specific choice in the development of the SAL and it is conditioned by the level of disaggregation of statistical data available. Spatial disaggregation should be such as to ensure the necessary detail of analysis of small-scale accessibility variation as well as the ability of central points to represent the entire sub-area (detailed discussion is found on p. 88).

The diversity of activity index is measured for each origin (one for each sub-area) and for each transport mode, namely non-motorized modes (NM), public transport (PT) and the private car (CAR). The assessment of the number of accessible activities is schematized in Figure 5.1. For each location, and each transport mode, an aggregate measure of accessibility to several activity types is produced (equation [1]). This index considers the potential use frequency of an activity in addition to the accessibility to each activity. Therefore, the access to activity types with higher frequency of use provides higher values of diversity of activities than the access to activity types with lower frequency of use. Thus, the diversity of activity index provides an average of the number of activity types accessible, weighted by the potential use frequency. The results of this index range from zero (no accessible activities) to one (all activities are accessible).

The accessibility measure of the SAL culminates in the production of three accessibility maps for the study region, one for each transport mode (NMDivAct, PTDivAct and CARDivAct). Accessibility levels of a given origin are represented by a colour scale in the sub-area of origin according to the accessibility level

---

2   This measure is based on a simplification, which considers that people choose the closest destination among the same activity type (regardless of quality, price and other personal preferences).

3   The potential frequency represents the potential use of an activity type in comparison to others, i.e., the average number of trips of a population for each activity type.

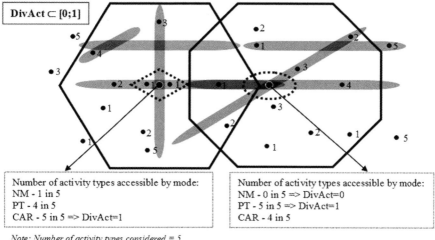

Number of activity types accessible by mode:
NM - 1 in 5
PT - 4 in 5
CAR - 5 in 5 => DivAct=1

Number of activity types accessible by mode:
NM - 0 in 5 => DivAct=0
PT - 5 in 5 => DivAct=1
CAR - 4 in 5

Note: Number of activity types considered = 5

Legend: Accessibility boundaries by ·:·: NM ⫢ PT ⬡ CAR
• 2 Location of an activity of type 2

Figure 5.1   Accessibility boundaries by transport mode drawn for two theoretical origin points[4]
Source: Silva, 2008.

available to a resident of that sub-area.[5] These geographical representations provide an overview of small-scale variations of accessibility levels to the diversity of activities by each transport mode.

An aggregate measure for the whole study area is made available by the regional diversity of accessibility index, providing an area wide average of accessibility for each transport mode, weighted by population,[6] as follows:

$$RDivAct = \frac{DivAct_i * P_i}{P} \qquad [2]$$

Where, $DivAct_i$ is the diversity of activity index for a given transport mode of the origin representing a spatial unit i, P_i is the population resident in the spatial unit i, and P the regional population.

---

4 Public transport boundaries are represented by continuous linear areas, to simplify the scheme; in reality they are a set of, approximately, circular areas around public transport stops of accessible routes.

5 In contrast to ordinary accessibility measures, where accessibility is generally represented by the limit of the accessibility area.

6 This is possible because accessibility is measured for a limited number of potential origin points and these points represent an approximate value of accessibility of all points in its spatial unit because of high spatial disaggregation of the measure.

The range of formulations used for the diversity of activity index is presented in Table 5.1.

Table 5.1   Formulations of the diversity of activity index

	NM	PT	CAR
Sub-area	$NMDivAct_i$	$PTDivAct_i$	$CARDivAct_i$
Study area	NM_RDivAct	PT_RDivAct	CAR_RDivAct

Source: Silva, 2008.

Accessibility Clusters

The *accessibility clusters* provide a comparative measure of accessibility levels by transport mode. These group land use and transport conditions favouring the use of the same transport mode (or modes). The use of a particular transport mode is considered to be favoured by land use and transport conditions when accessibility levels are perceived to be high by that particular transport mode, i.e., when an acceptable range of activities can be reached making its use competitive in comparison to the other modes.

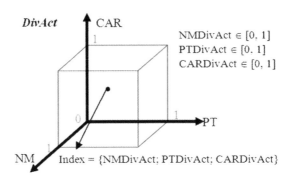

Figure 5.2   Potential combinations of accessibility values by three transport modes
Source: Silva, 2008.

The definition of accessibility clusters requires therefore the definition of the perception of high accessibility levels. This is brought about by *accessibility classes* which divide the theoretically unlimited combinations of accessibility levels by each transport mode, represented in the three dimensional (NM, PT, CAR) range of the diversity of activity index (Figure 5.2). Besides high accessibility (class A) the SAL uses two further classes, medium accessibility (class B) and low accessibility (class C), dividing the range of the diversity of activity index for the three transport modes into 27 *accessibility categories* (Figure 5.3). The use of accessibility classes aims to simplify the analysis of individual accessibility levels and, in addition, to facilitate the comparative analysis by developing a limited number of analysis categories (27). Accessibility class limits are defined, for each application, according to local perceptions of minimum accessibility requirements for each class (i.e., the amount of activities that should at least be accessible from any particular origin for accessibility to be considered high and medium). It is important to note that perception of accessibility is considered to depend solely on the amount of activities that can be reached and that, therefore, the same limits are considered for all transport modes. As a result, accessibility categories represent the different conditions provided by the land use and transport system for travel behaviour, with regard to potential choice of transport mode.[7] Clusters group these categories into nine groups. Clusters I to VII group land use and transport conditions favouring the use of the same transport mode (or modes).[8] For instance, cluster I provides land use and transport systems that enables high accessibility levels by non-motorized modes and solely by this mode, since accessibility levels by public transport or by car are, at most, medium or low (class B or C). This increases the competitiveness of this mode in comparison to the other and therefore the propensity to be used. Clusters VIII and IX group land use and transport conditions unable to provide high accessibility levels by any transport mode. These provide, at most, medium or low accessibility by any transport mode, respectively.

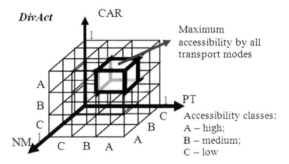

Figure 5.3   Benchmarking cube and accessibility classes by transport mode

Source: Silva, 2008.

---

7   For instance, if car and public transport provide higher accessibility class then walking, these transport modes are more competitive solutions and are, therefore, more likely to be used (providing the car is available). Therefore, the accessibility cluster reveals which transport mode is made more competitive by land use and transport conditions and therefore which transport mode is favoured for use choice.

8   For instance, cluster II represents land use and transport conditions favouring non-motorized modes and public transport use since accessibility levels by these two transport modes are high.

The 27 accessibility categories and the nine accessibility clusters are presented in Figure 5.4.[9] In this figure, accessibility categories are numbered from 1 to 27 and presented inside the benchmarking cube (one for each smaller cube). The nine clusters are numbered from I to IX and represented by the nine shades of grey of the benchmarking cube.

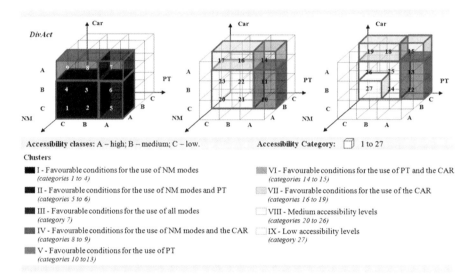

Accessibility classes: A – high; B – medium; C – low.   Accessibility Category: ⬜ 1 to 27

Clusters

■ I - Favourable conditions for the use of NM modes
(categories 1 to 4)

■ II - Favourable conditions for the use of NM modes and PT
(categories 5 to 6)

■ III - Favourable conditions for the use of all modes
(category 7)

■ IV - Favourable conditions for the use of NM modes and the CAR
(categories 8 to 9)

▨ V - Favourable conditions for the use of PT
(categories 10 to13)

▨ VI - Favourable conditions for the use of PT and the CAR
(categories 14 to 15)

▨ VII - Favourable conditions for the use of the CAR
(categories 16 to 19)

⬜ VIII - Medium accessibility levels
(categories 20 to 26)

⬜ IX - Low accessibility levels
(category 27)

Figure 5.4   Benchmarking cube and accessibility clusters
Source: Adapted from Silva (2008).

The benchmarking cube works as a synthesizing measure aggregating a large amount of the conditions given by the land use and transport system for potential mobility (specifically mode choice) to be sustainable. This measure enables the development of a geographical representation offering an overview of small-scale variations of relative competitiveness of transport modes, proving an instrument for the understanding of urban structure constraints on mobility choices. This geographical representation is done through a single aggregate map where different comparative accessibility conditions are represented through accessibility clusters.

Besides the usefulness of the benchmarking cube for the analysis purpose of the SAL (as synthesizing measure) it can also be used in decision support. With regard to the decision support role of the benchmarking cube, it can be used as a framework for the selection of accessibility objectives (among the accessibility categories and clusters) and as a framework for policy action choice. The selection of accessibility objectives is supported by the comparison of the current position

---

9   The figure represents the same benchmarking cube three times to provide a clear view of all categories and clusters, by representing three different slices of the cube.

and other potential position in the benchmarking cube (considering levels of comparative competitiveness between transport modes). It provides a support for the choice of objectives by defining a concrete and limited number of relative competitiveness for each transport mode, defined by the clusters. The selection of policy action (necessary to attain desired objectives) is supported by the benchmarking cube through: first, by supporting the development of different strategy and policy scenarios to bring about previously defined objectives; and second, by testing the outcomes of the developed scenarios. With regard to the former, the SAL supports the identification of major land use and transport features requiring action to attain the desired position in the cube (objective). This results from a direct relationship between the change of position in the benchmarking cube and specific variations in mode accessibility. These variations in accessibility by mode can be brought about by a variety of land use and transport policies. Thus, the SAL provides a somewhat objective relationship between relative competitiveness of transport modes and land use and transport features. This enables the development of strategy and policy scenarios to bring about the required changes in urban structure. With regard to the latter aspect of the framework for policy action choice, policy action scenarios can then be tested on the SAL for their ability to attain the desired change. The choice of concrete policy action from the variety of measures able to attain desired objectives is based on local political, social and economic constraints. At this stage the SAL works as a measurement instrument, assessing the results of potential policy action.

The intermediate step of strategy and policy development, although following general guidance from the results of the category map, must be based on further information. Guidance provided by the SAL is limited to its scope (land use and transport constraints on sustainable mobility) based on the assumption that, if urban structure conditions enabling mobility are not provided, sustainable travel behaviour cannot be brought about. Mobility management must consider a variety of complementary information for policy choice. The range of essential complementary information required for the development of land use and transport measures for mobility management should be locally defined for each case. It is important to highlight that policy action scenarios are not a direct result of the SAL, neither does the SAL develop strategies itself. Instead, SAL works as a framework of thought for the development of integrated land use and transport policies for mobility management.

Local Choices Required for Implementation of SAL

The SAL was conceived to be responsive to local conditions and perceptions of accessibility. Therefore, several aspects will have to be locally defined for each application in order to make SAL operational in the local context. These case-specific choices are summarized in Figure 5.5. This section presents some general recommendations for the development of a case-specific SAL.

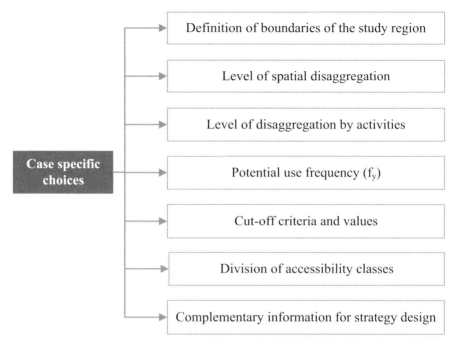

Figure 5.5　Case-specific choices
Source: Silva, 2008.

The exact **boundary of the study region** is the first aspect that has to be defined for each application of the SAL. The region must be wide enough to encompass the main potential mobility patterns of an urban agglomeration. The object of the SAL is travel behaviour enabled by urban structure and not real travel patterns. The study region must essentially comprise internal travel patterns (there are always some residual cross, entry and exit patterns). The choice of the study region should therefore be based on real travel behaviour, covering regional accessibility catchment areas.

The level of **spatial disaggregation** is another case-specific choice in the development of SAL. Spatial disaggregation is conditioned by the level of disaggregation of statistical data available in each case. Nevertheless, considering the soundness of the measure,[10] spatial disaggregation should be at least at the census track level (or even grid based, using cells of, at most, one square kilometre). Spatial disaggregation directly influences the soundness of the measure through both the detail of spatial data and the ability of the central point (potential origin) to be an adequate representation of the entire spatial unit.

While the disaggregation of transport mode is conceptually defined, the choice of **activity types** (and of the activities considered for each activity type) is case-

---

10　Soundness regards the detail of accessibility variations as well as the ability of central points to represent the entire spatial unit.

specific. Chosen activities should provide the most faithful portray of local travel demand (having to take into consideration statistical data constraints). In general, activities considered to have the most influence on travel behaviour are work, school, leisure and free-time activities, shopping, healthcare and other public and private services. Activity types should include these basic activities and, at least, at this disaggregation level. The use of more activity types or of higher disaggregation of the same activity types, provide a higher detail of land use conditions. The choice of activities to be included should rely on local data of the main travel generators.

Each application of SAL requires the definition of the **potential use frequency** of these activities (f_y). In order to enhance the soundness of the measure, this choice should be based on the knowledge of local travel behaviour, for instance, the percentage of trips per purpose. Therefore, and with regard to soundness, the choice of activity types to be included is also dependent on the data availability for the potential use frequency.

The use of a contour accessibility measure requires the definition of **cut-off criteria** and **respective values**. The cut-off criteria generally used are time and cost. The choice of each of these criteria as well as their values will have to be defined based on the knowledge of local travel behaviour. In the absence of this information, stated or revealed preference surveys may provide information for these choices. Table 5.2 shows some examples of time and cost cut-off criteria using the disaggregation by transport mode proposed by the SAL.[11]

Table 5.2   Examples of cut-off criteria

	NM	PT	CAR
Time	Walking time	Total travel time In-vehicle time Access time (to and from PT) Waiting time Walking interchange time Waiting interchange time	Total travel time Walking time (to and from the car) Parking time
Cost	Land slope Ratio between grid distance and straight line distance Existence of obstacles	Distance at interchange Comfort/quality Price	Total travel price (considering travel distance, petrol price, tolls, maintenance, parking, etc.) Price of tolls Parking price

Source: Silva, 2008.

---

11   Further detail may be used disaggregating cut-off criteria by activity type, since accessibility limits may vary across activity types. This choice is also case-specific and adds value to the soundness of the measure. Nevertheless, increased soundness should be balanced against increased costs and efforts.

Some of the examples presented in Table 5.2 can be included in each another. For instance, total travel time for public transport includes waiting time. Nevertheless, both may be used simultaneously for the same measure. For instance, people may consider destinations with total travel time, by public transport, higher than 30 minutes as inaccessible and simultaneously not consider the use of public transport if waiting time is higher than 10 minutes (with 10 minutes being included in the 30 minutes travel time).

The choice of the criteria for each case, as well as the maximum value of the criteria, is therefore a very important issue. Still, the balance between soundness and plainness of the measure must be considered for this choice.

The **division of accessibility classes** is one of the last choices in the development of a case-specific SAL. The limits of these classes should make the meaning of the accessibility classes operational, translating the local understanding and perception of high, medium and low accessibility levels.[12] These can be chosen involving experts on local mobility, land use, transport and mobility management.[13] Furthermore, the dispersion of spatial units' accessibility in the cube can be used to calibrate class limits. In any case, class A should be as narrow as possible to, first, ensure proximity of accessibility values in this class, thereby enabling high comparability between transport modes and, second, enhance the meaning of the accessibility clusters I to VII (which provide class A accessibility by at least one transport mode).

Finally, the range of **complementary information** required for the development of land use and transport measures for mobility management should also be locally defined. Complementary information must be chosen according to the local context as well as to the general purpose of policy design. Some examples of complementary information are population and employment distribution and density, land use and transport constraints, mobility patterns, as well as socioeconomic and political constraints. As have been referred to before, the SAL does not directly produce policy action scenarios; neither does it develop strategies by itself. Instead, the SAL works as a framework of thought for the development of integrated land use and transport policies for mobility management.

Theoretical Potentials and Limitations of the SAL

This section provides a brief discussion of the theoretical potentials and limitations of the SAL as an analysis and design support tool (Figure 5.6). This discussion will look at the contribution of a number of theoretical choices made during the

---

12   Therefore, accessibility class limits are the same for all three types of transport modes.

13   For instance, identifying the activity types which could be absent for a high accessibility level and defining the values of the class limit as the percentage of the potential use frequency (f_y) of the remaining activities.

development and analyse their individual contributions for the potential and limitation of the SAL.

The SAL is built upon the following main conceptual choices:

- geographical representation of measures;
- regional analysis scope (considering small scale variability);
- use of a simple accessibility measure;
- consider high disaggregation level of the land use and transport conditions;
- use of a single aggregate measure of comparative accessibility; and
- leave several aspects to be defined for each context of application.

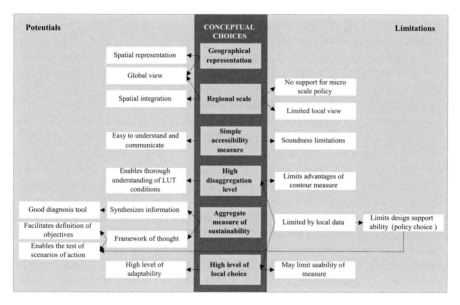

Figure 5.6   Potentials and limitations of the SAL
Source: Silva, 2008.

As has been mentioned before, the geographical representation of the results of accessibility clusters is used to enable the essential spatial comparison of accessibility levels. Furthermore it provides a global view of the entire territory in analysis. This measure has the advantage of supplying an image of the variability of how land use and transport conditions constrain mobility choices.

The SAL is conceptually defined for the regional scale. It is therefore not based on administrative divisions of the territory giving a view of mobility catchment areas. It is at this level that mobility policy must be defined and implemented. This approach enables the spatial integration of mobility policy, besides the integration of policy sectors (namely land use and transport) for which the SAL has been developed. On the other hand, the choice of the regional scale disables the support of the design of local, street level, actions. As a result, this tool excludes micro scale aspects of mobility such as urban design. Therefore, and in spite of the geographical representation of small-scale variations of accessibility levels, the SAL provides a limited local view.

The choice of a simple accessibility measure to baseline the development of the SAL is related to the potential given by these measures with regard to the ease of understanding and communicating the process and its results. As this is considered a requisite for the development of practical design support tools, aspects such as competition effects and accessibility decay with distance were not considered for the conceptual framework of the SAL.

The high disaggregation of land use and transport conditions (considering activity types and transport service) is used to enable a thorough understanding of local land use and transport constraints for mobility. This is naturally a fundamental feature of the SAL considering that this tool was developed with the aim of supporting the design of integrated land use and transport policies (Silva, 2008). Detail on existing conditions is therefore essential, although the extent of this detail is chosen for each case (and naturally dependent on the concrete objective of use of the SAL). Nevertheless, the choice of the level of disaggregation of land use and transport conditions is limited by the availability of local data (especially considering the high spatial disaggregation required). This is an important limitation of the SAL with regard to the soundness of the tool, threatening local applicability of the measure. The soundness of the SAL is limited not solely regarding its analysis purpose but also, and more importantly, regarding its design support purpose. The level of detail of land use and transport data used for the calibration of the accessibility measure influences the ability of the SAL to test certain policy scenarios. For instance, if parking effort is not considered for the car accessibility measure, the effect of parking management policies cannot be tested using the SAL. On the other hand, considering parking effort in car accessibility may require a high detail of data and the use of more complex measures (for instance generalized cost) to calibrate accessibility.

The use of one single (and simple) comparative accessibility measure represents one of the main advantages of the SAL as both, analysis and design support tool. For the analysis purpose, the use of accessibility clusters provides a synthesizing measure of land use and transport conditions constraining mobility choices. The benchmarking cube enables the combination of a variety of information and its analysis in a workable and understandable way. Therefore, the geographical representation of the accessibility categories and clusters potentially provides a good diagnosis tool.

For the design support purpose, the benchmarking cube is a potential framework for the development of integrated land use and transport policies. It facilitates the definition of objectives for sustainability of potential mobility and serves as a framework for policy action choice in order to attain desired accessibility objectives. Nevertheless, the ability to test action scenarios is limited by the detail used in the accessibility measure.

The choice to leave several aspects to be defined for each context of application was made in order to give the SAL a high level of adaptability to local conditions, which is essential for any policy design support tool as well as any accessibility measure.

Nevertheless, additionally to other limitations related to local choice presented before, the amount of choices required for the calibration of the SAL, as well as the potential controversy around these choices may limit the usability of the SAL. Lack of agreement around choices may hinder its application while disagreement with choices made during the calibration of the SAL may limit its use as a design support tool for mobility policy.

Case-Specific Applications

A number of choices are required for the application of the SAL to any case study. This section summarizes the main case-specific choices made for the application to Greater Copenhagen and Greater Oporto regarding the following aspect: spatial disaggregation for analysis level, disaggregation of activities and values of potential use frequency for the diversity of activity index, cut-off criteria (i.e., accessibility limits), and, finally, accessibility class limits.

Both case applications use a highly detailed spatial scale, with sub-areas of about 0.06 km². This enables high detail of spatial variations in accessibility conditions provided by the land use and transport system. In addition, it enables the analysis of accessibility conditions of each sub-area to be measured form its centroid. For Greater Copenhagen, sub-areas where defined based on a 250 × 250 m grid (approximately 0.06 km²).[14] Greater Oporto was disaggregated into census track sub-areas ranging from 125 m² to 6 km², and an average of approximately 0.06 km². Larger sub-areas (exceeding 1 km²) are rare resulting from areas with very low population density, therefore having a low constraint on the application of the SAL.

The application of the SAL considered a broad list of travel generating activities, namely, employment, schools, leisure, shopping, healthcare and other activities. The Portuguese case study used a total of 18 activities while the Danish used 15. There was an agreement between Portuguese and Danish researchers on the activity types to be included nevertheless differences in activity types were constrained by statistical data in each country. Activity types are presented in Table 5.3 and Table 5.4 including the aggregation used for both cases applications.

---

14   Only 33,378 of the total grid of 50,109 sub-areas of CMA were calculated. The remaining 16,731 correspond to sub-areas excluded for verifying simultaneously both the following conditions: no population and no access to road infrastructure (corresponding to cells whose centroid is more than 200 m away from the nearest road). These areas will from now on be referred to as non-urban (NU) areas.

Table 5.3   Activity types and frequency of use for Greater Oporto

Activity types		Activity Type	CAE[1]	Days in a month[2]	Percentage of trips[3]	f_y
Schools	Infant school and Elementary school	1	801	33%	12	4
	High school	2	802	45%		5
	University	3	803	22%		3
Leisure/ Entertainment	Parks, public gardens, squares	4		8	22	8
	Restaurants	5	553, 555	2		2
	Cinema	6	921	2		2
	Shows/theatre	7	923	2		1
	Sport	8	926	8		8
	Others (e.g., museums, libraries, night clubs, etc.)	9	521, 925, 927	2		1
Shopping	Food	10	521, 522	4	10	8
	Others	11	521, 524, 525, 526, 527	1		2
Healthcare	Pharmacies	12	523	1	15	2
	Hospitals and clinics	13	851	1		2
Other Activities	Public/municipal administration offices	14	751, 752, 753, 853	1		2
	Postal office	15	641	1		2
	Banks	16	65	1		5
	Others (ex: Insurance, Lawyers, Architects, financial advisers, etc.)	17	66, 67, 93	2		2
Employment	Employment	18		21	41	41

[1] CAE provides the Portuguese classification of economic activities. See details in section Table A.1.
[2] In case of school activities instead of presenting the days in a month the activity is engage, this table presents the percentage of student in each level since the number of days per month a student is at school is the same for all school levels. For more detail see Annex A2.
[3] INE (2000).
Source: Silva, 2008.

Table 5.4   Activity types and frequency of use for Greater Copenhagen

Activity types		Activity Type	NACE/DB03[1]	Days in a Month[21]	Percentage of trips[2]	f_y
Schools	Infant school and Elementary school	1	801000	18%	7	1
	High school	2	802000	66%		5
	University	3	803000	16%		1
Leisure/ Entertainment	Parks, public gardens, squares	4		12	35	18
	Restaurants	5	553009	3		5
	Cinema	6a	920000	8		12
	Shows/theatre					
	Sport					
	Others (e.g., museums, libraries, night clubs, etc.)					
Shopping	Food	10	158120 521100 522000	12	26	21
	Others	11	522909 524109 524409	3		5
Healthcare	Pharmacies	12	523000	1	5	1
	Hospitals and clinics	13	851100 851209	1		1
Other Activities	Public/municipal administration offices	14	751100 751209 752000	1		0.5
	Postal office	15	640000	1		0.5
	Banks	16	651000 652000	2		1.5
	Others (e.g., insurance, lawyers, architects, financial advisers, etc.)	17	660000 741100 742009	1		0.5
Employment	Employment	18			27	27

[1] NACE/DB03 provides the Danish classification of economic activities. See details in Annex A1.
[2] DTU-Transport (2006).
Source: Reis, 2009.

These tables also present the potential use frequency of activities f_y considered in the measurement of the diversity of activity index. This correction factor was based on real local travel behaviour data, namely on the distribution of trips by travel reason. Again disaggregation for both case studies was dependent on the data available in each case. According to the Portuguese National Institute of Statistics (INE, 2000; see Figure 4.40) trips of the Greater Oporto population were mainly related to work activities (41 per cent). The Danish Technical University (DTU-Transport, 2006; see Figure 4.18) found far less relevance for employment related travel in Greater Copenhagen (less than 30 per cent), with leisure being the most frequent travel generating activity (35 per cent). In Greater Oporto, leisure produces the second highest value of trips (22 per cent) although considerably lower than in Copenhagen. In both study areas, working and leisure hold around 60 per cent of travel purposes with the remaining 40 per cent divided between school, shopping and other activities.

Again here, differences between travel behaviour in both areas are very clear. Greater Oporto presents about the same amount of trips for all three travel purposes while in Greater Copenhagen, shopping is clearly dominant, with a quarter of trips. In order to define the values of the potential frequency of use of activities (f_y), the distribution of trips by travel reason were disaggregated according to activity types considered to be included in each travel reason.[15] Despite differences in the relevance of travel purpose between study areas the research team agreed on similar values for 'days in a month' by activity type for both cases. Independent of the average frequency of use the relative frequency within the same activity group (namely, school, leisure, shopping, employment and others) was considered similar.

The transport modes considered for each mode type are walking and bicycle for non-motorized modes, public and private collective transport (including road and rail) for public transport modes and the private car for car transport modes. Among non-motorized modes, only walking was considered for Greater Oporto; bicycles were not considered since local data on road slope were not available. Topography is generally considered as one of the main limitations to cycling in the GO. This data constraint considerably limits the soundness of the accessibility measure for the bicycle in this case study since GO is highly declivous. In these conditions, the bicycle was excluded from the analysis of non-motorized modes for this case study. For public transport all routes of the public road transport (STCP in GO and Movia in GC) and some routes of the private road transport operators in Greater Oporto[16] were considered. In addition, all rail, metro and light-rail routes were considered in both case studies.

15　For detail on distribution by activity types of the percentage of trips by travel reason, see Annex A2.

16　Among private road transport routes only 90 of approximately 250 existing private routes were considered due to lack of availability of GIS-based layout for the remaining routes.

Table 5.5   Total travel time cut-off values

	NM	PT	CAR
Total travel time cut-off value (min)	20	45	30

Source: Silva, 2008.

With regard to cut-off criteria, all three transport mode types use the criterion of total travel time (Table 5.5). These values were chosen for Greater Oporto based on the real average travel time by transport mode measured in 2000 (INE, 2000)[17] and considered to be similar for Greater Copenhagen in accordance with our Danish research partners. For the definition of the boundaries of accessibility by public transport, further detail was used, besides total travel time. For this transport mode, accessibility boundaries were also considered to be dependent of: walking time at entrance and exit of public transport system; the number of acceptable interchanges; the acceptable increase of travel cost with interchange; the acceptable walking distance at interchange; the acceptable waiting time at interchange; and, the total time from entrance to exit of the public transport system (Table 5.6).[18]

Table 5.6   Cut-off criteria and values for the public transport

Cut-off criteria	Value
Total travel time	45 min
Total time from entrance to exit of the public transport system	30 min
Walking time at entrance and exit of public transport system	5 min + 5 min
Number of interchanges	2
Increase of travel cost with interchange	€0
Walking distance at interchange	100 m
Waiting time at interchange	5 min

Source: Silva, 2008.

17   This study identified an average of 14, 24 and 35 minutes for walking, car use and public transport use for the study region. It seems reasonable that admissible travel time is higher than real average travel time. Based on this fact and on personal awareness, values in Table 5.5 were estimated to be slightly higher than real average travel time.

18   This limit was introduced due to GIS software limitations (network analyst of the ArcGIS 9.2), not being able to perform multi-criteria accessibility analysis. This led to the use of a combination of instruments in a complex sequence. In order to reduce complexity, the entrance and exit of the public transport system was simplified as the approximate 400 m radius around public transport stops. Therefore, instead of using the general criteria of maximum 45 minute travel time, a 30 minute travel time limit from entrance to exit of public transport system was used (excluding 15 minutes for access and exit distance and waiting time).

Total travel time is composed of the total time from entrance to exit of the public transport system (30 min), of walking time at entrance and exit of public transport system (5 + 5 min)[19] and of an average of 5 minutes waiting time at entrance of the public transport system.[20] The total time from entrance to exit of the public transport system includes the in-vehicle time as well as potential interchange waiting and walking time (5 + 1 min for each interchange). Interchange was only allowed to routes presenting maximum headways of 10 minutes[21] in order to grant an average maximum waiting time of 5 minutes at interchange.[22] Finally, assuming that any increase in travel price would be considered unacceptable,[23] interchange was only allowed between routes of public and private operators using the new integrated travel ticket in Greater Oporto called 'andante'. In Greater Copenhagen the whole pricing system is already integrated leaving no restrictions for transfer regarding travel price.

Finally, accessibility classes were defined for the following values of diversity of activity index:

- class C (low accessibility): ranging from 0 to 0.5;
- class B (medium accessibility): from 0.5 to 0.85 in Oporto and from 0.5 to 0.9 in Copenhagen; and
- class A (high accessibility): from 0.85 to 1 in Oporto and from 0.9 to 1 in Copenhagen.

The choice of the two values working as threshold of the three classes (0.5 and 0.85 in Oporto and 0.5 and 0.9 in Copenhagen) was based on the case-specific

---

19   Considering the generally used criteria for the catchment area of public transport stops of 400m, and an average walking speed of 5 km/h, it is reasonable to presume access and exit walking time to be around 5 min.

20   An average waiting time was considered for all public transport service instead of a waiting time of half the headway for each route because of required simplifications of the public transport accessibility problems due to limitations of the GIS technology used (network analyst of the ArcGIS 9.2). It seems reasonable to use 5 minutes as an average waiting time, considering both headway based routes and timetable based routes. In the first case because the majority of routes have headways of 10 minutes or less and in the second case because with timetable based routes people are expected, on average, to arrive 5 minutes earlier.

21   Exception was made for interchange to the s-bahn and metro in Copenhagen, to the light-rail in Oporto and to the train system in both cases. In case of the light-rail (Greater Oporto), s-bahn and metro (Greater Copenhagen), people were expected to render as acceptable higher interchange waiting times than 5 minutes. In case of the train, people were expected to know the timetable of the train service and therefore choose the public transport access service most suitable for interchange.

22   In accordance with the value found by Silva (2004) as limiting the acceptability of interchange in public transport service (for the STCP network).

23   Also based on the conclusions of Silva (2004).

diversity of activity index (activity types chosen and the potential frequency of use of each activity type). Furthermore, the dispersion of sub-regional results in the accessibility cube was also taken into consideration.

Following the recommendation stating that the accessibility class A should be as narrow as possible, its lower limit was defined in the Oporto case study for a diversity of activities index of 0.85. This value was defined based on the cumulative value of the potential frequency of use of each activity type not considered to be necessary at local level (walking distance), namely, activity types 3, 5, 6, 7, 9, 11, 15 and 17. These define 15 per cent of activities (considering the potential frequency of use) and thereby limit the accessibility class A to 0.85. In the case of Copenhagen activities 3, 5, 11, 15 and 17 were not considered necessary for a sub-area to have high accessibility level. The main difference to Oporto is the consideration of some leisure activities (namely activity 6a)[24] as necessary for high accessibility, justified by the higher proportion of leisure trips in Copenhagen.[25] In this case, the excluded activities define 12 per cent of the potential frequency of use, justifying the choice of 0.9 for the limit to accessibility class A (Figure 5.7).

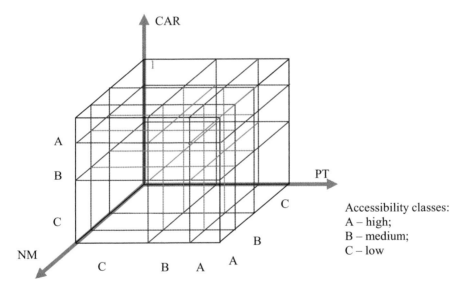

Figure 5.7   Case-specific benchmarking cube
Source: Silva, 2008.

24   Activity type 6a for Copenhagen includes activities 6, 7 and 9 used in the Oporto case study.

25   Contrarily to Oporto – where Employment is predominant – the activity type with the greatest proportion of trips in Copenhagen is leisure and entertainment, with 35 per cent of trips.

The value of diversity of activity index of 0.5 was found to be an acceptable upper limit for low accessibility levels in both case studies. This choice was based on the importance of employment for travel generation (41 per cent in Greater Oporto and 27 per cent in Greater Copenhagen). For this case the absence of employment and of a few other activities was considered to define low accessibility. In accordance the absence of activities accomplishing the same diversity of accessibility index (which implies a large amount of activity types) would also represent low accessibility.

Chapter 6

The Explanatory Qualitative-Quantitative Method

Petter Næss

Introduction

The so-called Explanatory Qualitative-Quantitative Method consists, as the name indicates, of a combination of qualitative and quantitative methods. It also purports to *explain* the phenomena investigated (in this case differences in travel behavioural patterns between residential areas differently located within the city/ metropolitan area and with different neighbourhood characteristics). The method thus aims at going beyond mere descriptions or identification of correlations. The purpose is to explain by documenting, in as plausible a way as possible, any causal relationships between the urban structural situation of residential areas and the inhabitants' travel behaviour. Precisely for that reason, the approach makes use of qualitative as well as quantitative research methods.

The method was first developed in a study of residential location and travel in the small Danish town of Frederikshavn (Næss and Jensen, 2004), further developed in a large and comprehensive study of the same topic in Copenhagen Metropolitan Area (Næss and Jensen, 2005; Næss, 2005, 2006a, 2006b, 2006c, 2007a, 2011), and has most recently been applied in a similar study in Hangzhou metropolitan area in China (Næss, 2007b, 2010b, 2013). All these three research studies have focused on the following research questions, of which the first could be characterized as the primary one and the following four as secondary questions:

- Which relationships exist between the location of the residence within the urban structure and travel behaviour (amount of transport and modal split), when taking into consideration demographic, socioeconomic as well as attitudinal factors?
- Does the location of the residence within the urban structure influence the range and frequency of activities in which people engage?
- On which rationales do people base their choices of activity locations and travel modes?
- Are the relationships between residential location and travel behaviour different among different sub-groups of the population?
- Is the effect of a residential situation where the need for everyday transportation is low, offset by a tendency to compensate for this by making more frequent and long trips during vacations and weekends?

In this volume the focus is on the first four of these questions, whereas the issue of possible compensatory long-distance travel will not be addressed. The latter question has been dealt with elsewhere, especially in Næss (2006c).

Urban Structures as Causes of Travel Behaviour

According to theories of transport geography and transport economy, the travel between different destinations is assumed to be influenced on the one hand by the reasons people may have for going to a place, and on the other hand by the discomfort involved when traveling to this location (Jones, 1978). By determining the distances between locations where different activities may take place, and by facilitating various modes of traveling, the urban structure makes up a set of conditions facilitating some kinds of travel behaviour and discouraging other types of travel behaviour.

The causes of travel behaviour of course also include personal characteristics of the travellers, such as age, sex, income, professional status, as well as values, norms, lifestyles and acquaintances. The emerging transportation pattern (choices of destinations, modes of traveling and trip routes) is a result of people's resources, needs and wishes, as modified by the constraints and opportunities given by the structural conditions of society.

In spite of decentralizing trends, most European cities still have a higher concentration of jobs, retail, public agencies, cultural events and leisure facilities in the historical urban centre and its immediate surroundings than in the peripheral parts of the urban area (among others, Newman and Kenworthy, 1999: 94–5). The inner and central parts of the metropolitan area include the largest supply of work opportunities, the broadest range of commodities in the shops, as well as the highest diversity of service facilities. For residents of the inner and central parts of the city the distances to this concentration of facilities will be short. Inner-city residents could thus be expected on average to make shorter daily trips than their outer-area counterparts, with a higher proportion of destinations within acceptable walking or biking distance.

Any study of the effects of urban structure on travel behaviour assumes – at least implicitly – that structural conditions have a potential to influence human actions. Ontologically and epistemologically, our study of residential location and travel in Greater Copenhagen and Greater Oporto is inspired by the philosophy of science position called Critical Realism (see, for example, Bhaskar, 1993, 1998, 2008; Sayer, 1992; Archer, 2000; Danermark et al., 2001).

Critical Realism could be regarded as an attempt to fuse important lines of thought within theory of science (e.g., hermeneutics, critical theory and realism), in opposition both to naïve empiricism and positivism but certainly also to postmodern relativism (Sayer, 1993). According to critical realism, the world exists independently of our knowledge of it, and this knowledge is both fallible and theory-laden. Moreover, what happens in the world – in nature as well as in society – is a result of causal powers working via a number of mechanisms.

Both in daily life and in science the term 'cause' is used in very different senses, for example, about a necessary condition and as a sufficient condition. Immediately, it seems clear that urban structural conditions cannot be attributed the status as a sufficient condition for a certain travel behaviour. Obviously, a number of other circumstances will play a part, among others, the wishes and preferences of the traveller, the state of her/his health, obligations of being present at specific places, and access to means of transport. It appears more reasonable to attribute urban structural conditions, e.g., the location of the residence, the status of contributory (partial) causes of travel behaviour, i.e., as one among several causes included in a causal relationship, but without the ability to produce the effect alone.

Some causal mechanisms may amplify each other while others may neutralize or reduce each other's influences. The causal powers influencing travel behaviour include, for example, the political and economic structures of society and the material structures, but also the cognitive and physical abilities of individuals. Which causal powers are relevant of course depend on which types of events we wish to explain. The causal powers have a potential to influence observable phenomena through a number of mechanisms. However, the mechanisms are only activated under certain conditions, dependent on the specific combination of influences from causal powers. Similarly, the events actually occurring (including the emerging state of things) depend on the combination of mechanisms at work in the particular situation.

Our studies are based – in line with Critical Realism – on the assumption that both structures and agents have particular properties and causal powers (Bhaskar, 1993; Archer, 2000; Sayer, 2000; Danermark et al., 2001). Apart from our natural environment, the structures surrounding us are in various ways 'socially constructed'. The 'constructs' may be physical artefacts like buildings or roads, or more immaterial structures like property relations, economic conditions or prevailing belief systems and cultural traditions. Once created, the various types of structures hold emergent powers and properties different from and beyond the aggregate sum of agential powers by which they were created. Not the least, it appears as highly reasonable to assume that material structures exert influence on human actions. These structures (e.g., roads, buildings, the natural topography) often have a high permanence, for example, the street network of the inner parts of many European cities is still characterized by the street pattern established several hundred years ago.

At the same time, the structures are being reproduced, modified and changed by human actions. Such changes most often occur gradually and slowly, but sometimes more dramatically and fast. The purpose of urban planning (as well as the knowledge production informing this planning) is precisely to influence these transformation processes in a way that is more favourable for society.

During much of the twentieth century, a dichotomy between *verstehen* (interpretive understanding) and *erklären* (causal explanation) has been a central issue in debates about the epistemological foundations, purposes and methods of the social sciences (Bransen, 2001; Lindlof, 2008). In line with this, causal explanations are sometimes contrasted with reason-explanations in the sense of explanations of 'purposeful action'. Such a reason-explanation of an action is to show that this action – according to the opinion of the acting subject – was the best means to realize her or his wishes (Føllesdal et al., 1996). In addition, the reason-explanation must show that this correspondence between action, wishes and opinions is not coincidental, and that the action was instead adapted to the wishes and opinions of the subject. It seems clear that reason-explanations are relevant in order to explain actions of traveling. As stated by Scheiner (2005: 167), 'action determinants' (including spatial frame conditions) only become relevant mediated by subjective patterns of interpretation. These interpretations therefore have to be considered by the researcher.

However, acknowledgment of the importance of interpretive understanding does not preclude causal explanations from being included as elements in reason-explanations. According to Critical Realism, reasons may be plausibly construed as causes (Bhaskar, 1998; Sayer, 2000). The dichotomy between explanation and understanding posited by classical hermeneutists like Weber and Dilthey appears to be rooted in a conception of causality as 'constant conjunction' stated by the eighteenth-century empiricist David Hume. However, as shown above, the Critical Realist conception of causality is fundamentally different from the Humean notion.

Causal mechanisms can, according to Critical Realism, involve the attitudes and knowledge resources of individuals, as well as the intersubjective production of meaning. Agents are defined in terms of their tendencies and powers, among which are their reasons for acting. Reasons are beliefs rooted in the practical interests of life. For every action there is a set of real reasons, constituting its rationale, which explains it. This does not mean that reasons are always rational, for beliefs may be false and also inconsistent. Moreover, reasons are not always followed by action, for what one wants to do may be prevented (Bhaskar, 1998).

To want something is for a human being the same as having a tendency to act in a specific manner (Johansson, 1984: 88). The want for employment is a basis for the tendency among people to seek jobs and travel to their workplaces. This want is, in its turn, strongly influenced by the wage labour system of our society and the need to earn money for subsistence.

For example, a resident of a peripheral residential area in Greater Copenhagen may choose to travel 19 kilometres by car in the morning because this action, according to the person's opinions, is the best mean to realize a wish to reach the workplace at the scheduled hour. Another person, living in the downtown area, may instead choose to ride two kilometres by bike in order to realize a similar wish. Thus, a common wish – to arrive at the workplace before the beginning of the working day – is realized by completely different means. Which mean is the best to realize a wish will depend on the conditions under which the wish is to be realized. These conditions are – along with the wishes and preferences of the actors – determinants of the actions a subject chooses to perform.

Linking Research Questions with Data

In principle, both time-series investigations (comparison of the same persons' travel behaviour before and after moving from one residential address to a different one) and cross-sectional studies (comparison of travel activity among different residents living in different geographical areas) are possible strategies in order to elucidate these issues empirically. In practice, recruiting participants of time-series investigations within this field has proved difficult, in particular due to the problems of identifying the participants and registering their travel behaviour *before* they move from the old to the new residence. Through retrospective questions it is still possible to obtain some information about possible changes in travel behaviour and activity patterns after moving from one residential location to another.

Table 6.1 provides an overview of the types of information considered necessary in order to answer each of the research questions mentioned in the beginning of this chapter (except the question about holiday trips, since this is not a topic addressed in the present volume). The table also shows the data sources used in order to acquire the desired information. In addition to trying to uncover whether, and to what extent, travel behaviour varies with urban structural conditions, a main purpose of the method is to gain more detailed comprehension of *how* and *why* such variation occurs: which are the *mechanisms* through which residential location influences transportation?

Quantitative surveys can only to a limited extent contribute to such comprehension. In order to uncover how and why urban structural conditions influence the inhabitants' travel, qualitative research methods are necessary. In particular, qualitative interviews are required to enable an answer to the questions concerning the residents' motivations and purposes for their ways of relating to their physical surroundings, notably the question about rationales for activity location and modal choice. Also for the other four research questions, qualitative interviews could contribute with deepening and more complex information than what is possible to obtain through quantitative questionnaire surveys.

However, the qualitative approach does not remove the need for quantitative analyses. Besides identifying the various causal powers and liabilities that activate the mechanisms leading to certain events, such as transport activity, there is a need for knowledge about the form of combination and proportions of causal powers and mechanisms typical for these processes. While the empirical identification of mechanisms affecting travel behaviour at the level of the individual could best be made by means of qualitative interviews, statistical analyses are needed in order to empirically identify the effects of urban structure on aggregate level travel patterns.

Among the various mechanisms involved, some of which amplifying each other and some counteracting each other's effects, we expect some mechanisms to be stronger and more common than other mechanisms. Our hypotheses and assumptions about the ways in which urban structure affects travel behaviour

Table 6.1   Research questions, information required and data sources

Research questions	Types of information required	Methods/sources for acquiring the information
Which relationships exist between the location of the residence within the urban structure and travel behaviour (amount of transport and modal split), when taking into consideration demographic, socioeconomic as well as attitudinal factors?	The location of the residence and its distances from various facilities.	Studies of and measurements on maps/GIS data.
		Municipal statistical data.
	The residents' travel activity during a period.	Address directories.
		Technical visits.
	Socioeconomic characteristics of the residents and their attitudes to relevant issues.	Questionnaire questions about the residents' travel and the distances travelled by their vehicles, and any changes in the amount of travel after moving.
	Travel behaviour before moving to the present dwelling.	Questionnaire questions about socioeconomic and demographic characteristics of the residents, and transport attitudes, environmental attitudes and leisure interests.
	Subjective opinions about needs of transport and car dependency.	Qualitative interviews, including questions about motives for choices of trip destinations and modal choices, and retrospective and hypothetical questions about travel behaviour in a different residential situation.
Does the location of the residence within the urban structure influence the range and frequency of activities in which people engage?	The activities in which the residents engage, their location, and possible changes compared to previous residential location and/or life situation.	Questions in questionnaires and qualitative interviews about activities, their location, and the meaning attached to different places in the city by the residents. Retrospective and hypothetical questions about activity patterns in a different residential situation.
On which rationales do people base their choices of activity locations and travel modes?	Location of activities, use of different modes of transport, and the considerations behind these choices.	Qualitative interviews including questions about destinations and travel modes, and the motivations for these choices
Are the relationships between residential location and travel behaviour different among different sub-groups of the population?	The information required for the above-mentioned questions.	The data sources of the above-mentioned questions.

concern *degrees* and *strengths* of relationships. In order to identify such tendencies and differences of degree, quantifiable information about the travel activity of a relatively high number of residents is necessary. The respondents also have to be recruited from areas reflecting the variation in the urban structural factors, the effects of which we want to investigate.

In accordance with the above, the studies in Greater Copenhagen and Greater Oporto, as well as the earlier studies where the EQQM method has been applied, all included a large travel survey among inhabitants of a number of residential areas and qualitative interviews with a number of households. The questionnaires included questions about travel behaviour, activity participation, socioeconomic characteristics of the respondents, residential preferences, and attitudes to transport and environmental issues. In the original Copenhagen Metropolitan Area study, a detailed travel diary investigation among some of the participants of the first survey was also carried out.

Recruiting participants of the investigation from a limited number of demarcated residential areas instead of, for example, drawing a random sample among the inhabitants of the metropolitan area, has mainly been motivated from the possibility of mapping a large number of urban structural properties in each area and include this broad range of characteristics as variables in the study. If the respondents were to be randomly sampled from all over the study area it would be far more difficult to get detailed information about the urban structural situation of each residential address. With a concentration of respondents to a limited number of areas the number of respondents might also be sufficiently high to make possible a meaningful comparison of average travel distances and modal shares (although the scope for random variation would be quite high, in particular for the areas with the fewest respondents). Pedagogically and with an eye to communication, we considered it important to be able to visualize relationships between urban structural conditions and travel by comparing concrete localities.

The participants of the qualitative interviews were recruited from a limited number of the residential areas, in order to illuminate distinctly different urban structural situations. The qualitative interviews were semi-structured, focusing on the interviewees' reasons for choosing activities and their locations, travel modes and routes, as well as the meaning attached to living in or visiting various parts of the city. An interview guide was produced in each study as an aid to the conversations. All interviews were tape recorded and thereupon transcribed in their entirety.

Analysis of the qualitative interviews was supported by *interpretation schemes*. These schemes comprised around 30 research sub-questions to be answered by the researchers, based on the information given by the interviewees. These questions were first answered with reference to each separate interviewee. Utterances potentially suited for being quoted in the research report were noted in a separate column, stating the relevant page and line numbers from the transcribed interviews. A comprehensive interpretation was then written for each of the research questions, summarizing the information from all the interviews.

By being required to make written interpretations of each interview in the light of each of the detailed research questions, the researchers were induced to read and penetrate the transcribed interview texts in a far more thorough way than what they would probably have done otherwise. Thus, in our opinion, the use of the interpretation scheme contributes significantly to increase the validity and reliability of qualitative interpretations.

As is evident from the above, the method aimed at 'triangulation' (Patton, 1987; Yin, 1994: 92), both regarding data sources (a combination, among others, of questionnaire data and data from personal, qualitative interviews) and methods of analysis (statistical analyses and qualitative interpretation of interview material). Thus, the method provides a broader and more nuanced understanding of the research questions and contributes to more reliable and robust conclusions.

Case-Specific Application

One of the main aims of this research is to assess the relationship between real travel behaviour and potential travel behaviour.[1] Indeed, this project explores the gap between the research on how urban structure constrains certain travel choices (represented by the SAL) and on how urban structure influences travel behaviour (represented by the EQQM). The main research question of EQQM is therefore of extreme importance to the general methodology of MOPUS. In addition, further detail will be discussed regarding the role of transport rationales as parts of the causal links between residential location and travel behaviour, the influence of residential location on the range and frequency of activities participation, and its influence on general travel behaviour among different sub-groups of the population. The EQQM method was applied to 18 selected residential areas in Greater Copenhagen and to 11 selected residential areas in Greater Oporto. With each residential area located within a local neighbourhood of about 800 m radius, these represent 6 per cent and 4 per cent of each study area. The selected areas have been chosen from different urban structure and socioeconomic contexts aiming to provide a good representation of each case study area.

In the original Copenhagen study, 29 residential areas selected from the whole Copenhagen Metropolitan Area were included. The most peripheral among these areas were located about 60 km away from downtown Copenhagen. Since Copenhagen Metropolitan Area covers an area nearly six times as large as Greater Oporto, we decided to include in the present study only the residential areas located within Greater Copenhagen. With this demarcation, Greater Copenhagen covers an area similar to that of Greater Oporto (GC is only 4 per cent smaller than GO), and the two case study areas are thereby much more comparable than they would have been if the original demarcation of the Copenhagen study area

---

1   Recalling the definition of potential travel behaviour as defined in Chapter 5: travel choices made available to inhabitants by the urban structure.

had been kept. Among the originally selected 29 residential areas, 18 are located within Greater Copenhagen.

Figure 6.1 and Figure 6.2 show the location of the selected local neighbourhoods in Greater Copenhagen and Greater Oporto, respectively. As can be seen, there is a mixture in both case cities of central and peripheral areas. In Greater Copenhagen, the outermost one is located 23 km away from the centre of Copenhagen. Most of the study areas are located along the different 'fingers' of Copenhagen's Finger Plan, including typical upper-income 'fingers' as well as more working-class-dominated corridors. Some of the residential areas are close to urban rail stations, while others are located further away from such stations. The dwelling types and densities also vary considerably, from the dense blocks of inner city Copenhagen to single family residences in lower density suburban settlements.

The selected local neighbourhoods of Greater Oporto include the main centre of Greater Oporto (Oporto city centre), several second order centres, lower level centres and rural areas. The most peripheral area is located 14 km away from the city centre. The selected areas represent locations near as well as far from motorways and main rail infrastructure. For instance, Miramar has very good access to motorways, has a main train station and low population density with very low amount of activities. On the other hand, Foz (Oporto) has high population density, and is located away from the main motorway system and the metro and rail system. As a final example, Maia has it all, from high population to excellent access to both light-rail and motorway systems.

The qualitative interviews were semi-structured, focusing on the interviewees' reasons for choosing activities and their locations, travel modes and routes, as well as the meaning attached to living in or visiting various parts of the city. In each of the city regions, the interviewees were recruited among the survey respondents from a selected number of the investigated residential areas. In Copenhagen Metropolitan Area, nine interviewees were chosen from three inner-city areas (Vesterbro, Kartoffelrækkerne and Frederiksberg North) and eight were recruited from two outer-suburban areas. These latter residential areas are located outside the demarcation of Greater Copenhagen, thus belonging to those 11 residential areas from the original Copenhagen Metropolitan Area study that were not included in the quantitative part of the present study. They are located some 5 to 10 km to the west and northwest of the demarcation of Greater Copenhagen shown in Figure 4.11. One of the peripheral interview areas (Stenløse) is located close to an urban rail station whereas the other peripheral interviewee area (Uvelse) has very poor accessibility by public transport. In Greater Oporto, 10 interviewees were recruited, representing typical inner-city neighbourhoods (one interviewee), suburban locations (five interviewees) as well as a location close to a second-order centre (four interviewees).

The interviews were in most cases conducted in the homes of the interviewees, usually lasting between one and a half and two hours. The interviews were based on a common interview guide originally produced in Danish for the Copenhagen study and later translated via English into a Portuguese-language version used in the

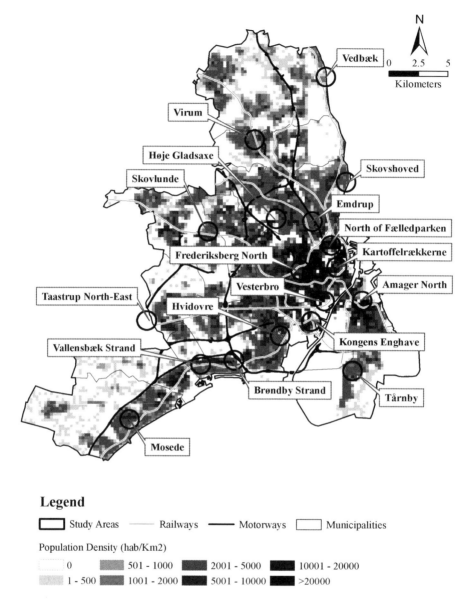

Figure 6.1   Location of the investigated residential areas (and population density) in Greater Copenhagen

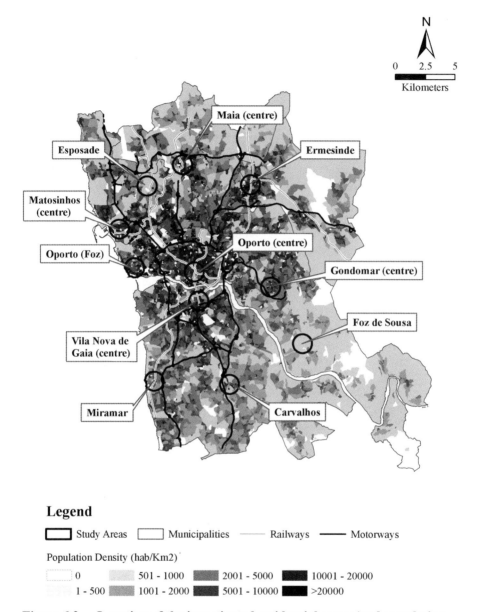

Figure 6.2   Location of the investigated residential areas (and population density) in Greater Oporto

Oporto study. All interviews in both city regions were tape recorded and transcribed. The interpretations were made by the respective research teams of Aalborg University and Oporto University, based on common templates for interpretation schemes.

Table 6.2 provides an overview of the research methods used in the empirical collection of data in the Greater Copenhagen and the Greater Oporto case. In accordance with the general methodology described earlier in this chapter, the Copenhagen area study included a large travel survey among inhabitants of the selected residential areas, a more detailed travel diary investigation among some of the participants of the first survey, and 17 qualitative interviews. For the comparison with Greater Oporto, discussion was centred on the results of the qualitative interviews, the large travel survey and on some information collected through the more detailed travel diaries.

The Greater Oporto study included a large travel survey among inhabitants of the 11 selected residential areas, very similar to the one used in Copenhagen. This survey included some extra questions meant to replace information provided by travel diaries in the Copenhagen study.

The concentration of respondents to a limited number of selected locations allows for a more in-depth account for contextual conditions in each of the chosen areas. But this method of selecting respondents also makes it problematic to carry out statistical generalizations from our sample of respondents to the populations of each study area. Therefore, the statistical levels of significance are only indicators of the certainty of the various relationships found *within* the sample.[2]

A generalization from our samples to the inhabitants of each study area must instead rely on *qualitative* arguments to a large extent (Sayer 1992: 103): To what extent do our residential areas, seen as a whole, deviate from the residential areas of Greater Copenhagen or Greater Oporto in general with respect to characteristics relevant to our research questions? To what extent do relevant characteristics of the individual respondents, also seen as a whole, differ from the total population of each study area? Does it appear likely and reasonable to assume that differences between the sample and the population of each study area have exerted decisive influence on the relationships found between residential location and travel behaviour?[3] For a more thorough discussion, see Næss and Jensen (2002) and Næss (2004).

---

2   Basically, social science studies aiming to throw light on relationships between outcomes and possible causes, as distinct from measuring the extension of a phenomenon at a given point of time, must be considered a kind of case studies. Judgments of the extent to which the relationships found in such studies can be generalized, must be based on the analytic generalization logic of case study research, not on the statistic generalizations of the 'context-independent' sciences. The fact that some time always passes between the collection of data and the publishing of the results of a study is in itself a reason for this: Even with perfect statistical representativeness during the phase of data collection, the world has already become different at the time of publishing.

3   A similar qualitative reasoning must be used when making generalizations from our case cities to other cities in Denmark, Portugal or the rest of Europe. And the same, of course, also applies to the generalizations drawn from the qualitative interviews with individual households.

Table 6.2   Applied research methods of Greater Copenhagen and the Greater Oporto studies

Research Method	Greater Copenhagen	Greater Oporto
Qualitative interviews	17 households[1]	10 individuals[2]
Semi-structured, each lasting about an hour and a half.		
Focus on the interviewees' reasons for activity participation, location of activities, travel modes and routes, as well as their opinions about different parts of the metropolitan area as places to visit and to live in.	✓	
Questionnaire survey among inhabitants of selected residential areas	18 selected residential areas (1,143 respondents)	11 selected residential areas (1,045 respondents)
Travel distances by different modes during one whole week.	✓	✓
Location of any workplace or place of education.	✓	✓
Annual driving distance with the household's car(s).	✓	✓
Changes in the amount of travel among respondents who have moved during the latest 5 years.	✓	✓
Perception of being dependent of car travel in order to reach daily activities.	✓	–
Frequency of participation in different activities.	✓	✓
Holiday trips.	✓	✓
Attitudes to transport and environmental issues.	✓	✓
Travel time by different modes during one whole week.	–	✓[6]
Number of trips by purpose during one whole week.	–	✓[7]
Detailed travel diary survey	Covering the four-day period from Saturday to Tuesday (273 respondents)	
Location of the various trip ends.	✓	–
Purpose, length, mode and travel time of each trip.	✓	–
Driving distance of the household's car(s) (based on odometer registration).	✓	–
Changes in activity participation and car ownership among respondents who have moved during the latest 5 years.	✓	–
Flights and other trips outside the local region.	✓	
Registration of urban structural conditions, including the distances from each respondent's dwelling to various centres and facilities.	✓	✓

[1] The qualitative interviews included nine households from three residential areas close to the city centre of Copenhagen (Vesterbro, Kartoffelrækkerne and Frederiksberg North), and eight households from two peripheral residential areas (Stenløse and Uvelse). The two latter areas are located in the outer part of the metropolitan area, outside the demarcation of Greater Copenhagen, as defined in this volume. However, we still think the situation of the interviewees from the two peripheral areas is fairly representative of the residents of the most peripheral among the residential areas included in the present study.

[2] The qualitative interviews included one interviewee living in the city centre of Oporto, four living close to second-order centres (Oporto Foz, Maia, Ermesinde and Matosinhos) and five living in more typically suburban locations (Gaia, Pedroso, Gondomar, Carvalhos and Miramar). Eight of the interviewees were female and two were men.

[3] Replacing 'purpose, length, mode and travel time of each trip' of travel diaries in Copenhagen.

[4] Replacing 'purpose, length, mode and travel time of each trip' of travel diaries in Copenhagen.

In Copenhagen, questionnaires were distributed by mail to the residents of the selected residential areas.[4] In the main survey, a total of 3,600 questionnaires were distributed to residents of the 18 areas included in the present study, of which 1,143 were completed and returned. Given the quite large questionnaire, requiring respondents to register daily transport over a whole week, the response rate of 32 per cent must be considered normal and acceptable. In Oporto, questionnaires were distributed to around 200 dwellings in each selected area of 800 m radius, and collected two weeks after distribution. This method was chosen to increase the response rate of the survey, considering that a lower number of resdential areas were used. To increase diversity of urban structures (using only 11 areas) each area was divided into three zones with different neighbourhood characteristics. In total, around 2,200 surveys were distributed of which 1,045 were collected. This corresponds to a response rate of 47 per cent among those who accepted to receive the questionnaire.

In addition to recording socioeconomic background variables and travel distances by different modes on each day during a week, the main survey included questions about frequency of participation in activities, attitudes to transport and environmental issues (only Copenhagen), residential preferences, perception of car dependency, and changes in the amount of transport among respondents who had moved recently. A large number of travel behaviour indicators were recorded for each respondent: total travelling distance, travelling distances by car, by bus, by train and by non-motorized modes, and the proportions of the total distance travelled by car, public transport, and non-motorized modes, respectively. Each of these eight aspects of travel behaviour was recorded for the weekdays (Monday–Friday), the weekend (Saturday–Sunday) and for the week as a whole, making up a total of 24 travel behaviour variables. In addition, annual driving distances of any cars belonging to the household were recorded, as well as flights and other long-distance holiday trips.

In the travel diary investigation for Copenhagen, a more detailed picture was given, including location of destinations for the various trips, trip purposes, trip lengths and travel times of all trips during a four-day period (from Saturday morning to Tuesday evening), changes in activities and car ownership due to moving, and flights and other trips outside the domestic region. In addition, the driving distances of the household's motor vehicles (if any) on the weekend (Saturday–Sunday) and on Monday–Tuesday were recorded, based on odometer monitoring. Distinct from the data from the main survey, which have been re-analyzed including only the respondents living within an area comparable to Greater Oporto (Greater Copenhagen, referred to by Statistics Denmark as 'Hovedstadsområdet'), no separate analyses of travel diary data were made for respondents living within this part of the metropolitan area. The present report thus does not contain any tables

---

4   The selected residential areas were demarcated so that each included approximately 200 households registered in the internet-based address directory Kraks Kort. The questionnaires were sent to all households within the demarcated areas.

or graphs based on the travel diary investigation. The travel diary study will still be referred to, along with the qualitative interviews, as a more general source of knowledge about the mechanisms through which residential location influences travel within the context of Copenhagen Metropolitan Area. In the travel diary investigation, 273 persons responded out of a gross sample of 775, i.e., a response rate of 35 per cent. Data of travel time and trip purpose was also collected in Oporto through the main travel survey (for seven days).

Table 6.3 shows a comparison of sample characteristics of respondents of the surveys and of census data for the 18 residential areas and for Greater Copenhagen as a whole. The biases found were largely the same in both surveys (large survey and travel diaries, the latter not shown in the table). Persons who were neither workforce participants nor students are clearly underrepresented among our respondents. The same applies to persons without a car in the household. In order to investigate what these distortions might imply, separate analyses have been carried out among each of the mentioned sub-groups of the respondents. The comparison with census data also shows that our respondents have higher incomes, higher car ownership and belong to somewhat larger households on average, than the population of the respective residential areas and of Greater Copenhagen. In general, apart from the two sub-groups mentioned above, the samples of the two

Table 6.3   Comparison of demographic and socioeconomic characteristics of the participants of the surveys with the inhabitants of the 18 residential areas and Greater Copenhagen as a whole

	Respondents of main survey (N = 1,143)	Inhabitants of the 18 residential areas	Inhabitants of Greater Copenhagen
Average number of persons per household	2.4	2.2	2.0
Average number of children aged 0–6 years per household	0.24	0.22	0.17
Average number of children aged 7–17 years per household	0.32	0.25	0.19
Average age among respondents	46 years		
Proportion of workforce participants among respondents	75%	70%	66%
Proportion of students/pupils among respondents	12%	12%	13%
Average household income (1,000 DKK)	521	414	337
Proportion with further education	37%		
Average number of cars per household	0.84	0.64	0.49

surveys must yet be considered fairly well representative for the inhabitants of the Copenhagen area and the selected residential areas.

Table 6.4 shows a comparison of sample characteristics of respondents of the survey and of census data for the 11 residential areas and for Greater Oporto as a whole. The 11 residential areas chosen are fairly representative of Greater Oporto regarding most household characteristics. Exception is made for the proportion of inhabitants with further education, which is already higher in the chosen areas than in Greater Oporto and reaches astonishingly high numbers when regarding the respondents of the survey. In addition, workforce participants and students are also overrepresented among respondents. This comparison reveals that respondents of the survey present higher average income and live in households with higher car ownership than the average in Greater Oporto. As mentioned before, the possible effect of these distortions will be studied through separate analysis of sub-groups of respondents, notably among respondents with high and low education levels and car ownership, respectively.

In order to identify the *separate* effects of the various, potential factors of influence, multivariate regression analyses were applied on the quantitative data. This multivariate control also makes it possible to neutralize any known

Table 6.4   Comparison of demographic and socioeconomic characteristics of the participants of the survey with the inhabitants of the 11 residential areas and Greater Oporto as a whole

	Respondents of main survey (N = 1,045)	Inhabitants of the 11 residential areas[1]	Inhabitants of Greater Oporto[2]
Average number of persons per household	2.8	2.7	2.9
Average number of children aged 0–6 years per household	0.20	0.18	0.21
Average number of children aged 7–17 years per household	0.34	0.32	0.36
Average age among respondents/ interviewees	45 years		
Proportion of workforce participants among respondents/interviewees	59%	58%	56%
Proportion of students/pupils among respondents/interviewees	15%	12%	12%
Average household income (€1,000)	15		12[3]
Proportion with further education	37%	12%	9%
Average number of cars per household	1.75		1.15

[1]   INE (2001).
[2]   Ibid.
[3]   GEP (2007).

biases between the sample and the population of the metropolitan area. If, for example, income is included among the independent variables in the multivariate analysis, the controlled relationship between residential location and travel will not be biased by any distortion in the income levels of the sample. In accordance with past applications (e.g., Næss, 2009b) the multivariate analyses included the following independent variables:

Urban structural variables (four in both Copenhagen and Oporto):

- the location of the residence relative to the main centre of the study area;[5]
- the location of the residence relative to the closest second-order centre;[6]
- the location of the residence relative to the closest urban rail station[7] (only in Copenhagen);

---

5   The main centre was defined as the City Hall Square. In the original Copenhagen Metropolitan Area study, where the outermost residential areas were located so far away from the city centre that a certain 'distance decay' in the use of central facilities was apparent, the distance from each residence to the city centre was measured by means of a non-linear transformation of the Euclidian distance. In the present study, where only neighbourhoods within the continuous urban area are included, Euclidian distances to the centre were found to be more closely related to the travel behaviour variables than the original non-linearly transformed distances. In both Greater Copenhagen and Greater Oporto, ordinary Euclidian distances have therefore been used.

6   Based on material from Greater Copenhagen Authority (Hovedstadens Udviklingsråd), the second-order centres for Copenhagen were defined as so-called 'urban centres with regionally oriented retail trade'. In the original study, these centres included the five outer-region towns of Køge, Roskilde, Frederikssund, Hillerød and Helsingør, as well as 14 other sub-regional centres, mainly in Copenhagen and the inner suburbs. The five outer-region towns and five other second-order centres are located in parts of the metropolitan area outside Greater Copenhagen and were thus not included in the study area of the present study, which included the following 14 urban centres with regionally oriented retail trade: 'København city' at Amagertorv, Vesterbrogade, Amagerbrogade, Kongens Lyngby, Ishøj Bycenter, Rødovre Centrum, Glostrup Hovedcenter, Ballerup-Centret, Hundige Storcenter, and Fiskertorvet. In the Oporto case study, we used urban areas classified as cities for second-order urban centres. The centre of each city was defined as a place near a facility of public interest commonly recognized as centre. In this case study a total of eight second-order centres were considered, namely, Matosinhos (town hall), São Mamede Infesta (church), Ermesinde (main train station), Valongo (Machado dos Santos square), Rio Tinto (church), Gondomar (town hall), Maia (town hall) and Vila Nova de Gaia (town hall). In the Oporto case study, distance to second-order centres was measured linearly, considering the better results of this variable in regression models.

7   Here, urban rail station refers to stations of the so-called S-trains. The S-train lines make up the backbone of the public transport system in Copenhagen Metropolitan Area. Distances to the closest urban rail station were measured logarithmically, from an assumption that the influence of a 100-metre increase in the distance would be stronger if the distance is short at the outset than if it is already long.

- the location of the residence relative to main regional retail centre (only in Oporto);[8] and
- the density of inhabitants and workplaces in the local area surrounding the dwelling.[9]

Variables describing demographic characteristics of the respondent and the household to which the respondents belongs (four in Copenhagen and Oporto):

- sex;
- age;
- number of household members below seven years old; and
- number of household members between 7 and 17 years old.

Variables describing socioeconomic characteristics of the respondent (seven in Copenhagen and eight in Oporto):

- workforce participation (three dichotomous variables for worker, student/ pupil and pensioner);
- personal income;
- driver's license;
- type of education (two dichotomous variables for medium and long education);
- attitudinal variables[10] (only in Copenhagen); and
- index for transport-related residential preferences.

In addititon, some other control variables indicating particular activities, obligations or social relations likely to influence travel behaviour during the period of detailed travel registration were included.

Regarding urban structure variables, distances to the main city centre and the closest second-order centre tell something about the location of the residence in relation to the metropolitan-scale hierarchy of centres. The distance to the closest urban rail station indicates the accessibility of the residence to the main public transport system of the region (and to local centres usually located around the stations). Correspondingly, the distance to the closest regional shopping centre

---

8   Measured logarithmically, for similar reasons as for the distance to urban rail stations.

9   Local area density was calculated as the sum of inhabitants and workplaces per hectare within a circle of two square kilometres (i.e., with a radius of 800 m) around the centroid of the residential area from which the respondents were recruited.

10   See Næss (2009a) for details. In analyses published earlier than 2009, two other attitudinal variables were used instead: Index for transport attitudes and index for environmental attitudes. In these earlier analyses, car ownership was also included among the control variables.

indicates the accessibility from the dwelling to key shopping opportunities. Local-area density tells something about the population base as a condition for local facilities.

The choice of the main urban structural variables to be included in the analysis was based mainly on theoretical considerations (including Christaller, 1966; Berry and Garrison, 1958) and the results from previous empirical studies (Næss et al., 1995; Næss, 2006). This choice was also supported by the qualitative interviews carried out as part of the Copenhagen study (see Chapter 8, pp. 151–9) and separate multivariate regression analysis of more than 30 urban structural variables (one at a time) considering all non-structural variables, aiming to study the role of more detailed urban structural conditions in travel behaviour (see Chapter 8, pp. 181–6). High multicollinearity between all these urban structure variables disables multivariate regression analysis of all these variables simultaneously. The choice of the urban structural variables to be included in the main analysis was based on the fact that, for most travel purposes, most residents choose among job opportunities and other facilities within a much larger area than just their local neighbourhood. The location of the dwelling relative to the citywide centre structure therefore generally tends to exert stronger influences than neighbourhood-scale built-environment characteristics on traveling distances and the proportions of travel carried out by different modes.

As can be seen from the above list of variables, car ownership was not included among the control variables of the main analyses. We are aware that much of the international research into influences of residential location on travel operates with car ownership as a control variable. However, from theoretical considerations (e.g., Hägerstrand, 1970) as well as according to a host of empirical studies, car ownership is influenced by urban structural conditions (Giuliano and Narrayan, 2003; Scheiner and Holz-Rau, 2007; Vance and Hedel, 2008; Næss, 2009a; Zegras, 2010; Aditjandra et al., 2010). Car ownership is therefore irrelevant as a control variable in analyses where income, driver's license possession, age and other socio-demographic variables have already been accounted for, and its inclusion will lead to biased results.

The same arguably also applies to transport attitudes and environmental attitudes, which are also likely to be influenced by residential location: Inner-city respondents who do not themselves need to use a car in their daily life but are exposed to the noise, fumes and risk of accidents imposed by suburbanites driving through their local environments may develop less car-friendly attitudes and a higher environmental awareness about pollution from car traffic than their suburban counterparts. We have, however, included transport-related residential preferences among the control variables of the Copenhagen study. Several researchers have pointed out that self-selection of residents into geographical locations matching their traveling preferences can be an obstacle to measuring the influences of residential location on travel. In order to throw light on the extent to which geographical differences in travel behaviour are a result of residential self-selection, respondents were asked to select and prioritize 3 out of 20 characteristics that would be most important if they were to move from their present residence to a new dwelling. Based on these answers, a dichotomous variable indicating whether or not the respondent showed a preference for residential locations enabling and facilitating shorter traveling distances and the use of public and/or non-motorized modes of travel was constructed. Respondents whose two highest-rated residential characteristics included 'short distance to the workplace', 'close to shopping facilities', 'close to rail station' or 'close to bus stop' were assigned a value of one, while the remaining respondents received a value of zero.

Since much of the international research into influences of residential location on travel operates with car ownership as a control variable, we have still included the number of cars per household member as a control variable in some additional sensitivity analyses. These analyses show that the results are robust also with the inclusion of car ownership as a control variable (see, for example, Næss, 2005, 2006a, 2006b, 2009b). The large number of independent variables might give rise to fear of multicollinearity problems. However, formal collinearity diagnostics do not indicate any such problems.[11] Notably, there is low multicollinearity between the urban structural and the non-urban structural variables.[12]

---

11   With all independent variables included in the regression models, the four urban structural variables in the Greater Copenhagen case have tolerance levels ranging from 0.43 to 0.86, and in the in Greater Oporto case ranging from 0.25 to 0.45.

12   If only one of the urban structural variables at a time is included in the regression model together with all the non-urban structural control variables, the four urban structural variables have tolerance levels varying from 0.77 to 0.93 in the Greater Copenhagen case and from 0.94 to 0.96 in the Greater Oporto case. Their lower tolerance levels in the models with all urban structural as well as control variables included are thus mainly due to mutual correlation between the urban structural variables.

Chapter 7

Mobility Choices Enabled by Urban Structure[1]

Cecília Silva and José Pedro Reis

This chapter presents the results of the application of the Structural Accessibility Layer (SAL) in the two areas of study: Greater Copenhagen (GC) and Greater Oporto (GO). The use of the SAL for the analysis of current land use and transport conditions for mobility encompasses two main results: first, the values of diversity of activities accessible by each transport mode group – non-motorized, public transport and car – and second, the analysis of accessibility clusters. The results for each of the case studies will be analyzed and discussed on pages 121–32 and 132–9, respectively. Later on (see pages 139–49), we carry out a comparative discussion of the two study areas.

Copenhagen

The following map (Figure 7.1) presents the spatial representation of the levels of accessibility by walking in Greater Copenhagen. A first analysis of the map shows that most of GC's territory (64 per cent of the area, according to Table 7.1) presents high levels of pedestrian accessibility (class A). These areas concentrate the great majority of the population: more than 93 per cent of the inhabitants live in areas with high accessibility conditions, 38 per cent of them live in sub-areas with pedestrian accessibility to all activities considered (DivAct = 1). Low accessibility areas (class C) have almost no population: only 0.2 per cent of Copenhagen's inhabitants.

The diversity of activity index by walking provides a comprehensive picture of the structure of centralities in a metropolitan area. Sub-areas with high levels of accessibility to activities (class A) can generally be found either around the city centre (in the municipality of Copenhagen and its closest vicinity) or along the 'fingers'. The existence of these high accessibility areas located along railway lines reveals a rather good coordination between land use and transport policies (notably the 'Finger Plan'), following the principles of a transit-oriented development.

---

1   The mobility choices enabled by the urban structure, as measured by SAL, have been presented and discussed in earlier publications (such as, Silva, 2008; Reis, 2009; Silva and Pinho, 2010; Silva, 2013; Silva et al. 2014). This chapter reproduced part of previous descriptions published in the referred publications.

Legend

☐ Municipalities ——— Railways (Train, S-Train, Metro)

DivAct

0.00	0.21 - 0.30	0.51 - 0.60	0.81 - 0.90
0.01 - 0.10	0.31 - 0.40	0.61 - 0.70	0.91 - 1.00
0.11 - 0.20	0.41 - 0.50	0.71 - 0.80	1.00

Figure 7.1   Diversity of activity index by walking in GC

Table 7.1   Accessibility classes for each transport mode by area and population

	Analysis by area (percentage of 542 km²)				Analysis by population (percentage of 1,201,390 inhabitants)			
	NM (walking)	NM (bicycle)	PT	Car	NM (walking)	NM (bicycle)	PT	Car
A	64.0%	81.0%	60.8%	81.3%	93.3%	99.9%	94.6%	100.0%
DivAct = 1	10.4%	45.9%	51.6%	81.3%	37.8%	80.4%	73.0%	100.0%
B	15.4%	0.1%	0.3%	0.0%	6.5%	0.0%	0.1%	0.0%
C	1.9%	0.1%	20.3%	0.0%	0.2%	0.1%	5.4%	0.0%
DivAct = 0	0.1%	0.0%	20.2%	0.0%	0.0%	0.0%	5.4%	0.0%
NU	18.7%	18.7%	18.7%	18.7%	0.0%	0.0%	0.0%	0.0%
Average regional level					0.97	1.00	0.95	1.00

The uppermost levels of accessibility (DivAct = 1) can be found in the centre of Copenhagen (municipality of Frederiksberg and the inner parts of the municipality of Copenhagen) as well as in a few peripheral centres, namely, Lyngby and Birkerød. The main reason for some of these areas not to have maximum accessibility levels by walking is due to lack of accessibility to activity 3 (universities).

Concerning the remaining territory (namely, the most peripheral areas), levels of accessibility by walking are significantly lower. This effect is mainly a result of low accessibility to activities 2 (high schools), 6 (theatre, cinema, sport, etc.) and 7 (Shopping – food), since these are more concentrated around a small number of centres and, at the same time, they have higher values of frequency of use (f_y). The suburbs to the south of Copenhagen also show some deficiencies regarding the accessibility to activities 2 (High schools) and 11 (Public administration offices). Sub-areas with no accessibility to activities (DivAct = 0) correspond to non-urban territories, which were not calculated. On average, the study region has a diversity of activity index by walking of 0.97.

There are a few zones within the centre of Copenhagen that present lower levels of accessibility (class B) when compared to surrounding areas, as a result of shortage of accessibility to activity 4 (parks, public gardens and squares, which represent about 12 per cent of travel). This information ought to be considered by the local authorities, since this problem could be easily solved by the provision of more public space.

Figure 7.2 presents the geographical distribution of non-motorized accessibility levels, but now considering the accessibility by bicycle. The map shows that, excluding the non-urban areas, the whole region has high accessibility conditions

Legend

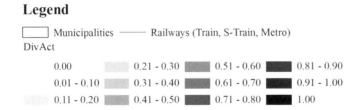

Figure 7.2   Diversity of activities accessible by bicycle in GC

(class A). In the Copenhagen city centre and in its closer periphery, all activity types are accessible by bicycle (DivAct = 1). This is also the case of some second-order centralities, like Lyngby, Birkerød (both to the north) and Ballerup (to the northwest), as well.

The analysis by population (Table 7.1) shows that almost all residents (99.9 per cent) live in sub-areas with high accessibility conditions (class A), and 80 per cent of the inhabitants have accessibility to all activity types considered. Moreover, GC presents the maximum value (1.00) for the regional average level of accessibility by bicycle. Comparing these results with the levels of accessibility by walking, we can conclude that, although pedestrian accessibility is already quite high, the conditions of accessibility to activities by non-motorized modes in GC improve significantly when the bicycle is considered.

Even though some centralities can be identified in this map – namely, considering sub-areas with DivAct = 1 – using the bike appears to make accessibility to activities less dependent on urban structure. It means that the mobility of Copenhagen's inhabitants is much higher by bicycle than by walking. This is normal considering not only the difference of speed between these two modes, but also the vast length of cycle tracks and the appropriate topography in GC (although the latter has not been considered in the model), which ensures the best conditions for the use of this transport mode.

In short, we may argue that Greater Copenhagen has a great potential for its residents to use non-motorized transport modes in their daily mobility patterns. However, we must bear in mind that accessibility by bicycle does not substitute the importance of the analysis of pedestrian accessibility, mainly the accessibility to everyday needs, because not everyone has the ability (for reasons of health, age, etc.) to use a bicycle.

With regard to accessibility by public transport modes, the geographical distribution of the diversity of activities index (Figure 7.3) clearly marks the spatial distribution of public transport availability. A large proportion of GC's area (39 per cent) has no access to public transport service, considering both non-urban areas and sub-areas with DivAct = 0 (see Table 7.1). However, these territories only concentrate 5.4 per cent of the overall population: the great majority of GC inhabitants (95 per cent) live in sub-areas with high accessibility conditions (class A). The proportion of population with accessibility to all considered activities is almost as high, representing a share of 81 per cent. Sub-areas with medium accessibility conditions by public transport are largely absent, representing less than 1 per cent of the area and the population of the study region. The average value of diversity of accessibility for the study region is 0.95.

Sub-areas with high accessibility by public transport are generally located in the centre ('the palm of the hand') and in the vicinity of public transport routes, including the S-Train (along the 'fingers'), local and regional train, some bus routes and also the Metro in the south of the centre.

The diversity of activity index by public transport gives us a representation of spatial distribution of public transport network as well as of public transport

Legend

 Municipalities ———— Railways (Train, S-Train, Metro)
DivAct

0.00	0.21 - 0.30	0.51 - 0.60	0.81 - 0.90
0.01 - 0.10	0.31 - 0.40	0.61 - 0.70	0.91 - 1.00
0.11 - 0.20	0.41 - 0.50	0.71 - 0.80	1.00

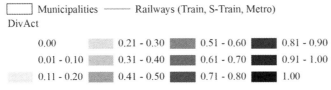

Figure 7.3   Diversity of activities accessible by public transport in GC

service level and activity density around public transport access points. Public transport operators generally follow objectives of profit maximization resulting in routes along both high population and activity densities. Therefore, the fact that most of the population has access to public transport and that accessibility levels in these areas are high, comes with no surprize.

The geographical distribution of accessibility levels by car is represented in Figure 7.4. Excluding the non-urban areas, accessibility conditions by this transport mode are high in the entire study area. Moreover, most of these sub-areas (81.3 per cent of the territory, the whole study region if we exclude non-urban areas) provide accessibility by car to all activity types considered, and encompass the entire population (see Table 7.1). Considering these conditions, the average value of 1.0 for the study region is not surprising.

Figure 7.5 represents the geographical distribution of accessibility clusters. As the entire study region provides high accessibility level by car (class A), only nine of the accessibility categories defined by the benchmarking cube can be found. Consequently, only the following four of the nine accessibility clusters (see Figure 5.4) are attainable in these conditions:

III – favourable conditions for the use of all modes;
IV – favourable conditions for the use of NM modes and the CAR;
VI – favourable conditions for the use of PT and the CAR; and
VII – favourable conditions for the use of the CAR.

The map clearly shows areas of the study region providing land use and transport conditions which enable travel behaviour to be sustainable – areas in cluster III, IV and VI – although real travel patterns may still have low levels of sustainability since car use is an available mode choice. The remaining region does not provide the necessary land use and transport conditions to foster sustainable travel behaviour. Even if inhabitants would be willing to pursue more sustainable travel behaviour land use and transport conditions would avert them from doing so (without loss of quality of life).

According to the map and to Table 7.2, more than half of the study area provides high accessibility levels by all transport modes (cluster III). Throughout GC several sub-areas are found in clusters III or IV (favourable conditions for the use of all modes or for the use of NM modes and the car), representing about 10 per cent of the territory. These areas are normally located near centralities with most activities, but lacking public transport availability. Sub-areas with favourable conditions for the use of the car and public transport (cluster VI) are more rare (7 per cent of the territory).

Sub-areas offering only favourable conditions for car use are generally located in more peripheral areas. These areas correspond to 10 per cent of GC and concentrate less than 1 per cent of the population (see Table 7.2). The great majority of GC residents (95 per cent) live in sub-areas with favourable conditions for the use of all modes (cluster III). The remaining inhabitants of GC live in places with favourable conditions for the use of car and NM modes (5 per cent).

Legend

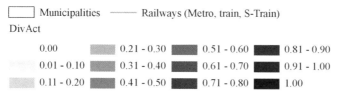

Figure 7.4   Diversity of activities accessible by car in GC

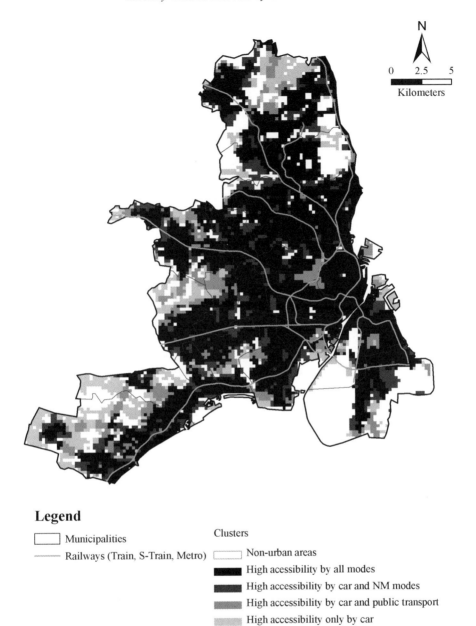

Legend

Municipalities

Railways (Train, S-Train, Metro)

Clusters

Non-urban areas

High acessibility by all modes

High accessibility by car and NM modes

High accessibility by car and public transport

High accessibility only by car

Figure 7.5   Clusters of accessibility in GC

Table 7.2   Categories and clusters by area and population

Clusters	Area (km²)	Percentage	Population	Percentage
III	290	53.5%	1,063,847	88.5%
IV	57	10.5%	57,372	4.8%
VI	39	7.3%	72,218	6.0%
VII	54	10.0%	7,953	0.7%
NU	101	18.7%		
Total	542	100.0%	1,201,390	100.0%

Figure 7.6 shows a similar map, but now using the bicycle for non-motorized accessibility. A first analysis of the map shows that the areas with favourable conditions for car use only (cluster VII) as well as sub-areas in cluster VI (high accessibility by car and PT modes) shrinks considerably and almost disappears. On the contrary, sub-areas in clusters III and IV increase significantly. This is in accordance to what could be expected. With the increase in accessibility levels by NM modes attained by the use of the bicycle, several sub-areas with high accessibility levels by car (cluster VII) have now also high accessibility by NM modes (cluster IV), while sub-areas with favourable conditions for car and PT use (cluster VI) will now offer good accessibility conditions by all transport modes.

Examining the population (Table 7.3), we see that almost 95 per cent of GC residents live in sub-areas with favourable conditions for the use of all modes, while less than 1 per cent of the population lives in sub-areas only favouring car use – hence with land use and transport offering insufficient conditions for sustainable travel behaviour – and the same happens with cluster VI.

Table 7.3   Comparison of the proportion of area and population in each accessibility cluster using bicycle or walking as non-motorized mode

Clusters	Area (%)		Population (%)	
	Bicycle	Walking	Bicycle	Walking
III	60.7%	53.5%	94.5%	88.5%
IV	20.3%	10.5%	5.3%	4.8%
VI	0.1%	7.3%	0.1%	6.0%
VII	0.2%	10.0%	0.1%	0.7%
NU	18.7%	18.7%		

Moreover, almost the entire population lives in sub-areas with high accessibility conditions by bicycle (clusters III and IV). This does not mean that real travel patterns are necessarily sustainable (since car use is also an available mode choice), but it is definitely a positive indicator.

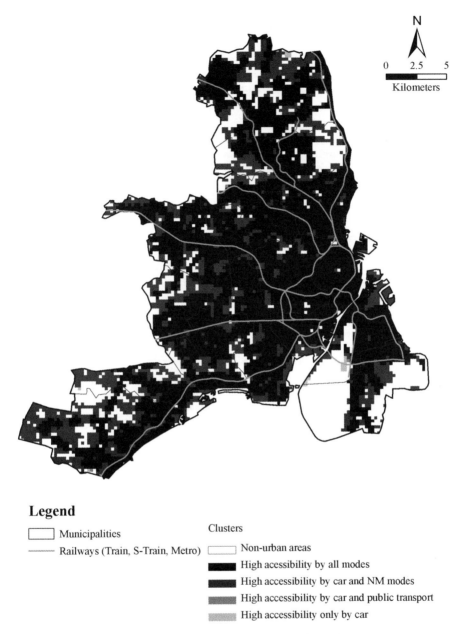

Legend

Municipalities

Railways (Train, S-Train, Metro)

Clusters

Non-urban areas

High acessibility by all modes

High accessibility by car and NM modes

High accessibility by car and public transport

High accessibility only by car

Figure 7.6   Clusters of accessibility in GC (with bicycle)

In summary, Greater Copenhagen seems to provide rather good conditions for sustainable travel behaviour, namely by non-motorized modes and primarily when accessibility by bicycle is considered. On average, the study region presents quite positive results, falling into cluster III (high accessibility conditions by all transport modes). All four considered transport modes have indeed average accessibility levels above 0.95, two of them (bike and car) even provide maximum accessibility levels.

Although accessibility conditions by public transport and non-motorized modes are quite favourable in Copenhagen, the car is still the transport mode with higher accessibility levels and the bicycle is the only mode which appears to be capable of competing with it.

Oporto

The diversity of activities accessible by each transport mode in Greater Oporto is presented in the following three figures, while Table 7.4 provides an overview of the accessibility classes for each transport mode, presented by area and population.

Table 7.4   Accessibility classes for each transport mode by area and by population

	Analysis by area (percentage of 563 km²)			Analysis by population (percentage of 1,089,118 inhabitants)		
	NM	PT	CAR	NM	PT	CAR
A	435%	47.8%	100.0%	77.6%	83.4%	100.0%
DivAct = 1	7.3%	31.3%	86.5%	25.2%	71.2%	98.1%
B	48.6%	4.0%	0.0%	21.3%	1.7%	0.0%
C	7.9%	48.2%	0.0%	1.1%	15.0%	0.0%
DivAct = 0	0.0%	48.2%	0.0%	0.0%	15.0%	0.0%
Average regional level				0.91	0.84	0.99

Source: Silva, 2008.

Figure 7.7 presents the geographical distribution of accessibility levels by non-motorized modes. A first analysis of the map shows almost no area with low accessibility levels (class C) and a more or less even distribution of high and medium accessibility levels (see Table 7.4). However, analyzing the population shows that the large majority of the study area inhabitants (78 per cent) live in good accessibility conditions by non-motorized modes, while less than 22 per cent live in medium accessibility conditions. On average the study region provides high accessibility conditions by non-motorized modes with a regional value of diversity of activity index higher than 0.9.

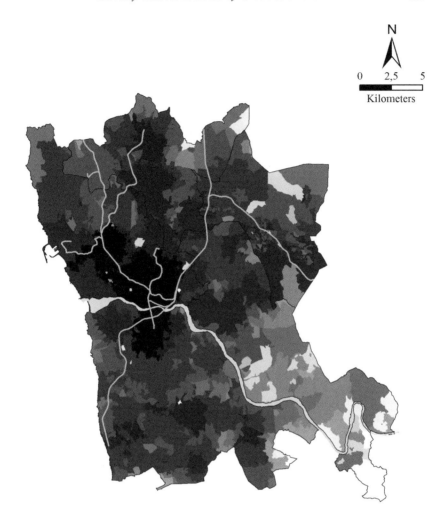

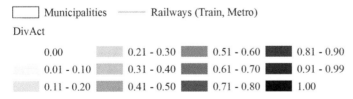

Figure 7.7 Diversity of activities accessible by non-motorized modes in GO

Source: Adapted from Silva (2008).

Good accessibility conditions can be mainly found in Oporto and several corridors stretching north and east from this municipality. To the south, good accessibility conditions are more scattered with a larger continuum stretching from Oporto to the northern part of the municipality of Vila Nova de Gaia.

The diversity of activity index by non-motorized modes provides a clear picture of the urban centres' structure of Greater Oporto. This outline of the main urban centres seems to be strongly related to traditional urban agglomerations along the main national road network (excluding motorways). While to the north these agglomerations are closer together forming urban corridors instead of centres, urban development has been more disperse to the south enabling a clear recognition of boundaries of each urban centre.

The best accessibility conditions (with accessibility to all activity types by walking) are presented in an area stretching from the municipality of Oporto north to the city centre of Matosinhos and south to the city centre of Vila Nova de Gaia. One quarter of the population of the study region lives in this privileged area (representing only 7 per cent of the study region area), where all activity types are accessible by foot and in theory all main daily activities could be pursued within the neighbourhood.

Sub-areas with diversity of activity index between 0.9 and 1.0 are generally lacking activity types 3, 6 and 7, referring to graduate schools, cinemas and theatres. In some cases other activity types, such as parks or public gardens (4), postal offices (15) or sport facilities (8) are also missing. Although these areas still give good conditions for the use of non-motorized modes for most daily activities they force their inhabitants to choose other less sustainable modes to reach other activities (although, with the exception of sport facilities, these have generally low frequency of use).

Less than 22 per cent of the population of the study area lives in areas presenting medium accessibility levels, being unable to walk to several every-day activities. The remaining 1 per cent of population living in conditions of low non-motorized accessibility is scattered on an area representing 8 per cent of the study region.

Figure 7.8 presents the geographical distribution of accessibility levels by public transport modes. As referred before, this measure is a good indicator for the spatial distribution of public transport availability. Although almost half of the study region has no access to public transport service, this area only holds 15 per cent of the overall population (see Table 7.4). The vast majority of the remaining population lives in areas with high levels of accessibility to diversity of activities by public transport (83 per cent). 71 per cent live in conditions of maximum accessibility to activities by public transport. Only 2 per cent of the population lives in medium accessibility conditions by public transport in 4 per cent of the study area. On average, the region presents an accessibility index of 0.84 (accessibility class B but very close to class A).

The best accessibility conditions (with accessibility to all activity types by public transport) can be found in almost the entire municipality of Oporto, stretching mainly to the north along the main public transport corridors and in

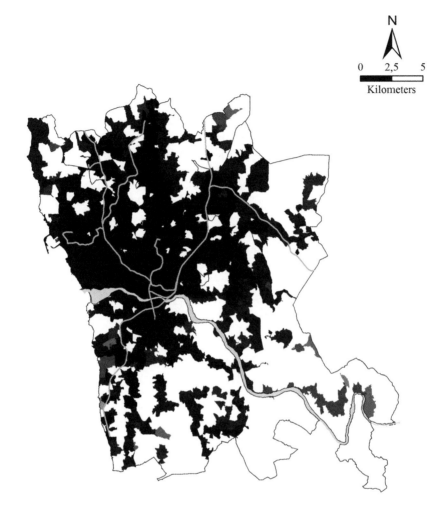

Legend

☐ Municipalities   ⎯⎯ Railways (Train, Metro)

DivAct

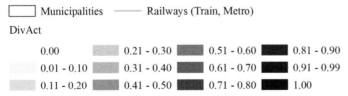

Figure 7.8   Diversity of activities accessible by public transport in GO
Source: Adapted from Silva (2008).

a small part to the south. The remaining area with high accessibility conditions (containing 12 per cent of the population) shows accessibility restrictions mainly to graduate schools (3).

Figure 7.9 presents the geographical distribution of accessibility levels by car. Almost the entire study area provides their inhabitants with accessibility to all activity types by car (98 per cent of the population living in 87 per cent of the study area). Excluded from these conditions are two peripheral areas, one at the northeast and the other at the southeast, and several small areas scattered across the study area. Almost 93 per cent of the study region presents high accessibility levels giving good conditions to 99 per cent of the population for the use of the car as access mode for everyday activities. On average, the study region present almost maximum accessibility level, with a value of 0.99 regarding activities accessible by car.

The remaining 7 per cent of the territory mainly includes sub-areas with medium accessibility levels on the far south-eastern side of the study area. The low values of accessibility for these sub-areas seem to be a result of severe artificial boundary effects. Low accessibility levels are presented by a residual number of sub-areas scattered across the study area, resulting from network errors. In these conditions it is fair to say that the entire study area provides high accessibility levels to all its inhabitants (class A), with 98 per cent having access to all activities by this transport mode.

Figure 7.10 represents the accessibility clusters, resulting from the comparison of mode accessibility. This map illustrates the land use and transport conditions constraining the higher or lower sustainability of mobility. In other words, it represents the sustainability of potential mobility.

Recalling that the car offers the same accessibility class for the entire study area (class A), only nine of the accessibility categories defined by the benchmarking cube can be found. Consequently, and similarly to the results reached in Copenhagen, only four of nine accessibility clusters – clusters III, IV, VI and VII – are represented in the map.

While diversity of activity maps by transport mode efficiently pictures our image of the urban structure, the comparative map provides a new image of the same urban structure. This map reveals, in detail, the modal choice limitations brought upon by the urban structure of Greater Oporto. Generally speaking it reveals two main territories: one where people have more sustainable mode choices made available by urban structure (clusters III, IV and VI) and another that does not provide the necessary land use and transport conditions to foster sustainable travel behaviour (cluster VII, were mode choice is structurally limited to the car).

As Figure 7.10 shows, nearly the entire municipality of Oporto provides high accessibility by all transport modes (cluster III), as well as its closer periphery and several corridors stretching north and east. We can also find some sub-areas with high accessibility by all transport modes in the south, more scattered along the southern part of the municipality of Vila Nova de Gaia. In this area, sub-areas

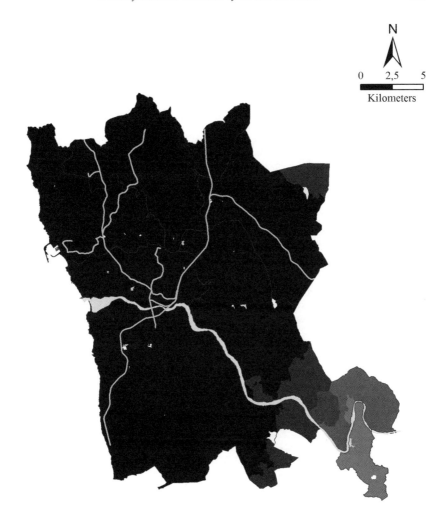

Legend

☐ Municipalities ------- Railways (Train, Metro)

DivAct

0.00	0.21 - 0.30	0.51 - 0.60	0.81 - 0.90
0.01 - 0.10	0.31 - 0.40	0.61 - 0.70	0.91 - 0.99
0.11 - 0.20	0.41 - 0.50	0.71 - 0.80	1.00

Figure 7.9   Diversity of activities accessible by car in GO
Source: Adapted from Silva (2008).

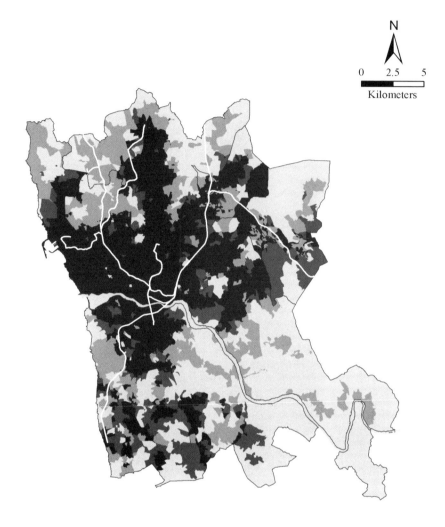

Legend

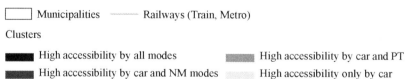

Figure 7.10   Clusters of accessibility in GO
Source: Adapted from Silva and Pinho (2010).

with good accessibility conditions by car and non-motorized modes (cluster IV) are also common, suggesting deficiencies in public transport supply. As to the sub-areas with car favouring conditions (cluster VII), they can generally be found in the most peripheral zones of Greater Oporto, notably in the southeast.

The clear majority of the population (71 per cent) lives under land use and transport conditions providing high accessibility by all transport modes (cluster III), in an area smaller than 33 per cent of the study region (Table 7.5). The remaining population lives mainly in public transport and car favouring conditions (cluster VI, 13 per cent of population). Around 7 per cent of the population live in non-motorized and car favouring conditions (cluster IV) while almost 10 per cent live in favouring conditions only for the use of the car (cluster VII).

Table 7.5   Categories and clusters by area and population

Clusters	Area (km²)	Percentage	Population	Percentage
III	181	32.1	769,691	70.7
IV	63	11.3	74,327	6.8
VI	87	15.5	137,892	12.7
VII	231	41.0	107,208	9.8
Total	562	100	1,089,118	100

Source: Silva and Pinho, 2010.

Summarizing, the region has clearly two distinct areas with regard to land use and transport conditions for sustainable travel behaviour. Nevertheless, on average, it is fair to say that the region provides already good conditions for the use of both non-motorized modes and the car, although conditions for car use are considerably better than for walking. On the other hand public transport accessibility is still not at acceptable levels and considerably lower than car accessibility, offering a clear advantage for car use and therefore for non-sustainable travel behaviour.

Discussion

In this section, a comparative analysis of the results of the SAL for the two regions of study: Greater Oporto and Greater Copenhagen is presented. As referred before, Greater Oporto and Greater Copenhagen are fairly similar both in area and in population. Therefore, the average population density is not very different, although slightly higher in Copenhagen (Table 7.6). These two areas have, however, quite different patterns of urbanization, as a result of different dimensions (Copenhagen is a larger metropolis than Oporto) as well as different planning practices and traditions.

In addition, lifestyles in these two cities are also very different and this fact has mobility implications, namely in the distribution of trips per purpose and in the modal split. The importance of trips related to leisure and shopping is higher in Copenhagen, as well as the use of the bike, which is almost non-existent in Oporto. Moreover, the transport infrastructure is also different in the two study regions, as well as the urbanization patterns, as referred to in Chapter 4. Table 7.6 summarizes some of these main characteristics of the two study regions.

Despite these differences, two of the transport mode types considered show fairly similar results in both case studies: the car, which has maximum accessibility levels in almost the entire regions of Oporto and Copenhagen, and also the public transport, which provides the highest accessibility conditions in the centre and along the main public transport routes in both study areas (see Figure 7.3 and Figure 7.8).

Table 7.6   Characteristics of the two study regions

Greater Copenhagen		Greater Oporto
1.2 million	**Population**	1.1 million
542 km²	**Area**	563 km²
2,215 hab/km²	**Average population density**	1,936 hab/km²
Car: 42.9 Public transport: 11.2 Walking: 21.4 Cycling: 23.2 Others: 1.3	**Modal split (%)**	Car: 47.6 Public transport: 26.2 Walking: 20.2 Others: 6.1
Work: 27.1 School: 6.8 Leisure: 35.5 Shopping: 25.9 Others: 4.6	**Trips per purpose (%)**	Work: 40.8 School: 11.6 Leisure: 21.7 Shopping: 10.4 Others: 15.6
Public transport network based on railway system (mainly radial) complemented by a wide radial and circular bus network. Radial and circular motorways (0.57 km/km²).	**Transport infrastructure**	High density radial and circular motorway network (0.64 km/km²). Public transport mainly based on bus. Railway network (Metro and train) is radial and, in Oporto municipality, limited to the city centre.
Traditionally monocentric structure with high concentration of population and employment in the city core and a radial pattern of development along the 'fingers'. Today shows some signs of polycentric decentralization due to an efficient transport system and restrictive land use policies since the 1950s.	**Urban structure**	Historically polycentric structure related to the location of industrial activities. Today shows a high concentration of jobs in the city centre, but is experiencing a process of population and employment decentralization towards the surrounding municipalities.

There is also – both in Oporto and in Copenhagen – a significant positive correlation between population density and accessibility by public transport (Table 7.7), which was to be expected since PT operators normally plan routes along territories with high population and activity densities, as to follow objectives of profit maximization. For this same reason, it is only natural that in the two studied regions most population has access to public transport and that accessibility levels in these areas are high. The analysis by population and area, however, shows more positive results in Copenhagen, which has a higher share of residents living in high accessibility conditions (95 per cent against 83 per cent in Oporto) by PT modes and these areas cover more than 60 per cent of the study area, while in Oporto high accessibility sub-areas represent less than half of the territory. This again comes as no surprize considering the transit oriented development of the 'Finger Plan' and thus of the Copenhagen Region urban structure.

Table 7.7   Population and population density by classes of accessibility by PT modes

PT class	Population percentage		Population density (residents/km²)	
	Copenhagen	**Oporto**	**Copenhagen**	**Oporto**
A	94.6%	83.3%	3,452	3,376
B	0.1%	1.7%	613	829
C	5.4%	15.0%	587	600
Regional average population density			2,218	1,936

Figure 7.11 shows the spatial distribution of the diversity of activity index by walking in the two study regions. GC and GO are represented in the same spatial scale (1:350,000), to enable a better comparison between the levels of accessibility and to provide a more comprehensive picture of the urban structures. Figure 7.12 represents, in a similar way, the population density in the two study regions.

Looking at what these two metropolitan regions have in common, it is evident that both Oporto and Copenhagen show the highest levels of accessibility by walking in their centres. At the same time, there are in both cases several peripheral areas that have also high accessibility levels.

Moreover, the analysis of the two maps together suggests a close relationship between density and pedestrian accessibility: the areas with higher population density normally match the places with better accessibility conditions. Table 7.8 supports this observation, showing much higher values of population density in areas with high accessibility by walking (class A), both in Oporto and in Copenhagen. The positive correlation between population density and accessibility to activities is indeed widely supported by both theoretical and empirical literature (see, for example, Cervero and Kockleman, 1997; Kenworthy and Laube, 1999; Stead et al., 2000).

Figure 7.11 Diversity of activity index in the two regions of study (full-page pictures are available in Figure 7.1 and Figure 7.7)

Source: Adapted from Silva et al. (2014).

Legend

Municipalities   Population Density (hab/Km2)
Railways
        0   501 - 1000   2001 - 5000   10001 - 20000
        1 - 500   1001 - 2000   5001 - 10000   >20000

**Figure 7.12   Population density in the two regions of study
        (full-page pictures are available in Figure 4.11 and Figure 4.35)**
Source: Adapted from Silva et al. (2014).

Table 7.8   Population and population density by classes of pedestrian accessibility

	Population percentage		Population density (residents/ km²)	
NM class	Copenhagen	Oporto	Copenhagen	Oporto
A	93.3%	77.5%	3,232	3,461
B	6.5%	21.5%	940	849
C	0.2%	1.0%	180	261
Regional average population density			2,218	1,936

Whereas the results both in Oporto and in Copenhagen hold for this positive correlation between population density and level of accessibility to activities, the exercise of comparing these two areas is not that linear. Despite having fairly similar population densities (slightly higher in Copenhagen) the average regional level of pedestrian accessibility is higher in Greater Copenhagen (0.97) than in Greater Oporto (0.91). The analysis of the levels of accessibility by population (see Table 7.8) confirms this idea. In Copenhagen there is a higher share of population (93.3 per cent) with high level of pedestrian accessibility (class A) to activities than in Oporto (77.6 per cent).

Furthermore, sub-areas with high accessibility conditions represent 64 per cent of Greater Copenhagen's surface, while in Oporto these areas cover less than half of the territory. Interestingly, the major differences appear when we analyze the remaining accessibility classes. In Oporto, almost half of the territory has medium accessibility conditions while in Copenhagen the proportion of class B sub-areas is only 15 per cent of the surface. Conversely, low accessibility areas are only 8 per cent of GO's territory, while in Copenhagen more than 20 per cent of the region does not provide satisfactory accessibility conditions (including Class C and non-urban areas). This means that accessibility levels in Oporto are more homogeneous, while in Copenhagen there is a larger gap between high and low accessibility areas. The same happens when looking at the population distribution. In Oporto the proportion of inhabitants with medium levels of accessibility is higher than in Copenhagen (21.3 per cent in GO against 6.5 per cent in Copenhagen).

These effects reflect different patterns of urbanization in these two metropolitan areas, in part as a result of different planning traditions. They suggest that, even though there is a link between higher population densities and higher levels of pedestrian accessibility, there are other structural factors influencing the accessibility conditions in a metropolitan area.

In Oporto, for instance, population is more scattered throughout the urban area, making it more difficult to locate a wide variety of activities closer to a larger number of households. Activities in Oporto are also more scattered resulting in more homogeneous levels of accessibility.

In Copenhagen, on the other hand, efficient land use and transport policies during the past decades provided for a more balanced location of population, jobs and activities, resulting in a pattern of 'concentrated decentralization' of the Copenhagen Metropolitan Area (see Chapter 4). Urbanization has followed a strategy of transit-oriented development, associating urban development to main public transport nodes (specifically main train stations). This means that population is concentrated around several centralities all over the metropolitan region and developed around main train stations, making it possible for activities to locate closer to the places where people live and, therefore, providing better pedestrian accessibility conditions at the same time as providing better access to public transport. This also challenges the first assumption that Greater Copenhagen has a monocentric urban structure, since the 'concentrated decentralization pattern' can be seen as a type of polycentric development.

Although the study area does not provide a clear picture of this 'concentrated decentralization' pattern (because it only represents the central part of the metropolitan area) we can see several high accessibility areas outside the inner city. Contrarily to the case of Oporto – where second-order centres are clearly visible – the very high accessibility levels all across Greater Copenhagen somehow conceal the structure of centralities. However, as referred before, it is still possible to identify a few secondary centres (for instance Lyngby or Birkerød) as well as concentrations of high accessibility centralities outside the centre, mainly along the 'fingers'.

Summarizing, we may conclude that the results of the SAL – notably the geographical distribution of pedestrian accessibility levels – support the idea that Greater Oporto and Greater Copenhagen do not have so different urban structure characteristics. In both cities the highest accessibility levels can be found in the centre but there are also several important secondary centres with good accessibility conditions around it. In Oporto these centralities generally appear around old towns or former industrial settlements and along the national roads; in Copenhagen they are concentrated in the 'fingers', along railway lines, as a result of planning policies.

It is, nevertheless, important to recall that there are some limitations regarding the spatial scale. We chose to study two regions similar both in area and in population. However, being Copenhagen a larger city than Oporto, the two study areas do not represent exactly the same thing. While Greater Copenhagen is the urban centre of a metropolis, Greater Oporto includes the metropolitan centre but also some suburban areas, some of them even rural. This effect partially explains the higher average population densities and accessibility levels in Copenhagen.

The final part of this section concerns the comparative analysis of accessibility clusters for the two study regions. Figure 7.13 represents the geographical distribution of this measure in GC and GO using the same scale.

In both study regions, areas within cluster III (high accessibility by all transport modes) normally match the territories with high pedestrian accessibility. In Copenhagen these areas are generally located in the city centre as well as in the second-order centres, along the 'fingers'. Sub-areas with favourable conditions for

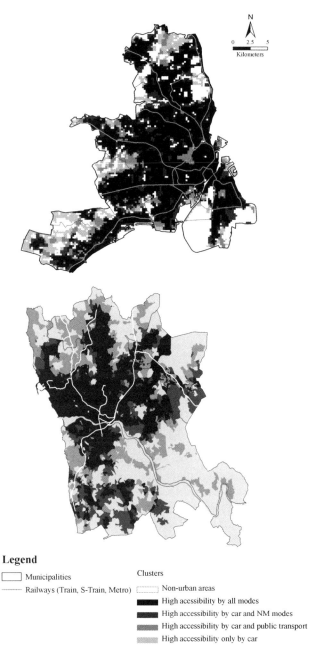

Legend

☐ Municipalities

------- Railways (Train, S-Train, Metro)

Clusters

▢ Non-urban areas

■ High accessibility by all modes

■ High accessibility by car and NM modes

▦ High accessibility by car and public transport

▒ High accessibility only by car

Figure 7.13   Clusters of accessibility in GC and GO
                (full-page pictures are available in Figure 7.5 and Figure 7.10)

Source: Adapted from Silva et al. (2014).

car and PT use (cluster VI) are normally located in peripheral territories along the main public transport routes and also in a few areas within the inner city with lower pedestrian accessibility (which were identified before). Sub-areas with favourable conditions for walking and car use can usually be found in the vicinity of cluster III territories, corresponding to places further away from PT stops.

In Oporto the picture is somewhat different, as sub-areas with favourable conditions for the use of all modes tend to be more centralized in Oporto municipality and its closest periphery. There is a first ring around this central area corresponding to sub-areas in cluster VI (mainly to the north and to the south) and cluster IV (mainly to the east, in Gondomar). Territories that only favour car use are normally located in the more peripheral parts of Greater Oporto. There are however some exceptions to this tendency, notably Maia (in the north, with high accessibility by all transport modes) and the southern area of Gaia municipality with more scattered sub-areas belonging to clusters III and IV.

Both in Oporto and in Copenhagen most of the population lives in sub-areas with favourable conditions for the use of all transport modes and the proportion of residents living with favourable conditions just for car use (cluster VII) is rather limited (Table 7.9). However, conditions in Copenhagen are more positive, with almost 90 per cent of its residents living in areas providing favourable conditions for the use of all modes (against 71 per cent in Oporto), while less than 1 per cent of Copenhagen's population lives with favourable conditions for car use only (in Oporto this share is 9.8 per cent).

Regarding the proportion of territory, the results are similar: both cities present positive results but conditions in Copenhagen are better. Sub-areas in cluster III represent 54 per cent of Greater Copenhagen and 32 per cent of Greater Oporto's territory. On the other hand, 41 per cent of GO corresponds to sub-areas in cluster VII (car favourable conditions), while in Copenhagen this territories are less than 30 per cent (already including non-urban areas).

Similar to what happened with pedestrian accessibility, there is a positive connection in both study areas between density and accessibility, with territories with high accessibility conditions by all transport modes clearly presenting the highest levels of population density, opposite to sub-areas with high accessibility only by car. However, as it was referred before, population density by itself does not explain the huge differences in accessibility conditions between the two case studies.

On average, Oporto falls into accessibility cluster IV, with high accessibility by car and non-motorized modes and medium accessibility by public transport modes, while Copenhagen has on average high accessibility conditions by all modes (cluster III, Table 7.10). Therefore, we can argue that the two studied regions already provide good conditions for the use of non-motorized modes, namely by walking and to a higher extent in GC. Moreover, if we consider travelling by bicycle in Copenhagen, the level of non-motorized accessibility will be much higher (with a regional value of 1.0). On the other hand, Greater Oporto does not

Table 7.9　　Population and population density by accessibility clusters

	Population percentage		Population density (residents/km^2)	
Clusters	Copenhagen	Oporto	Copenhagen	Oporto
III	88.5	70.7	3,670	4,263
IV	4.8	6.8	1,006	1,175
VI	6.0	13.8	1,841	1,435
VII	0.7	8.7	147	443
Regional average population density			2,218	1,936

Source: Silva et al., 2014.

provide acceptable levels of accessibility by public transport yet, which offers a clear advantage for car use and therefore for non-sustainable travel behaviour.

Copenhagen's pattern of concentrated decentralization (a result of the transit oriented development strategy followed by the 'Finger Plan') appears to provide accessibility conditions with the potential to encourage more sustainable travel patterns, by promoting both non-motorized and public transport use. This idea is supported by the proportion of the population with favourable accessibility conditions by sustainable modes, which is always higher in Copenhagen, even with more restrictive criteria for the definition of the high accessibility class.

However, it is important to assess if this higher potential for sustainable mobility in Copenhagen actually corresponds to more sustainable travel behaviour of its residents.

Table 7.10 compares two accessibility measures resulting from the SAL (proportion of population living in sub-areas with high accessibility conditions and average regional level of accessibility) with the real modal distribution of trips made by the residents of GC and GO.

The main difference in transport mode choice between these two cities is the use of the bike, which represents over 23 per cent of trips made by Copenhagen's residents but it is almost inexistent in Oporto. Such a high importance of the bicycle in Copenhagen has implications on the travel shares of the remaining transport modes, limiting the comparison with Oporto. That is, if conditions for travelling by bike were not so favourable, modal shares of the other transport modes would certainly be higher.

In fact, public transport appears to be the mode losing more trips to the bicycle in Copenhagen. Even with better accessibility conditions – Copenhagen has a higher proportion of population living in class A sub-areas and also a higher average level of accessibility – public transport represents only 11.2 per cent of trips in this region, less than half of the share in Oporto (26.2 per cent). Regarding pedestrian mobility, on the contrary, the higher accessibility conditions in Copenhagen correspond to higher proportion of trips made by walking. Although the difference is relatively small – 24.1 per cent in GC against 20.2 per cent in GO – this difference in mode choice is quite relevant considering that probably a significant proportion of bike users would travel by walking if the bicycle was not available.

Table 7.10   Comparison between accessibility conditions and real modal distribution in Greater Copenhagen and Greater Oporto

Greater Copenhagen				Greater Opoto		
Modal split[1]	Population with high accessibility	Average regional DivAct		Modal split[2]	Population with high accessibility	Average regional DivAct
24.1%	93.3%	0.97	**NM (walking)**	20.2%	77.5%	0.91
11.2%	94.6%	0.95	**PT**	26.2%	83.3%	0.84
42.9%	100%	1.00	**CAR**	47.6%	100%	0.99
23.2%	99.9%	1.00	**NM (Bike)**	-	-	-

[1]   Number of trips by transport mode according to a travel survey carried out by DTU Transport (2006–2009). These data do not refer to Greater Copenhagen, but to a slightly different region corresponding to the municipalities of Copenhagen and Fredriksberg plus the former county of Copenhagen.
[2]   Data concerning the number of trips per person by transport mode in Oporto in 2001, retrieved from INE. The values do not refer to the study area, but to the metropolitan area of Oporto.

The car has fairly similar results in Oporto and Copenhagen, matching the similar accessibility conditions (maximum accessibility levels in both the study regions). Even though the bicycle is probably not the most direct competitor of the car, the proportion of trips by car in Copenhagen (42.9 per cent) would most likely increase slightly to values closer to Oporto's (46.7 per cent) if the bicycle was not considered.

In summary, we can conclude that people living in areas with high accessibility conditions by non-motorized modes tend to use these modes more often. There is also a stronger tendency for car use in territories where urban structure constraints on non-motorized modes and public transport are higher.

Furthermore, both study regions present quite high proportions of car trips, much above any of the other transport modes. In fact, considering accessibility levels, we reach the conclusion that, whatever the accessibility conditions by sustainable modes, accessibility conditions by car are always similar or even higher. This means that policies aiming to promote sustainable travel behaviour (related to urban structure or not) would probably have to promote not only better accessibility conditions by sustainable modes, but they would also have to consider constraints on car use, in order to increase competitiveness of the more sustainable modes of transport.

Chapter 8

Residential Location and Travel Behaviour

Petter Næss

Introduction

This chapter presents the results of the application of the Explanatory Qualitative-Quantitative Method (EQQM) to the Greater Copenhagen and the Greater Oporto cases. First, the results of the analyses of the qualitative interviews will be presented, with a particular focus on the interviewees' rationales for location of activities, travel modes and frequency of activity participation (see pp. 151–9). Thereafter, material from the questionnaire surveys will be presented, investigating the effects of the main urban-structural variables while controlling for relevant demographic and socioeconomic variables (and in the Copenhagen case also for transport-related residential preferences). Here, the overall relationships found when all population groups are considered together will be presented first (see pp. 159–75), followed by separate analyses for sub-groups of the population, notably women and men and persons with a high and with a low level of education (see pp. 175–81). The role of more detail-level (neighbourhood-scale) urban structural conditions will then be analyzed, comparing the effects of such characteristics with those of the main urban structural variables (see pp. 181–6).

Explaining the Causal Links: Examples from the Qualitative Material

In order to substantiate that residential location is a (contributory) cause of differences in travel distances and modes, we must show the basic mechanisms by which the location of dwellings influences travel behaviour. Examples illuminating the transport rationales of residents and how these rationales interact with spatial conditions in shaping routines for travel behaviour make up important elements in this endeavour. Transport rationales are here understood as the backgrounds, motivations and justifications that agents draw on when they make transport-relevant decisions about their participation in activities, location of these activities, modes of transportation and the routes followed (Næss and Jensen, 2005; 165). The concept, which includes instrumental, safety-based, comfort-based, aesthetic as well as affective dimensions (see Scheiner and Holz-Rau, 2007, and Steg et al., 2001, among others), has some overlap with the notion of 'mobility view' coined by Beckmann (2001). Combined with the spatial configuration of residences, employment and other facilities in a city or metropolitan area, the transport rationales produce some characteristic relationships between residential location and travel found in a number of different urban contexts.

Rationales for Location of Activities

In both city regions, the interviewees' choices of locations for their activities seem to be influenced by two main, competing rationales which are balanced against each other in different ways, depending on a number of circumstances. These two rationales are:

* Choosing the best facility; and
* Minimizing the friction of distance.

Each of these two rationales includes several more detailed aspects or sub-rationales. The rationale of choosing the best facility thus includes criteria related to the instrumental purpose of the activity (e.g., job content, salary, qualification requirements, etc., of workplaces, and range of commodities, prices, etc., of shops), but also to some extent criteria related to cultural, symbolic or aesthetic properties of the locations (e.g., the 'atmosphere' of a particular place). The rationale of minimizing the friction of distance (Lloyd and Dicken, 1977) includes an aspect of minimizing the spatial distance that must be travelled in order to reach the facility (e.g., measured in km); an aspect of minimizing the traveling time; an aspect of minimizing the stress or physical efforts of traveling to the location (e.g., in the form of changing between different means of transport); and an aspect of minimizing the economic costs of the trip. To a considerable extent, the sub-rationales under the rationale of minimizing the friction of distance overlap each other, but under certain conditions (e.g., congested roads, scarce parking, or a particular configuration of the public transport lines) the fastest, least costly or most conveniently accessible locations may be different from the physically closest ones.

When talking about traveling distances, the interviewees in both case regions were usually not very explicit regarding the way(s) in which distance matters. Some interviewees explicitly referred to time consumption for traveling, but most often no particular reasons were stated why travel distance was important. Despite national differences, imperatives of not wasting away either money or time are probably quite pervasive in the contemporary social and cultural contexts of both case regions, especially among the interviewees facing the strongest economic and time-geographical constraints. Arguably, the fact that so few interviewees mentioned money saving or time saving explicitly as underlying motivations for distance minimizing most likely reflects the hegemonic status of these concerns, rendering it unnecessary to refer to them explicitly. Both these rationales were also more often mentioned as concerns influencing choices of travel mode (see below).

Among our interviewees in both city regions, the sub-rationale of choosing facilities where the instrumental purpose of the activities can best be met is clearly more common than the sub-rationales associated with cultural, aesthetic and symbolic preferences and atmosphere. The two latter sub-rationales exert some influence on the destinations of shopping and leisure trips among some interviewees.

Choice of Out-of-Home Activity Locations   Among the different travel purposes, trips to workplace or higher education, along with visits to friends and relatives, are the trip purposes where 'choosing the best facility' rationale dominates most strongly over the 'minimizing friction of distance' rationale. For visiting trips, the 'best facility' should here be understood as the places where precisely those people you want to visit are living or staying. The destinations of visiting trips are thus defined entirely by the traveller's family relations and circle of acquaintances. For jobs, the formal qualifications of the worker must match the qualification requirements of the employer, the job content, working conditions and salary must be acceptable, seen from the point of view of the worker, and the worker must be able to actually be employed in competition with other applicants for the job. The 'best facility' in the context of choice of workplaces should therefore be understood as the best attainable opportunity. The interviewees usually admit that there is a balancing between choosing the best attainable opportunity and minimizing the distance (in travel time or kilometres) from the dwelling, but they generally seem to be willing to travel quite far, if necessary, in order to find a job matching their qualifications, interests and expectations regarding salary level.

Because the workplace or school/university is usually visited each weekday, while long visit trips are carried out far less frequently, journeys to work or education are the travel purposes accounting for the largest proportion of the travel distance on weekdays. The acceptable travel distance to work or education appears to increase the more specialized work qualifications you have, the more mobility resources you have at your disposal and the further away you live from the largest concentrations of work and education opportunities. For those with specialized job qualifications, the whole metropolitan area is usually considered as a relevant job market.

For example, an economist living in a peripheral suburb of Copenhagen Metropolitan Area told that he preferred to commute all the way to downtown Copenhagen instead of finding a less challenging job in a municipality closer to the residence:

> Surely, I would like something closer to home, but there are no such [relevant] jobs available to me here in the vicinity. Then it would have to be if I were interested in working in a municipal administration. … But that would be such a small workplace, and I simply want some more challenges. … Yes, for sure, most work opportunities for economists are in the city of Copenhagen. (Male economist, 38 years old)

For non-work activities, distance minimizing gains higher importance, especially for everyday activities. For some interviewees, distance minimizing applies to all activities. This mainly occurs among non-participants of the workforce (retired or unemployed persons) who at the same time have few mobility resources (non-car-owners and low income). For most interviewees, there is still a trade-off between the 'best facility' rationale and the 'distance minimizing' rationale also for non-work activities. For shopping, distance minimizing is the most important for grocery shopping on weekdays, but the 'best facility' rationale gains importance for weekend shopping, especially for purchases of non-food commodities.

In daily-life travel, some trips are more fixed and basic than other trips. Often, such a trip makes up the stock of a trip chain. Other travel purposes are then 'hitched' on this stock trip. For workforce participants, the journey to work is the most basic trip on weekdays. Distance minimizing is then sometimes applied with the workplace as a base instead of the home. For example, several interviewees carry out some shopping and leisure activities close to the workplace. This is especially mentioned by Oporto interviewees who live in suburbs and work in the downtown area. One female 42-year-old economist tells that she uses to take breaks from work to do some shopping or going to gym, and another woman, a 44-year-old psychologist, takes breaks from work to do some shopping or going for a walk. In the Copenhagen case, suburban interviewees from a low-density neighbourhood with poor provision of local facilities often choose a well-assorted store along the route followed anyway on the way home from work. In this way, the rationale of distance limitation can be combined with the rationale of choosing the best facility even for suburbanites' shopping trips.

When it comes to leisure trips, the choice among facility categories depends strongly on the interests and lifestyle of the person in question, but quality differences within each facility category matter as well. For example, a distant, but larger and more beautiful forest may be preferred for outings rather than a local forest.

As regards non-work trips, a male 32-year-old architect/builder previously living in the downtown area of Oporto said that he usually chooses non-local destinations because he does not like the suburban neighbourhood where he now lives. Instead of looking for the 'best facility', it is in this case apparently a matter of avoiding the 'worst facility', where the facility qualities in question have to do with the 'atmosphere' of the neighbourhood. Such an 'escape' rationale (Kaiser, 1993) could thus be seen as negative variant of the 'best facility' rationale, as it will motivate people to choose facilities other than the closest ones. Another suburban Oporto interviewee (an unemployed 30-year-old woman) also disliked the neighbourhood she had moved into a few years ago. She preferred locating many of her activities to a downtown neighbourhood to which she had family and emotional ties, although her mobility was quite restricted since she had not got a car. Such an emotional 'pull' effect was to some extent apparent also for the above-mentioned architect/builder in addition to the 'push' effect of not liking his present neighbourhood. Among persons who have moved, an 'emotional ties' sub-rationale could thus be identified.

In particular for the most basic trip purposes on weekdays (workplaces and places of higher education), our respondents and interviewees emphasize the possibility of a choice of facilities over proximity. This means that the amount of travel is influenced to a greater extent by the location of the residence in relation to concentrations of facilities than by the distance to the closest single facility within a category. This is evident also for cultural and entertainment facilities, specialized stores and, to some extent, grocery shopping in the weekend. For leisure activities, the 'atmosphere', emotional ties and the aesthetic qualities of a destination may also play a role. Since the largest concentrations of workplaces, as well as other facilities, are in the city centre and the inner districts of the city, the above-mentioned circumstances imply that the amount of quotidian travel is influenced by how far away the interviewees live from the city centre rather than by the distance from their dwelling to lower-order centres.

Our material from the Copenhagen study shows that the propensity for using local facilities depends partly on which facilities exist in the proximity of the dwelling, and partly on the competition from non-local facilities. In the districts next to the downtown area, a relatively broad supply of local facilities often exists, but at the same time there is a strong competition from facilities in the city centre. Conversely, the local supply of facilities is often more modest in the outer parts of the metropolitan area, but the long distance to the concentration of facilities found in inner city at the same time weakens the competition from the latter facilities.

Choice of Residential Location   In the qualitative interviews of the studies in Copenhagen Metropolitan Area and Greater Oporto, a clear tendency can be found that interviewees living in inner districts and/or close to main public transport lines mention accessibility or reduced needs for transport as important positive features of the neighbourhood and/or reasons for living there, while interviewees living in neighbourhoods with poor availability of facilities do not. The only exception is one suburban interviewee in Oporto who points at the proximity of her employer-provided dwellings to her workplaces.

The fact that most of the interviewees living in central districts or sub-centres well-served by public transport mention accessibility or reduced needs for transport as important elements of their residential preferences, while those living in neighbourhoods with poor transit provision and low availability of facilities do not, could be interpreted as an indication of transport-related residential self-selection. But such self-selection hardly undermines the causal relationships between urban structures and travel behaviour. Rather, emphasis on accessibility to jobs and other facilities is an example of the rationale of minimizing the friction of distance. Similar to how this rationale, together with a rationale of choosing the best facility, influences residents' locations of their activities, the rationale of minimizing the friction of distance will also, when key trip destinations (particularly the workplace) are seen as the base, influence people's choices about where to live, together with the rationale of choosing the best facility. In this case, 'the best facility' refers to amenities of the residence other than its distance to the workplace and other frequent trip destinations, such as housing costs, availability of a private garden, absence of noise and air pollution, socioeconomic characteristics of the neighbourhood, etc.

Rationales for Modal Choice

The interviewees' choices of travel modes are influenced by a number of different and interconnected rationales. These rationales could be classified into two main groups:

- Rationales concerning the efficiency of the movement from origin to destination; and
- Rationales concerning the process of moving from origin to destination.

The first of these two groups includes concerns related the time consumption, economic costs and accessibility benefits of traveling by different modes. The second group includes concerns related to physically, psychologically and socially positive or negative aspects associated with traveling by a particular mode.

Among the rationales concerning the efficiency of the movement from origin to destination, the following appear to be the most important ones to our interviewees:

- Time-saving;
- Flexibility;
- Expansion of the radius of action; and
- Money-saving.

The rationales concerning physical, psychological and social aspects associated with the process of traveling include:

- Comfort;
- Limitation of physical efforts;
- Relaxation;
- Safety;
- Aversion against frustrations;
- Physical exercise;
- Enjoyment of surrounding environment;
- Affective dislike or preference for a particular mode;
- Lifestyle signalling;
- Habits; and possibly also
- Demonstration of wealth and status.

The rationale of time saving generally leads interviewees to choose those modes of travel that can bring them as fast as possible from their origin to their destination. Among interviewees who do not have a car at their disposal, this implies a preference for bike on short trips, public transport for long trips, and, if the time of the trip is not fixed, avoiding the rush hours when traveling by bus. Among car owners, the time-saving rationale encourages the choice of car for long trips and non-motorized modes for short trips where car driving (including walking time to and from parking) would be more time-consuming than biking or walking. The time-saving rationale strengthens the influence of proximity to the main city centre on the choice of travel mode, since the more slowly-moving traffic in inner-city areas makes up an incentive for residents of these areas to choose non-motorized modes or public transport.

Since long trips will be very time-consuming as well as physically exhausting if they are made by non-motorized modes (in particular by foot), rationales of time-saving and limitation of physical efforts will logically imply a dependence of travel modes on trip distances. Trip distance thus appears to have the role of an intermediate rationale through which residential locations leading to shorter traveling distances are also conducive to a higher share of non-motorized travel.

The rationale of flexibility generally leads to a preference for individual modes of travel rather than public transport (due to the rigid layout of lines and time schedule of the latter). For short and medium-long trips, this implies a preference for bike (or walking for the shortest distances) rather than bus, tramcar or metro for longer trips the flexibility rationale leads to a preference for car or motorcycle. The flexibility rationale may strengthen the influence of proximity to the main city centre on modal choice, since public transport is less flexible in the periphery and car traffic more hampered in the inner city.

The rationale of expanding the radius of action is related to a rationale for activity location of choosing the best facility (see the previous section), as the use of motorized modes, in particular car, expands the geographical area within which relevant facilities can be chosen. For a particular trip, e.g., with the purpose of shopping, the car may be chosen in order to visit a broader range of shops than would otherwise be possible within an acceptable level of time consumption. The radius of action rationale strengthens the relationship between proximity to the city centre and modal choice, since the incentive to increase the radius of action is higher in outer areas where a more narrow range of facilities is available within a short distance from the dwelling. To some extent, this rationale also contributes to more car trips when living far away from the closest local centre.

The rationale of money-saving strengthens the influence of a central residential location (especially proximity to the main city centre) on modal choice, since gasoline consumption per km is higher and parking more expansive in inner-city areas, and because the money-saving rationale may act as a catalyzer realizing the potential for non-motorized travel among residents living close to relevant destinations. The latter also applies to the rationales of physical exercise, experience of surroundings and aversion against frustration, which may contribute to realizing a potential for walk/bike when distances to facilities are moderate.

Although interesting in themselves, the remaining rationales for modal choice appear to be of lesser importance to the ways in which residential location influences travel behaviour. We shall therefore not elaborate on these rationales here.

Rationales for Activity Participation

Our interviews indicate that people's activity patterns are to some extent adapted to the availability of facilities in the proximity of the dwelling, but their total level of activity participation shows little geographical variation. In particular, this applies to workforce participation. According to our survey data, there is no tendency among either the Greater Copenhagen or the Greater Oporto respondents of reduced employment frequencies among people living far away from the main concentrations of workplaces. In the Copenhagen study, where frequencies of 'teleworking' were also investigated, only a very modest tendency of teleworking was found among respondents with long commuting distances.

For leisure activities, distance decay occurs to a greater extent. For example, a non-car-owning female interviewee who had some years ago moved from the downtown area of Oporto to a suburb lamented the poorer activity opportunities in her new neighbourhood. She considered that if she could return to living in the centre of the metropolitan area, she could recover many habits that she once had. Another Oporto interviewee, a male car-owner, who had also moved from the inner city to a suburb, considered that his quality of life would be improved if he moved back to a more central neighbourhood. Usually, however, the total amount of leisure activity participation does not vary much with residential location, although the composition of activities does, depending on where the relevant facilities can be found. Trip frequencies are therefore not varying much between inner-city residents and suburbanites. Activities which would be conducted more rarely if living in a more peripheral area include evening classes, gym team exercise, badminton, socializing with neighbours, visits to restaurants, and going to the cinema. On the other hand, some suburban interviewees, especially in Copenhagen Metropolitan Area, consider that they would visit forests and other green areas less frequently, make fewer jogging trips, invite friends home more rarely and – perhaps needless to say – spend less time on gardening if they were to live in an inner-city neighbourhood.

Since the total amount of out-of-home activity participation is not much influenced by residential location, 'distance decay' only to a small extent counteracts the overall tendency of increased traveling distances and more frequent car trips when living far away from the main concentrations of facilities.

Rationales for Route Choice

The relationships between the amount of travel and the distance from the dwelling to the city centre and local centres is theoretically based on the assumption that there is no systematic difference between inner-city and outer-area residents in the extent of any deviations from the shortest route. The rationales for route choice generally support this assumption, apart from the rationale of physical exercise. Since the need for extending the length of bike or walking trips in order to obtain sufficient exercise is higher if the destination is close than if it is located far away, the tendency to exercise-motivated detours is likely to be more widespread among inner-city dwellers than among their outer-area counterparts. However, from an environmental and greenhouse gas perspective, this compensatory mechanism contributing to somewhat increased traveling distances among exercise-minded inner-city residents is unimportant, as these non-motorized trips consume no fossil energy and generate no greenhouse gas emissions whatsoever.

Results from the Main Questionnaire Surveys

As mentioned in Chapter 6, a large number of travel behaviour indicators were recorded for each respondent: total traveling distance, traveling distances by car and motorcycle, by bus, by train and by non-motorized modes.[1] These data were used to determine the proportions of the total distance travelled by car, public transport, and non-motorized modes, respectively. These aspects of travel behaviour were recorded for the weekdays (Monday–Friday), the weekend (Saturday–Sunday) and for the week as a whole, making up a total of 24 travel behaviour variables. Below, we shall concentrate on factors influencing the following aspects of travel behaviour:[2]

- Total traveling distance during the week;
- The traveling distance carried out by car and motorcycle; and
- The traveling distance carried out by non-motorized modes.

---

1   The recorded travel distances were based on information from the respondents about how far they had travelled by each mode during each day of the week. This of course represents a source of inaccuracy. However, we do not believe that this inaccuracy leads to any systematic bias of the results.

2   In the analyses, any respondents with extreme weekly traveling distances (i.e., more than three interquartile intervals above the upper quartile) and respondents who have not travelled at all during the investigated period have been excluded. In Greater Copenhagen, six respondents who had not at all travelled and 15 with extreme traveling distances (over 1,103 km) were excluded from the analyses. In Greater Oporto, no respondents had travelled extremely long distances, and there were no respondents who had not at all travelled during the week. However, three respondents had recorded implausibly long travel distances by non-motorized modes (more than 500 km each over the week). Since we suspected these respondents' traveling distances to be unreliable, they were excluded from the analyses. All the remaining respondents in each case city (except those with missing values) were included in the analyses.

It might also have been interesting to present the corresponding results from analyses of factors influencing traveling distances by public transport. Especially, such results would be relevant for the comparison of EQQM and SAL results. However, neither in Greater Copenhagen nor in Greater Oporto did we find any significant effects of the residential variables on the distances travelled by public transport. Most likely, this reflects the fact that the respondents living in the parts of the cities where the availability of public transport services is highest, often have their regular trip destinations within a relatively short distance. So even if they may travel more frequently by transit, their overall traveling distances by public transport may still not differ much from the average. The short distances to regular trip destinations also implies that many such trips are carried out by foot or by bike rather than by transit. Instead of presenting separate graphs and tables for the relationships between the residential location variables and travel by public transport, the effects found in multivariate analyses of residential location variables on traveling distances by transit will only briefly be mentioned.

The following residential location and density variables were included in the main analyses:

- The linear distance from the dwelling to the main city centre, measured in kilometres;
- The linear distance from the dwelling to the closest second-order centre, measured in kilometres;
- The logarithmic distance to the closest urban rail station (Greater Copenhagen) or main regional retail centre (Greater Oporto); and
- Density of inhabitants and jobs in the local neighbourhood, measured within an 800 m radius.

The non-urban-structural control variables were those mentioned in Chapter 6. It should be noted that transport-related residential preferences were not included among the control variables of the Oporto study, since the number of responses to this question was too low to be considered valid for the analysis. However, since the effects of the urban structural variables of the Greater Copenhagen study turned out to be affected only to a very small degree depending on whether or not the residential preferences variable was included, we believe the possible bias in the Greater Oporto study due to the lack of control for residential preferences to be not very serious. Moreover, as argued by Næss (2009a), the fact that people to some extent 'self-select' into areas matching their transport attitudes is in itself a demonstration of the importance of urban structure to travel behaviour. If there were no such influence, people who prefer not to travel by car might as well settle in the peripheral part of the metropolitan area, far away from public transport stops and the city's main concentrations of workplaces and service facilities.

In Greater Copenhagen, the respondents have on average travelled 247 km during the week investigated, of which 168 km was by car or motorcycle, 50 km by public transit, and 25 km by non-motorized modes. The Greater Oporto respondents have on average travelled 171 km during the week investigated, of which 141 km was by car or motorcycle, 22 km by public transit, and 7 km by non-motorized modes.

Some respondents have travelled by all these modes during the week, but many have only used one single mode or have combined two modes, e.g., walking and public transport. The distribution of traveling distances by the different modes is thus highly different from the ideal, bell-shaped normal distribution. Also, the total travel distances are non-normally distributed. For example, in Greater Oporto, half of the respondents have travelled less than 120 km during the week while the 10 per cent who have travelled the longest distances have on average travelled more than 550 km over the seven days investigated. These non-normal distributions pose some specific challenges to the statistical analyses. In order to cope with the fact that considerable proportions of respondents had not at all used either car/motorcycle or non-motorized modes of transport during the investigated week, the traveling distances by different modes and in total were logarithmically transformed in order to meet the requirements of linear regression in a more satisfactory way. In the multivariate analyses presented below, the residuals for the travelling distances by car or motorcycle are still 'moderately skewed' (Bulmer, 1979, quoted from Brown, 2012) with skewness coefficients of -0.607 (Greater Copenhagen) and 0.589 (Greater Oporto). In the analyses of total weekly travel distance and the travelling distance by non-motorized modes in Greater Copenhagen, skewness is less pronounced, with skewness coefficients of -0.430 and -0.219, respectively. According to Bulmer (ibid.), the latter distributions could hence be characterized as 'approximately symmetrical'. In Greater Oporto, residuals for total weekly travel distance as well as travel by non-motorized modes is more skewed, with coefficients of -0.862 and 0.874, respectively, which again fall under the range characterized by Bulmer (ibid.) as 'moderately skewed'. Although these latter values may give rise to some concern about the reliability of the calculated levels of significance, we still consider the results shown in the following sections to be sufficiently robust for the purpose of this presentation, which is to show the urban structural characteristics influencing various aspects of travel behaviour and indicate their order of magnitude, rather than purporting to provide a basis for precise predictions (see Næss, 2004, for a further discussion).

Bivariate Correlations

Before turning to the main statistical analyses we will present a few graphs (Figures 8.1 and 8.2) showing bivariate correlations in Greater Copenhagen and Greater Oporto between each residential location variable and one selected transport variable: the total weekly travelling distances (including all modes of transport). Distinct from the multivariate analyses presented later, the traveling distance has not been logarithmically transformed in these graphs.

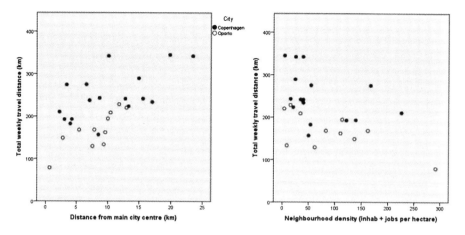

Figure 8.1   Mean weekly total travel distances among respondents living in residential areas in Greater Copenhagen (black dots) and Greater Oporto (white circles), located at different distances from the city centres (left), and with different neighbourhood densities (right)

As we can see, the respondents of both the Greater Copenhagen and the Greater Oporto studies tend to travel longer distances the further away they live from the main city centre as well as from the closest second-order centre. Conversely, traveling distances tend to decrease, the lower is the density of population and jobs in the local neighbourhood. In Oporto there is also a clear tendency of longer traveling distances the further away the respondents live from a regional retail centre, whereas what could be considered the corresponding relationship in Greater Copenhagen (travelling distance as a function of the distance to the closest urban rail station) is less clear.

Similar relationships as those shown in Figure 8.1 and Figure 8.2 exist for the weekly distance travelled by car or motorcycle. The distances travelled by non-motorized modes show correlations with the residential location and density variables inverse to those of the total traveling distances and the distances travelled by car or motorcycle: Residents living close to any of the three categories of centres or in a high-density area tend to walk or bicycle longer distances than their counterparts living further away from such centres or in lower-density areas.

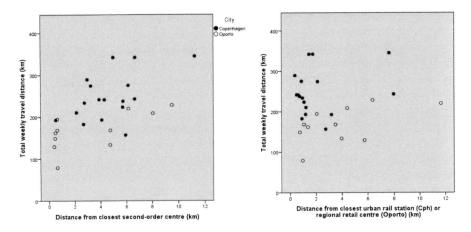

Figure 8.2   Mean weekly total travel distances among respondents living in residential areas in Greater Copenhagen (black dots) and Greater Oporto (white circles), located at different distances from the closest second-order centre (left), and from the closest urban rail station (Copenhagen) or main regional retail centre (Oporto) (right)

Multivariate Analyses

The relationships shown in the previous section are only bivariate. A number of individual characteristics of the respondents also influence travel behaviour, some of which are correlated with residential location. There are also mutual correlations between the different residential location variables. Let us therefore turn to the multivariate analyses, where statistical control for mutual correlation between the different independent variables has been made. The multivariate regression analyses have been carried out by means of a so-called 'backward elimination method'. First, a regression analysis is conducted, including all independent variables of the model (most often 17 variables in the Greater Copenhagen study and 16 variables in the Greater Oporto study, cf. Chapter 6). Unless all variables show effects satisfying a required significance level (in our analyses normally set at $p = 0.100$), the variable with the weakest significance level is excluded. The process continues until the model includes only variables meeting the required significance level.

Total Weekly Traveling Distances   Table 8.1 shows the results of the multivariate analysis of factors potentially influencing the Greater Copenhagen and Greater Oporto respondents' average total traveling distance during the investigated week (logarithmically measured). Clear relationships between residential location and weekly traveling distances exist, also when controlling for a number of relevant

Table 8.1 Results of a multivariate linear regression analysis of factors potentially influencing the logarithm of the weekly total travelling distance among Greater Copenhagen and Greater Oporto respondents

	Unstandardized coefficients		Standardized coefficients		Level of significance (p values)	
	Copenhagen	Oporto	Copenhagen	Oporto	Copenhagen	Oporto
Residential location variables:						
Distance from the dwelling to the main city centre (km)	0.0235		0.167		0.000	N.S. (p = 0.235)
Population and job density (persons and jobs per hectare)		−0.000026		−0.160	N.S. (p = 0.542)	0.000
Distance from the dwelling to the closest second-order centre (km)					N.S. (p = 0.270)	N.S. (p = 0.470)
Logarithm of the distance (in km) from the dwelling to the closest urban rail station (km) (Copenhagen study only)					N.S. (p = 0.411)	
Logarithm of the distance (in km) to the closest main regional retail centre (Oporto study only)						N.S. (p = 0.521)
Control variables:						
Whether the respondent holds a driver's license for car (yes = 1, no = 0)	0.423	0.593	0.162	0.180	0.000	0.000
Personal annual income (in Copenhagen: measured in 1000 DKK, in Oporto measured in classes of income)	0.00043	0.097	0.121	0.146	0.001	0.001
Sex (female = 1, male = 0)	−0.200	−0.375	−0.107	−0.145	0.001	0.000
Workforce participation (yes = 1, no = 0)	0.217	0.334	0.097	0.122	0.005	0.010

Whether the respondent is a pensioner (yes = 1, no = 0)	−0.726	−0.189	N.S. (p = 0.638)	0.000
Whether the respondent has a long education (yes = 1, no = 0)	0.358	0.136	N.S. (p = 0.281)	0.003
Whether the respondent is a student/pupil (yes = 1, no = 0)	−0.213	−0.075	0.031	N.S. (p = 0.281)
Number of household members below seven years	−0.100	−0.062	0.052	N.S. (p = 0.538)
Whether the respondent had moved to the present dwelling less than five years ago (yes = 1, no = 0)	0.109	0.056	0.086	N.S. (p = 0.525)
Age			N.S. (p = 0.576)	N.S. (p = 0.253)
Number of household members aged 7–18			N.S. (p = 0.327)	N.S. (p = 0.619)
Regular transport of children to school or kindergarten (yes = 1, no = 0)			N.S. (p = 0.343)	N.S. (p = 0.711)
Index for transport-related residential preferences (preference for locations facilitating short traveling distances and/or public transport usage = 1, no such preference expressed = 0) (Copenhagen study only)			N.S. (p = 0.868)	
Constant	4.386	4.342	0.000	0.000

Note: Only variables meeting a required significance level of 0.10 were included in the final regression model. N.S. = not significant at the 0.10 level. N = 902 (Copenhagen) and 442 (Oporto). Adjusted R^2: 0.142 (Copenhagen) and 0.332 (Oporto).

demographic and socioeconomic variables. There are, however, some interesting differences between the two cities in the aspects of residential location exerting the strongest influences on the amount of travel. In Greater Copenhagen, the strongest locational effect is found for the distance from the dwelling to the main city centre (Beta = 0.167, p = 0.000), with no significant effects found of either the distance from the dwelling to the closest second-order centre, the logarithmic distance from the dwelling to the closest urban rail station, or the density of population and jobs in the local neighbourhood. In Greater Oporto, the only significant effect of residential location on the weekly traveling distance is of the latter variable (Beta = −0.160, p = 0.000), with no significant effects found of the distances from the dwelling to the main city centre, the closest second-order centre, or the closest regional retail centre.

The effects of demographic and socioeconomic variables are in line with what could be expected from theoretical considerations and conform to the results of a number of previous empirical studies. In both cities, traveling distances tend to increase if the respondent holds a driver's license, has a high income, is male, and/or is a workforce participant. Apart from this, traveling distances in Greater Copenhagen (but not in Greater Oporto) tend to be shorter if the respondent is a student/pupil, belongs to a household with children less than seven years old, and/or has lived in the present dwelling for five years or more. In Greater Oporto (but not in Greater Copenhagen), travelling distances tend to decrease if the respondent is a pensioner and increase if the respondent has a long education. It should be noted that the lack of significant effects of some variables does not necessarily mean that they do not exert any influence at all, only that their effects are too weak and uncertain to rule out the possibility that they are the results of mere chance.

Based on the various sets of multivariate regression analyses in this and the next sub-chapters, calculations have been made of the controlled effects of residential location on the traveling distances of each respondent. This has been done by keeping all variables with effects meeting the required significance level (p = 0.100) constant at mean values, while inserting the respondent's actual values for all urban structural variables included in the regression model. Based on the estimates thus derived of expected travelling patterns emanating from the various residential addresses, average, expected values for weekly travelling distances have been calculated for each of the investigated areas, adjusted for bias in the overall mean values generated through the logarithmic transformation process.[3]

---

3 The predicted mean total travelling distances of each residential area generally show lower values (on average 31 per cent in Greater Copenhagen and 42 per cent in Greater Oporto) than those based on actually measured travel distances. Predicted mean travelling distances by non-motorized modes also differ from the actual mean travelling distances, but in this case the predicted non-motorized travel is underestimated in Copenhagen (by 60 per cent) while overestimated in Greater Oporto (more than twice as high as the actual means). Apparently, the transformation of travelling distances into logarithmic values and the transformation of predicted logarithmic travel distances back to Euclidian distances

Figure 8.3 shows the results of these analyses for each city, where the estimated mean traveling distances for each area have been plotted against the distance to the city centre as well as with the local area density.

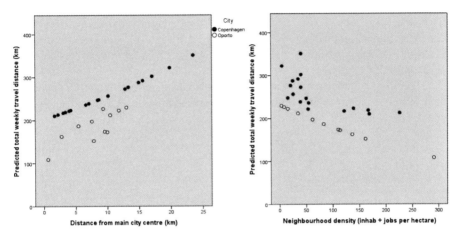

Figure 8.3   **Predicted average weekly total travel distances among respondents living in residential areas in Greater Copenhagen (black dots) and Greater Oporto (white circles), located at different distances from the city centres (to the left), and with different neighbourhood densities (to the right)**

In both cities, weekly travelling distances tend to be considerably longer if the respondent lives in a low-density neighbourhood at the outskirt of the city than if the dwelling is located in a high-density, central part of the city. As can be seen, the predicted travelling distances in Greater Copenhagen follow a smooth curve when plotted against the distance between the dwelling and the city centre, whereas the pattern is more 'jumpy' when plotted against neighbourhood density, yet with a clear tendency of increasing travelling distances as densities get lower. This reflects the fact that the distance from the dwelling to the city centre is the only urban structural variable showing a statistically significant effect on weekly travelling distances, but neighbourhood densities at the same time tend to be higher in the central parts, so there is also a tendency of increasing travelling distances

has caused a certain shrinking of the predicted values, compared to the raw data. Such shrinking when using logarithmic dependent variables has been observed also in other studies of land use and travel (e.g., Næss, 2010a). In Figure 8.2, we have applied 'uplift factors' corresponding to the above-mentioned degrees of under- or overestimation in order to make the overall predicted means consistent with the means reported in the introduction of section 8.3 and in Figure 8.1.

when densities get lower. In Greater Oporto, the roles of these two urban structural variables (distance from the dwelling to the city centre and neighbourhood density) have been switched, compared to Greater Copenhagen, so the smooth curve is now found when travelling distances are plotted against neighbourhood densities.

In Greater Oporto too, densities tend to decrease with increasing distances from the city centre, so there is a clear tendency of increasing travelling distances the more peripherally the dwelling is located also in Greater Oporto, yet with a somewhat 'jumpy' pattern reflecting the variation in densities between neighbourhood located at the same distance from the city centre.

Travelling distances are on average somewhat longer in Greater Copenhagen than in Greater Oporto, but this difference between the cities is smaller than the differences between central and peripheral locations in each city.

Travel by Car and Motorcycle   Table 8.2 shows the results of a multiple regression analysis of factors influencing the distance travelled by car or motorcycle during the investigated week. Relatively high proportions of the respondents (22 per cent in Greater Copenhagen and 21 per cent in Greater Oporto) had not at all travelled by car or motorcycle during the week, and their traveling distances by car and motorcycle were accordingly recorded as zero. The ideal requirement of ordinary least square regression analysis of normally distributed dependent variables is therefore not met. Similar to the analyses of total weekly travelling distances, the traveling distances by car or motorcycle were logarithmically transformed in order to meet the requirements of linear regression in a more satisfactory way.

In Greater Copenhagen, travelling distances by car or motorcycle tend to increase the further away the residence is located from the main city centre as well as from the closest second-order centre. Of these two effects, the distance to the main city centre exerts the strongest influence (Beta = 0.110, p = 0.001). The effect of the distance to the closest second-order centre is weaker and somewhat more uncertain (Beta = 0.064, p = 0.071). No significant effects were found of either neighbourhood density or the location of the dwelling relative to the closest urban rail station. In Greater Oporto, living in a dense local area tends to reduce the weekly distance travelled by car or motorcycle during the week (Beta = −0.132, p = 0.000), whereas no significant effects are found of the other locational variables. Since Greater Oporto is a relatively polycentric city, it appears plausible that local neighbourhood density, with the higher level of public transport services and greater availability of service facilities and also job opportunities usually found in dense areas, plays a more important role in influencing car travel in Greater Oporto than in the more monocentric Greater Copenhagen, where residential location relative to the main concentration of jobs and services found in the inner districts is of high importance to the need for motorized travel.

In both cities, travelling distances by car or motorcycle are influenced to a considerably higher extent by socio-demographic variables than by residential location. In particular, possession of a driver's license exerts a strong influence.

Table 8.2   Results of a multivariate linear regression analysis of factors potentially influencing the logarithm of the weekly travelling distance by car or motorcycle among Greater Copenhagen and Greater Oporto respondents

	Unstandardized coefficients		Standardized coefficients		Level of significance (p values)	
	Copenhagen	Oporto	Copenhagen	Oporto	Copenhagen	Oporto
Residential location variables:						
Logarithm of the distance (in km) to the closest main regional retail centre (Oporto study only)		0.294		0.132		0.000
Distance from the dwelling to the main city centre (km)	0.0378		0.110		0.001	N.S. (p = 0.163)
Distance from the dwelling to the closest second-order centre (km)	0.0584		0.064		0.071	N.S. (p = 0.947)
Population and job density (persons and jobs per hectare)					N.S. (p = 0.678)	N.S. (p = 0.256)
Logarithm of the distance (in km) from the dwelling to the closest urban rail station (km) (Copenhagen study only)					N.S. (p=632)	
Control variables:						
Whether the respondent holds a driver's license for car (yes = 1, no = 0)	2.144	2.052	0.335	0.393	0.000	0.000
Personal annual income (in Copenhagen: measured in 1000 DKK, in Oporto measured in classes of income)	0.00119	0.133	0.136	0.126	0.000	0.002
Workforce participation (yes = 1, no = 0)	0.348	0.401	0.064	0.092	0.074	0.037
Sex (female = 1, male = 0)	−0.225	−0.310	−0.049	−0.076	0.096	0.043
Whether the respondent has a long education (yes = 1, no = 0)		0.563		0.136	N.S. (p = 0.913)	0.001

continued

Table 8.2 *concluded*

	Unstandardized coefficients		Standardized coefficients		Level of significance (p values)	
	Copenhagen	Oporto	Copenhagen	Oporto	Copenhagen	Oporto
Whether the respondent is a pensioner (yes = 1, no = 0)		−0.754		−0.124	N.S. (p = 0.538)	0.003
Whether the respondent is a student/pupil (yes = 1, no = 0)	−0.643		−0.093		0.010	N.S. (p = 0.995)
Age	−0.0107		0.069		0.064	N.S. (p = 0.693)
Number of household members aged 7–18					N.S. (p = 0.352)	N.S. (p = 0.993)
Regular transport of children to school or kindergarten (yes = 1, no = 0)		0.362		0.082	N.S. (p = 0.155)	0.029
Index for transport-related residential preferences (preference for locations facilitating short traveling distances and/or public transport usage = 1, no such preference expressed = 0) (Copenhagen study only)	−0.251		−0·055		0.059	
Number of household members below seven years					N.S. (p = 0.366)	N.S. (p = 0.690)
Whether the respondent had moved to the present dwelling less than five years ago (yes = 1, no = 0)					N.S. (p = 0.848)	N.S. (p = 0.385)
Constant	0.560	1.465			0.183	0.000

Note: Only variables meeting a required significance level of 0.10 were included in the final regression model. N.S. = not significant at the 0.10 level. N = 903 (Copenhagen) and 442 (Oporto). Adjusted R^2: 0.270 (Copenhagen) and 0.442 (Oporto).

Travelling distances by car or motorcycle also tend to increase in both cities if the respondent has a high income, is a workforce participant and/or is male. In Greater Copenhagen, we also find tendencies toward shorter travelling distances by car or motorcycle if the respondent is a student/pupil, is old and/or has preference for residential locations facilitating short traveling distances and/or public transport usage. In Greater Oporto, residential preferences were not included in the analysis, and neither age nor being neither a student/pupil shows any significant effect on the distance travelled by car or motorcycle. Instead, we find significant tendencies toward longer travelling distances by car if the respondent has a high education level, is not a pensioner, and/or regularly transports children to/from school or kindergarten.

None of the effects of the non-urban-structural variables are surprising from a theoretical point of view. The fact that a high education level tends to increase travelling distances by car/motorcycle in Greater Oporto but not in Greater Copenhagen might reflect the presence of a stronger discourse among the educated middle-class in Greater Copenhagen than in Greater Oporto in favour of transport modes perceived as environmentally friendly and health-bringing. The reason might, however, also be a more decentralized and car-oriented location of white-collar and academic jobs in Greater Oporto than in Greater Copenhagen.

Travel by Non-Motorized Modes Similar to the analyses of travel by car and motorcycle, Table 8.3 shows the result of an analysis of factors influencing non-motorized travel during the investigated week. Again, logarithmic transformation of travelling distances has been applied, since the originally measured distances by non-motorized modes were far from normally distributed, especially in Greater Oporto, where more than half of the respondents had not at all travelled by foot or by bike during the week, non-motorized travel being almost non-existent among respondents living in the suburbs. This low usage of non-motorized modes is in stark contrast to the situation in Greater Copenhagen, where especially the bike plays an important role in intra-urban travel. With the logarithmic transformation, the deviation from the requirements of linear regression is less pronounced, although the level of skewness is still rather high in the Greater Oporto data (cf. the discussion on pp. 161–2).

In both Greater Copenhagen and Greater Oporto, travelling distances by non-motorized modes tend to increase the closer the respondents live to the main city centre (Beta = −0.071, p = 0.063 in Copenhagen; Beta = −0.120, p = 0.095 in Oporto). Although the distance to the main city centre is the only urban structural variable showing significant effects in both cities, other urban structural variables exert stronger influences in each city on the non-motorized travel distances. In Greater Copenhagen, the strongest effect is found of the distance from the closest second-order centre (Beta = −0.157, p = 0.001). A clear effect, but with an opposite sign, is also found of the location of the dwelling relative to the closest urban rail station (Beta = 0.097, p = 0.010). While the distance travelled by non-motorized modes tends to increase with proximity to the main city centre as well as to the

Table 8.3 Results of a multivariate linear regression analysis of factors potentially influencing the logarithm of the weekly travelling distance by non-motorized modes among Greater Copenhagen and Greater Oporto respondents

	Unstandardized coefficients		Standardized coefficients		Level of significance (p values)	
	Copenhagen	Oporto	Copenhagen	Oporto	Copenhagen	Oporto
Residential location variables:						
Distance from the dwelling to the main city centre (km)	−0.0174	−0.0375	−0.071	−0.120	0.063	0.095
Population and job density (persons and jobs per hectare)		0.0000203		0.145	N.S. (p = 0.647)	0.044
Distance from the dwelling to the closest second-order centre (km)	−0.102		−0.157		0.001	N.S. (p = 0.528)
Logarithm of the distance (in km) from the dwelling to the closest urban rail station (km) (Copenhagen study only)	0.364		0.097		0.010	
Logarithm of the distance (in km) to the closest main regional retail centre (Oporto study only)						N.S. (p = 0.520)
Control variables:						
Whether the respondent holds a driver's license for car (yes = 1, no = 0)	−0.441	−0.239	−0.096	−0.084	0.003	0.071
Workforce participation (yes = 1, no = 0)		−0.665		−0.282	N.S. (p = 0.134)	0.000
Whether the respondent has a long education (yes = 1, no = 0)	0.467		0.144		0.000	N.S. (p = 0.253)
Age	−0.0152		−0.138		0.000	N.S. (p = 0.698)
Personal annual income (in Copenhagen: measured in 1000 DKK, in Oporto measured in classes of income)	−0.00065		−0.103		0.003	N.S. (p = 0.201)

Regular transport of children to school or kindergarten (yes = 1, no = 0)	−0.429	−0.088	0.006	N.S. (p = 0.373)
Index for transport-related residential preferences (preference for locations facilitating short traveling distances and/or public transport usage = 1, no such preference expressed = 0) (Copenhagen study only)	0.207	0.063	0.046	
Number of household members aged 7–18			N.S. (p = 0.962)	N.S. (p = 0.223)
Sex (female = 1, male = 0)			N.S. (p = 0.626)	N.S. (p = 0.670)
Whether the respondent is a pensioner (yes = 1, no = 0)			N.S. (p = 0.614)	N.S. (p = 0.344)
Whether the respondent is a student/pupil (yes = 1, no = 0)			N.S. (p = 0.724)	N.S. (p = 0.410)
Number of household members below seven years			N.S. (p = 0.863)	N.S. (p = 0.693)
Whether the respondent had moved to the present dwelling less than five years ago (yes = 1, no = 0)			N.S. (p = 0.839)	N.S. (p = 0.976)
Constant	2.896	1.603	0.000	0.000

Note: Only variables meeting a required significance level of 0.10 were included in the final regression model. N.S. = not significant at the 0.10 level. N = 900 (Copenhagen) and 441 (Oporto). Adjusted R²: 0.142 (Copenhagen) and 0.187 (Oporto).

closest second-order centre, living close to an urban rail station tends to reduce the amount of walking and biking. The two former effects reflect the higher availability of potential trip destinations within acceptable walking or biking distances when living close to the main city centre or one of the second-order centres.

The tendency of shorter travelling distances by non-motorized modes when living close to an urban rail station probably partly reflects that the availability of good public transport opportunities makes some respondents prefer to travel by transit to destinations that might otherwise have been reached by bike. Partly, the effect may also reflect that those living close to an urban rail station do not need to walk so long distances to get on the train.

In Greater Oporto, the variable exerting the strongest influence on the non-motorized travelling distances is the local neighbourhood density (Beta = 0.145, p = 0.044). The amount of non-motorized travel (which in the case of Oporto refers mainly to walking, as biking is an almost non-existing travel mode in Oporto) tends to increase the higher is the density of inhabitants and jobs in the local area. This is hardly surprising, as a high local density provides for a greater availability of shops, other services and job opportunities within acceptable walking distances.

Apart from the residential location variables, we find in both Greater Copenhagen and Greater Oporto a tendency of increased non-motorized travel among respondents who do not possess a driver's license. This is the only non-urban-structural variable showing a significant effect in both cities. In Greater Copenhagen, non-motorized travelling distances also tend to increase if the respondent has a long education, is young, has a low income and/or has preference for residential locations facilitating short traveling distances and/or public transport usage. Especially the effect of education level is rather strong (Beta = 0.144, p = 0.000) and is interesting in that it shows another aspect of the above-mentioned difference between Greater Copenhagen and Greater Oporto in the discourses on modes of urban travel among educated middle-class people. In Greater Oporto, no effect of education level on the amount of non-motorized travel can be seen. Instead, we see a very strong negative effect of workforce participation (Beta = −0.282, p = 0.000). This may reflect poor facilitation for bike commuting, but there may also be a prevailing transport culture in Greater Oporto discouraging the use bike for journeys to work, cf. above.

Similar to Figure 8.3, Figure 8.4 shows average expected values for weekly travelling distances by non-motorized modes for each investigated residential area in the two cities, plotted against the distance to the city centre as well as with the local area density.

In both cities, respondents living in dense and central districts tend to travel about three times as long distances by non-motorized modes as their outer-area counterparts. Just as striking is the great difference between the two cities in overall non-motorized travelling distances, with Greater Copenhagen respondents travelling on average nearly four times as long by foot or by bike than their Greater Oporto counterparts. The more hilly terrain of Greater Oporto may be part of the

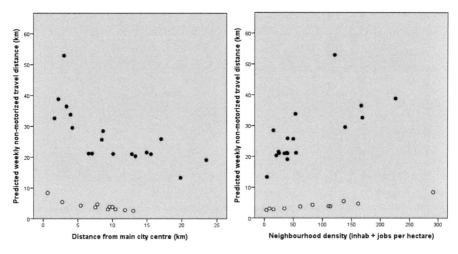

Figure 8.4   **Predicted average weekly travel distances by non-motorized modes among respondents living in residential areas in Greater Copenhagen (black dots) and Greater Oporto (white circles), located at different distances from the city centres (left), and with different neighbourhood densities (right)**

explanation for this, but more important are probably Copenhagen's much more extensive infrastructural facilitation for bike travel and the strong bike culture of the Danish capital.

Influences of Residential Location on Travel among Sub-Groups of the Population

In the previous sections, influences of residential location characteristics on travel behaviour among the whole samples of respondents has been analyzed and discussed. There are, however, some interesting differences between population groups in the ways in which residential location influences travel behaviour, in particular between women and men and across education levels. In this section, some of these differences will be highlighted. Due to space constraints, only the effects of residential location on the total weekly travelling distances will be presented. Similar differences do, however, also exist for travel by car and motorcycle and for the modal split between different means of transport (Næss, 2006a, 2008).

Table 8.4 shows differences between men and women in each city in the influences of urban structural as well as demographic and socioeconomic variables on weekly travelling distances. In Greater Copenhagen, the only urban structural variable showing a significant influence on female respondents' weekly travelling distances is the distance from the dwelling to the closest second-order

Table 8.4 Results of a multivariate linear regression analysis of factors potentially influencing the logarithm of the total weekly travelling distance among female and male respondents in Greater Copenhagen and Greater Oporto

	Women		Men	
	Copenhagen	Oporto	Copenhagen	Oporto
Residential location variables:				
Distance from the dwelling to the main city centre (km)	N.S. (0.489)	0.169 (0.003)	0.305 (0.000)	N.S. (0.632)
Population and job density (persons and jobs per hectare)	N.S. (0.853)	N.S. (0.768)	N.S. (0.437)	−0.190 (0.002)
Distance from the dwelling to the closest second-order centre (km)	0.094 (0.039)	N.S. (0.730)	N.S. (0.722)	N.S. (0.408)
Logarithm of the distance (in km) from the dwelling to the closest urban rail station (km) (Copenhagen study only)	N.S. (0.971)		N.S. (0.659)	
Logarithm of the distance (in km) to the closest main regional retail centre (Oporto study only)		N.S. (0.987)		N.S. (0.791)
Control variables:				
Whether the respondent holds a driver's license for car (yes = 1, no = 0)	0.150 (0.001)	0.244 (0.000)	0.192 (0.000)	0.169 (0.006)
Workforce participation (yes = 1, no = 0)	N.S. (0.135)	0.176 (0.007)	0.148 (0.001)	0.178 (0.012)
Personal annual income (in Copenhagen: measured in 1000 DKK, in Oporto measured in classes of income)	0.172 (0.000)	N.S. (0.108)	N.S. (0.289)	0.230 (0.000)
Whether the respondent is a student/pupil (yes = 1, no = 0)	N.S. (0.518)	0.139 (0.020)	−0.115 (0.013)	N.S. (0.988)
Whether the respondent is a pensioner (yes = 1, no = 0)	N.S. (0.221)	N.S. (0.161)	N.S. (0.909)	−0.276 (0.000)

Whether the respondent has a long education (yes = 1, no = 0)	N.S. (0.226)	N.S. (0.958)	0.214 (0.001)	N.S. (0.362)
Number of household members below 7 years	N.S. (0.229)	N.S. (0.429)	N.S. (0.734)	N.S. (0.158)
Whether the respondent had moved to the present dwelling less than five years ago (yes = 1, no = 0)	N.S. (0.158)	N.S. (0.430)	N.S. (0.479)	N.S. (0.777)
Age	N.S. (0.472)	N.S. (0.577)	N.S. (0.642)	N.S. (0.295)
Number of household members aged 7–18	N.S. (0.490)	N.S. (0.762)	N.S. (0.363)	-0.105 (0.076)
Regular transport of children to school or kindergarten (yes = 1, no = 0)	N.S. (0.847)	N.S. (0.502)	N.S. (0.485)	N.S. (0.781)
Index for transport-related residential preferences (preference for locations facilitating short traveling distances and/or public transport usage = 1, no such preference expressed = 0) (Copenhagen study only)	N.S. (0.890)	N.S. (0.872)		

Note: Standardized regression coefficients, levels of significance in parentheses. Only variables meeting a required significance level of 0.10 were included in the final regression model. N.S. = not significant at the 0.10 level. N = 468 women and 435 men in Greater Copenhagen, and 237 women and 205 men in Greater Oporto. Adjusted R^2: 0.075 (women, Copenhagen), 0.202 (men, Copenhagen), 0.299 (women, Oporto) and 0.328 (men, Oporto).

centre, and with a rather modest effect (Beta = 0.094, p = 0.039). Among male Greater Copenhagen respondents, we instead find a strong influence on travelling distances from the location of the dwelling relative to the city centre (Beta = 0.305, p = 0.000). Looking at Greater Oporto, the gendered pattern observed in Greater Copenhagen is virtually reversed. In Greater Oporto, the only urban structural variable showing significant effect on female respondents' travelling distances is the distance from the dwelling to the city centre (Beta = 0.169, p = 0.003). Among Greater Oporto male respondents, population and job density is instead the only urban structural variable showing a significant effect (Beta = −0.190, p = 0.002).

As mentioned earlier, there is considerable mutual correlation between the urban structural variables. In the multivariate statistical analyses, this implies a risk that the urban structural variable most closely correlated with the travel behavioural variable 'captures' the effects of the other urban structural variables whose effects do not satisfy the required significance level. Such an 'all-or-nothing' outcome of the backward elimination regression method may exaggerate the differences between the influences of different urban structural variables on a given travel behaviour variable. Nevertheless, our material suggests that the travelling distances among female respondents in Greater Copenhagen are influenced mainly by the distance from the dwelling to more local facilities, whereas the amount of travel among women participating in the Greater Oporto survey is mainly influenced by the distance from the dwelling to the main city centre. Among male respondents, this difference between Greater Copenhagen and Greater Oporto is reversed. A possible explanation could be a higher degree of decentralization of male-dominated workplaces in Greater Oporto than in Greater Copenhagen, where on the other hand a number of female-dominated workplaces within retail, health care, education and nursing exist in the second-order (and also lower-order) centres just as much as in the downtown area. In the parts of Greater Copenhagen located not very far away from the centre there are, on the other hand, a number of workplaces within banking, finance, a range of consulting trades and other services where men are in the majority.

In a similar way as the former table, Table 8.5 shows differences between respondents with a high and low education level in each city in the influences of urban structural and socio-demographic variables on weekly travelling distances. Again, we see some interesting differences across population groups but also between the two cities.

Among Greater Oporto respondents with a high education, the urban structural variable showing a significant effect on the weekly travelling distance is the distance between the dwelling and the main city centre (Beta = 0.175, p = 0.011). Travelling distances among Greater Oporto respondents with a low level of education are instead mainly influenced by the distance from the dwelling to the closest regional retail centre (Beta = 0.162, p = 0.003). Since respondents with a high education live on average a bit further away from the city centre than the low-education group, this may in itself result in a higher proportion of inward-directed trips to central facilities and hence a stronger positive correlation between trip

Table 8.5 Results of a multivariate linear regression analysis of factors potentially influencing the logarithm of the total weekly travelling distance among respondents in Greater Copenhagen and Greater Oporto with low and high education level

	Low education		High education	
	Copenhagen	Oporto	Copenhagen	Oporto
Residential location variables:				
Distance from the dwelling to the main city centre (km)	0.232 (0.000)	N.S. (0.558)	N.S. .(0.481)	0.175 (0.011)
Logarithm of the distance (in km) to the closest main regional retail centre (Oporto study only)		0.162 (0.003)		N.S. (0.934)
Population and job density (persons and jobs per hectare)	N.S. (0.136)	N.S. (0.349)	−0.114 (0.013)	N.S. (0.389)
Distance from the dwelling to the closest second-order centre (km)	N.S. (0.145)	N.S. (0.520)	N.S. (0.472)	N.S. (0.695)
Logarithm of the distance (in km) from the dwelling to the closest urban rail station (km) (Copenhagen study only)	N.S. (0.347)		N.S. (0.258)	
Control variables:				
Whether the respondent holds a driver's license for car (yes = 1, no = 0)	0.232 (0.000)	0.174 (0.005)	0.088 (0.049)	0.209 (0.003)
Personal annual income (in Copenhagen: measured in 1000 DKK, in Oporto measured in classes of income)	0.148 (0.001)	0.172 (0.001)	0.139 (0.005)	N.S. (0.149)
Workforce participation (yes = 1, no = 0)	N.S. (0.436)	0.125 (0.054)	0.098 (0.042)	0.131 (0.086)
Whether the respondent is a pensioner (yes = 1, no = 0)	N.S. (0.490)	−0.187 (0.003)	N.S. (0.654)	−0.234 (0.003)

continued

Table 8.5   *concluded*

	Low education		High education	
	Copenhagen	**Oporto**	**Copenhagen**	**Oporto**
Sex (female = 1, male = 0)	-0.160 (0.000)	-0.183 (0.001)	N.S. (0.352)	N.S. (0.118)
Whether the respondent is a student/pupil (yes = 1, no = 0)	N.S. (0.333)	N.S. (0.355)	-0.166 (0.001)	N.S. (0.575)
Number of household members below 7 years	N.S. (0.380)	N.S. (0.748)	-0.074 (0.100)	N.S. (0.504)
Whether the respondent had moved to the present dwelling less than five years ago (yes = 1, no = 0)	0.072 (0.090)	N.S. (0.448)	N.S. (0.587)	N.S. (0.750)
Age	N.S. (0.658)	N.S. (0.536)	N.S. (0.498)	N.S. (0.839)
Number of household members aged 7–18	N.S. (0.368)	N.S. (0.297)	N.S. (0.612)	N.S. (0.370)
Regular transport of children to school or kindergarten (yes = 1, no = 0)	N.S. (0.743)	N.S. (0.770)	N.S. (0.378)	N.S. (0.142)
Index for transport-related residential preferences (preference for locations facilitating short traveling distances and/or public transport usage = 1, no such preference expressed = 0) (Copenhagen study only)	N.S. (0.469)		N.S. (0.807)	

Note: Standardized regression coefficients, levels of significance in parentheses. Only variables meeting a required significance level of 0.10 were included in the final regression model. N.S. = not significant at the 0.10 level. N = 444 with low education and 459 with high education in Greater Copenhagen, and 257 with low education and 185 with high education in Oporto. Adjusted R²: 206 (low education, Copenhagen), 117 (high education, Copenhagen), 0.305 (low education, Oporto) and 0.171 (high education, Oporto).

distances and distance between the dwelling and the city centre. Probably, there is also a larger concentration of blue-collar jobs around the suburban retail centres, making the commuting trip lengths of low-education respondents more dependent on the distance from the dwelling to such centres than to the main city centre.

In Greater Copenhagen, local neighbourhood density is instead the influential urban structural variable among the high-education group of respondents. Given the location of a high concentration of office jobs within banking, insurance, governmental administration, etc., in downtown Copenhagen and adjacent districts, the absence of any significant effect of the distance between the dwelling and the city centre may seem surprising. However, although many jobs requiring a high education level are centrally located and the workplaces of respondents with a long education are on average located somewhat closer to the city centre than those of the respondents in the low-education group, Greater Copenhagen respondents with a high education tend to live on average closer to the city centre (7.9 km) than the location of their workplaces (9.6 km). Outward commutes are therefore more common than inward commutes among this group of respondents, distinct from the situation among Greater Copenhagen respondents with a low education, whose workplaces are on average located closer to the city centre (10.2 km) than where they live (11.5 km).

Moreover, a more detailed differentiation between employment groups (not shown here) shows that travelling distances among persons with a high education within technical or economic subjects are strongly influenced by the distance from the dwelling to the city centre, whereas travelling distances among those Copenhagen respondents with a high education within other subjects are mainly influenced by the distance from the dwelling to local (notably second-order) centres, where a number of relevant jobs exist within schools, kindergartens, hospitals, nursing homes and town halls. When all high-education respondents are grouped together, local-area density comes to the fore as a variable incorporating the effects of proximity to downtown Copenhagen as well as to second-order centres.

The Role of More Detailed Urban Structural Conditions

In the United States, research into land use and transport relationships has for a long time been predominantly directed towards the influence of local-scale urban structural conditions on travel behaviour, comparing traditional suburban residential areas with areas developed according to the so-called 'New Urbanism' and 'Transit Oriented Development' principles (Cervero, 2003; Krizek, 2003). In our studies in Greater Copenhagen and Greater Oporto too, a number of detail-level urban structural characteristics were investigated.

Local-scale urban design principles, such as street pattern, availability of sidewalks and bike paths, etc., and aesthetic neighbourhood qualities, can influence the attractiveness of different travel modes and can for some travel purposes also affect trip destinations. Boarnet and Crane (2001b: 37) mention the following six urban features as urban form and land use measures that might influence travel behaviour: density (residential or employment, or more complex accessibility measures); extent of land use mixing; traffic calming; street pattern; jobs-housing balance (or land use balance); and pedestrian features such as the availability of sidewalks. According to Handy et al. (1998), built environment characteristics can potentially reduce car travel partly by encouraging walking as a substitute for car driving, and partly by facilitating shorter car trips than what would be the case if a certain facility type is not available in the neighbourhood. The built environment features that can encourage walking include 'objective' factors (like how close the facility is located to the dwelling, or the availability of sidewalks) as well as more subjective factors (e.g., how pleasant and safe the walking route is perceived to be).

This section presents a separate analysis of the relationships between a number of urban structure variables and travel behaviour. Table 8.6 shows the results from analyses of the relationships of 4 metropolitan-scale and 12 detail-scale urban structural variables (selected from a total of 38 urban structural variables analysed in Copenhagen and 31 in Oporto)[4] with the logarithm of the respondents' weekly traveling distance by car or motorcycle. The table shows the bivariate relationships as well as partial correlations of each urban structural variable with the logarithm of the distance travelled by car or motorcycle. In the partial correlation analysis, control has been made for the distance from the dwelling relative to the main city centre as well as 11 demographic and socioeconomic variables.

The urban structural variables have been grouped into six categories: location of the residence relative to the overall centre structure in the metropolitan area, location of the residence in relation to rail-bound public transport, local area density, service facility accessibility in the proximity of the dwelling, availability of local green recreational areas, and local street structure.

As can be seen in Table 8.6, with a few exceptions, most of the urban structural variables, also those at a detailed scale, show clear bivariate associations with the amount of car traveling. This applies to Greater Oporto as well as Greater Copenhagen. However, when controlling for demographic and socioeconomic variables as well as for the location of the dwelling relative to the main city centre, most of the correlations of the detail-scale urban structural variables become insignificant. In Greater Copenhagen, the only urban structural variables showing significant correlations (understood as $p < 0.1$) with the amount of car traveling when controlling for socio-demographic variables and the location of the dwelling relative to the city centre are the distances from the residence to the closest second-order centre ($r = 0.070$, $p = 0.025$), the closest grocery shop ($r = 0.104$, $p = 0.001$), the closest post office ($r = 0.091$, $p = 0.004$), the closest primary school

---

4   The original analyses also included a number of variables generated through logarithmic and other non-linear transformations of the Euclidian distances from the dwelling to different kinds of centres and facilities, as well as several indices for the availability of different kinds of public services and shopping opportunities. These variables have not been included in this presentation.

Table 8.6   Results for Oporto and Copenhagen from separate analysis of the effects of various detail-level urban structural variables on the logarithm of the weekly travelling distance by car or motorcycle

	Bivariate correlations (Pearson's r)		Partial correlations (Pearson's r)	
	Greater Copenhagen	Greater Oporto	Greater Copenhagen	Greater Oporto
Location of the dwelling relative to the metropolitan-level centre structure:				
Distance along the road network from the dwelling to the main metropolitan centre	0.219*** (0.000)	0.243*** (0.000)		
Distance along the road network from the dwelling to the closest second -order centre	0.252*** (0.000)	0.178*** (0.000)	0.070* (0.025)	0.040 (0.407)
Logarithmic distance along the road network from the dwelling to the closest regional shopping mall / regional retail centre	0.168*** (0.000)	0.155*** (0.000)	0.026 (0.404)	0.062 (0.197)
Location of the dwelling relative to railway stations:				
Distance along the road network from the dwelling to the closest urban railway station	0.124*** (0.000)	0.148*** (0.000)	0.016 (0.617)	0.134** (0.005)
Density in the surroundings of the dwelling:				
Density of inhabitants and jobs in the local area of the dwelling (inhabitants and jobs within a radius of 800 m)	-0.152*** (0.000)	-0.226*** (0.000)	-0.018 (0.573)	-0.052 (0.276)
Population density in the local area of the dwelling	-0.135*** (0.000)	-0.110** (0.002)	0.001 (0.978)	0.001 (0.979)
Job density in the local area of the dwelling	-0.152*** (0.000)	-0.214*** (0.000)	-0.032 (0.317)	-0.028 (0.564)
Availability of service facilities in the proximity of the dwelling:				
Total number of shops (grocery as well as non-food) within 1.5 km distance from the dwelling	-0.159*** (0.000)	-0.270*** (0.000)	-0.013 (0.679)	-0.045 (0.347)

continued

Table 8.6 *concluded*

	Bivariate correlations (Pearson's r)		Partial correlations (Pearson's r)	
	Greater Copenhagen	**Greater Oporto**	**Greater Copenhagen**	**Greater Oporto**
Linear distance along the road network from the dwelling to the closest grocery shop	0.293*** (0.000)	0.052 (0.148)	0.104** (0.001)	0.073 (0.126)
Linear distance along the road network from the dwelling to the closest post office	0.247*** (0.000)	0.090* (0.013)	0.091** (0.004)	0.128** (0.007)
Linear distance along the road network from the dwelling to the closest local authority main building (city hall)	0.093** (0.002)	0.151*** (0.000)	−0.005 (0.879)	0.019 (0.687)
Linear distance along the road network from the dwelling to the closest primary school	0.240*** (0.000)	0.094** (0.009)	0.057 (0.070)	0.051 (0.287)
Linear distance along the road network from the dwelling to the closest kindergarten	0.213*** (0.000)	0.108** (0.003)	0.054 (0.087)	0.044 (0.362)
Diversity of Activities Accessible by non-motorized modes (walking) (only Oporto)		−0.073* (0.044)		0.029 (0.542)
Diversity of Activities Accessible by public transport (only Oporto)		−0.081* (0.026)		−0.123* (0.010)
Local green recreational areas:				
Availability of a recreational area of at least 10 hectares within 0.5 km distance from the dwelling	0.041 (0.175)	0.131*** (0.000)	0.010 (0.740)	0.027 (0.566)
Local street pattern:				
Grid structure (1) or other street patterns (0)	−0.144*** (0.000)	0.127*** (0.000)	0.049 (0.118)	−0.083 (0.083)

Note: N = 756 for Oporto and 1,117 for Copenhagen in the bivariate correlation analyses; N = 450 for Oporto and 1,022 for Copenhagen in the partial correlation analyses. Levels of significance (p-values, two-tail) in parentheses. P-values below 0.0005 are marked with three asterisks, p-values between 0.0005 and 0.01 are marked with two asterisks, and p-values between 0.01 and 0.05 are marked with one asterisk.

(r =0.057, p = 0.070), and the closest kindergarten (r = 0.054, p = 0.087). In Greater Oporto, even fewer urban structural variables show significant correlations with the amount of car traveling when controlling for socio-demographic variables and the location of the dwelling relative to the city centre. These variables are: the distance from the dwelling to the closest urban railway station (r = 0.134, p = 0.005), the distance from the residence to the closest post office (r = 0.128, p = 0.007), an index for the diversity of activities accessible by public transport (r = −0.123, p = 0.010) and whether the streets in the local neighbourhood are based on a grid structure (r = −0.083, p = 0.083).

The effects of the more local-scale variables all have the expected signs, which indicate that they tend to influence the amount of car travel in accordance with what would be presupposed from theoretical considerations. It should, however, be noted that the local street structure only shows the expected kind of correlation in Greater Oporto (i.e., less car travel if the street network has a grid pattern). In Greater Copenhagen, a slight opposite correlation is found, albeit not statistically significant (p = 0.118). The significant partial correlations of local service facilities variables with the amount of car traveling in both cities suggests that availability of facilities like grocery shop, post office, primary school and kindergarten in the proximity of the dwelling does contribute to reduced needs for car travel for non-work purposes. Grocery shops are facilities usually visited several times a week and also one of the facility categories where people, according to the transport rationales discussed earlier, often prefer the closest opportunity. The same applies to primary schools, kindergarten and not the least post offices.

The fact that the distance to grocery shops and the other above-mentioned facilities show stronger correlations with car travel in both cities than neighbourhood densities (when controlling for socio-demographic variables and the distance to the city centre) suggests that local-area density, although important for providing a population base for local services, cannot alone explain the provision of these facilities. In the suburbs, supermarkets have during recent decades been established along the road network instead of integrated in the old urban fabric, and this may explain why accessibility to grocery stores (and also post offices, which increasingly are located inside supermarkets) to some extent seems to be 'decoupled' from local-area density – at least when controlling for the distance to the city centre.

In Oporto, we also see a clear, negative correlation between car travel and the index for the diversity of activities accessible by public transport. This is a clear indication that the quality of the public transport provision matters to the modal split between car and transit. The negative correlation between this accessibility variable and car travel is consistent with the correlation (in Oporto) between the amount of car travel and the distance to the closest urban rail station. We do, however, not find any similar controlled correlation between the amount of car traveling and the accessibility index for walking. Neither do we find any partial correlation in Greater Copenhagen between the distance to the closest urban rail station and the amount of car travel. There are a much larger number of urban rail stations in Greater Copenhagen than in Greater Oporto, and they are also more evenly distributed over Greater Copenhagen. These circumstances might be a plausible reason for the difference across cities in the relationships found between automobile travel and distance to rail station.

In the above analyses of partial correlations, the distance from the dwelling to the city centre has, as already mentioned, been included as a control variable. Controlling for the distance from the city centre is based on the assumption that, for example, the local area density and the distance from the dwelling to the closest grocery store is influenced by how centrally or peripherally the neighbourhood is located (and not the other way round, that for example the distance to the closest grocery store determines how far from the city centre a dwelling is located). This assumption about the direction of influence is in accordance with location theories, e.g., Christaller (1966) and Alonso (1964). As mentioned in Chapter 4, there are clear centre-periphery gradients in both Greater Copenhagen and Greater Oporto for neighbourhood densities, and the same also applies for the distances from dwellings to most of the local service facilities. This also means that the distance from the dwelling to the city centre, in addition to its direct effects shown on pp. 159–81, exerts indirect influences on travel behaviour via the other urban structural variables showing significant effects.

Chapter 9

Mobility Patterns and Urban Structure

Paulo Pinho and Cecília Silva

The research project reported in this book started with our interest in applying and testing two complementary research methods concerned with the relationships between urban structure and travel behaviour – SAL and EQQM. The potential of comparing results through the cross analysis of two metropolitan areas – Greater Copenhagen and Greater Oporto – were, in the end, very satisfactory and fulfilled with important lessons learned from the simultaneous application of both methods. This final chapter summarizes the main findings from the cross analysis of the two case studies by each method, as well as the general conclusions and recommendations.

Lessons Learned from the Cross Analysis of the Two Case Studies

Lessons Learned from EQQM

The application of the EQQM method allowed the study of particular relationships between urban structure and travel behaviour. More specifically, the method made possible the study of the influence of certain urban structure factors, namely the distance of residence to several types and levels of centralities (main urban centre, second-order centres, well served rail centres, main regional retail centres) and local density levels, on particular travel choices, specifically, travel distance (total and by mode) and mode share (distance-based). All urban structure variables represent different centrality features. For instance, rail stations considered in Copenhagen were chosen for their activity density, working as urban centres which in addition are well served by the public transport system. Furthermore, considering the public transport oriented development around the main urban rail stations of Copenhagen, adopted by the 'Finger Plan', these stations are naturally part of the structure of centralities of this urban metropolis. In Oporto, retail centres were also chosen for their density of activities. However, in this case, not all retail centres work as urban centralities with some of them being only shopping malls apparently disconnected from their surroundings. These retail centres concentrate many activities and opportunities but most of them are shopping malls on the outskirts of the city of Oporto. This characteristic of the Oporto urban structure illustrates specific local development patterns and local travel habits in opposition to Copenhagen. Finally, local density is also clearly a measure of centrality identifying population centres, employment centres and mixed population and employment centres.

Both case studies make evident significant influences of urban structure on travel behaviour. Although all variables revealed significant influences in, at least, one of the analysed situations, some seem to be more relevant than others. This research project showed, in particular, the importance of the following urban structure factors:

- location of residence relative to main centres;
- location of residence relative to second-order centres; and
- local density.

However, overall, comparison between the complete set of results of both case studies seems to reveal more consistent results in Copenhagen then in Oporto. In Copenhagen travel depends more consistently on the distance to the main centre and to the second-order centres. These variables show higher significance and stronger influence in most of the analyzed regression models in Copenhagen.

In Oporto there is clearly a less significant influence of urban structure on travel behaviour, although local density seems to have a somewhat stronger and more significant influence on total travel distance and walking while the distance to the main regional retail centres has a stronger and highly significant influence on car use.

In any case, the research results show a strong influence of urban structure variables on travel behaviour, but each case study reveals different patterns of influence according to different local travel characteristics. It is important to point out that public transport use is not influenced by any of these urban structure variables in our two case studies (Table 9.1).

It is important to highlight that differences in the results found in multivariate regressions are consistent with the differences in the urban structures of these two case studies. Copenhagen is a capital city and therefore has higher densities of activities and opportunities, which may justify a stronger influence of the main centre on travel behaviour. This urban metropolis also has a richer tradition of spatial planning with a long-standing and consistent plan of transit oriented development around the main centre and the main rail system, the 'Finger Plan'. It is therefore not surprising that the main and second-order centres, and also the main rail stations, have a clearer influence on travel.

Finally, the results of the EQQM analysis in these two case studies seem to suggest that more consistent urban structures shaped by long established planning policies have a clearer influence on travel behaviour (the case of Greater Copenhagen) while, on the other hand, less consistent urban structures shaped by weaker or more liberal planning policies have a less clear and significant influence on travel behaviour (the case of Greater Oporto, in comparative terms).

Table 9.1   Positive and negative influence of urban structure variables on weekly travel distance totally and by different modes (only direct effects included)

Multivariate regression models for weekdays	Urban structure variable							
	Copenhagen				Oporto			
	1st centre	2nd centre	Rail station	Local density	1st centre	2nd centre	Retail centre	Local density
Total travel distance	+							−
Non-motorized travel distance	−	−	+		−			+
Car and motorcycle travel distance	+	+	+				+	

Note: Darker shading show a stronger influence and lighter colours a weaker influence.

Lessons Learned from SAL

Conceptually, SAL allows the study of the relationships between urban structure and potential mobility. More specifically, the method provides a geographical representation of how urban structure, namely the spatial distribution of activities and transport, constrains travel choices and, specifically, mode choice. Therefore this method is able to study the influence of the location and the diversity of activities (opportunities) on residents' model choices.

Contrary to EQQM, which has already been applied in a number of different countries and city contexts (see, for instance, Næss and Jensen, 2004; Næss, 2006a, 2007b) we should recall that SAL was more recently developed and only applied to the case study of Greater Oporto (Silva, 2008; Silva and Pinho, 2010). In this way, this research project provided the opportunity to apply and test SAL in another metropolitan area. This application proved to be quite successful as far as data requirements and data handling are concerned. Indeed, the available Copenhagen database could perfectly respond to the specific needs of SAL. In addition, and more importantly, the overall results are consistent and meaningful. In other words, SAL passed the test of its second application on a large-scale case study.

Furthermore, results show that the Copenhagen urban structure provides more sustainable mode choice conditions than the Oporto one (in proportion of area and population served). Transit oriented development brought about by the famous 'Finger Plan' produced urban structures able to provide more environment friendly mode choices to inhabitants, than dispersed developments that, although scattered around a traditional polycentric structure (the initial spatial matrix of

Greater Oporto), seem to show less efficient and consistent planning controls, in most cases serving localized private investment interests to the detriment of a global and more energy efficient territorial organization.

In addition, we would like to emphasize that in these similar metropolitan areas, as far as territorial sizes and resident populations are concerned, Greater Copenhagen is able to offer larger areas of higher accessibility levels by slower transport modes than Greater Oporto. While differences in the population served can be explained by better organization of the urban structure, differences in area result from a higher concentration (density) of activities and a better geographical distribution. Indeed, in this respect, there are important differences between these two study areas. First it is important to point out that Copenhagen is the capital of Denmark and therefore there are some good reasons why, in the same territory and for the same population, more areas can be found with high accessibility levels than Oporto. Being a capital city, many more activities are likely to be concentrated there. Greater Oporto cannot expect to have the same amount of activities with high accessibility, in such a wide area, with a lower population. In addition, it is important to point out that these two case studies are slightly different in terms of the respective mobility catchment areas. In Oporto, around 94 per cent of trips are made within the study area; while in Copenhagen this proportion decreases to around 81per cent. Although in both cases the respective study areas have an acceptable size for the application of the SAL or the EQQM, this difference must be taking into consideration in a more detailed and fine-tuning comparison of results.

Finally, it is important to point out that results from both case studies corroborate a clear connection between local accessibility and local density. Areas with higher accessibility levels (diversity of activities) invariably correspond to higher local densities (population).

Potential (SAL) vs Real (EQQM) Mobility

The comparison of results from both case studies shows a consistent influence of potential mobility (mobility choices enabled by different urban structures) on real mobility. In comparison to Oporto, the better conditions, in global terms, provided by the Greater Copenhagen urban structure correspond to more energy efficient travel behaviour in this study area, with a higher use of non-motorized modes and a slightly lower level of car use.

Whereas the better pedestrian accessibility conditions in Copenhagen are reflected in the higher share of travel by walking, the same relationship is not found when comparing mobility by public transport. Oporto residents tend to travel by public transport more often than their Danish counterparts, although accessibility conditions by this mode are considerably better in Copenhagen. Even though this might seem inconsistent, it is probably a consequence of the very different levels of bicycle use in these two cities. The much higher use of the bike in Greater Copenhagen has two effects in travel behaviour that help to explain these results. On the one hand, if a new transport mode is available and if it is highly used, as it is the case of the bike in Copenhagen, the modal share of the other transport modes will automatically drop. On the other hand, the literature shows that the bicycle tends to compete with public transport, in particular. Nevertheless, the car is by far the most used transport mode in both study areas, which is very much in accordance with the maximum levels of accessibility to activities by car found in both cities.

For a more comprehensive picture of the relationships between potential mobility and actual travel behaviour in the different urban areas of Greater Oporto and Greater Copenhagen, the remaining part of this section will focus on the comparison between the results of the SAL and real mobility patterns for each investigated area of EQQM, based on the survey data.

Table 9.2 summarizes some of the data concerning actual travel behaviour in the set of areas investigated in both Greater Copenhagen and Greater Oporto.

The table confirms the idea that the choice of these particular areas for each case study aimed to represent diversified situations in both Copenhagen and Oporto. The considerable differences found between minimum and maximum levels (for all variables in the two case studies) indicate a range of diverse travel behaviours. Generally speaking, Danish respondents travel more kilometres from Monday to Friday than their Portuguese counterparts. However, Oporto residents travel, on average, a longer distance by car. Travel distances by non-motorized modes are much higher in Copenhagen, which is obviously a consequence of the high use of the bicycle in Copenhagen, while in Oporto, with its irregular topography, this mode is practically non-existent. The values regarding modal share are consistent with the data presented earlier for the whole study regions: car use is higher in Oporto, while in Copenhagen people tend to travel by non-motorized modes more often.

Table 9.2   Travel behaviour in the EQQM investigated areas (values referring to weekdays) and average levels of accessibility by walking (from SAL)

Greater Copenhagen				Greater Oporto		
Min.	Max.	Average[1]		Min.	Max.	Average[2]
84.1	221.8	142.4	Total travel distance (km)	37.9	158.1	112.8
28.9	192.6	87.6	Travel distance by car (km)	22.3	132.9	92.0
10.8	78.5	31.3	Travel distance by public transport (km)	10.1	26.2	16.8
6.4	30.9	20.5	Travel distance by NM modes (km)	1.5	6.1	3.7
22%	84%	49%	Car share	25%	77%	63%
6%	47%	20%	Public transport share	14%	32%	20%
6%	58%	30%	Share of non-motorized modes	4%	48%	15%
0.86	1.00	0.97	Average NM accessibility level (SAL)	0.33	1.00	0.95

[1] Mean value weighted by the number of respondents in each investigated area.
[2] Mean value weighted by the number of respondents in each investigated area.
Source: Silva et al., 2014.

Furthermore, not only is mobility in Copenhagen higher than in Oporto (average travel distance is longer on weekdays) but it is also less carbon intensive (distance by car is lower and there is a higher use on non-motorized modes). In other words, low carbon travel patterns do not necessarily mean less mobility.

The analysis of the use of non-motorized modes in the specific areas studied located in different parts of Greater Oporto and Greater Copenhagen produces, again, quite interesting results. Figure 9.1 and Figure 9.2 double-crosses the spatial distribution of walking accessibility levels with the average share of NM modes in each investigated area.

In Oporto, the main city centre has by far the highest share of walking, representing almost half of all trips. The proportion of trips by foot is also substantially high (between 13 per cent and 20 per cent) in areas located near second-order centres. All these areas have high accessibility levels: DivAct = 1 in Oporto centre and Vila Nova de Gaia and over 0.9 in Matosinhos, Maia, Ermesinde and Gondomar. The remaining study areas have lower shares of NM modes, which, in some cases, correspond to lower accessibility levels. Data concerning travel distance by NM modes are consistent with these results, with Oporto centre presenting the highest travel length during weekdays (6.1 km). Respondents of the five study areas located near second-order centres also travel significant distances, between 3.3 and 4.9 km.

In Copenhagen, the highest use of NM modes can also be found in central areas, a couple of them having a proportion of trips by these modes over 50per cent. Along with this positive relationship between travelling by foot or bike and living close to the main metropolitan centre, some considerably high shares of NM modes use can also be found in outer parts of Greater Copenhagen, in study areas located near secondary centralities.

The comparison between use of NM modes and diversity of activities is quite difficult, since all the study areas are located in territories with high accessibility levels (DivAct higher than 0.9). However, study areas with higher shares of car use, such as Vesterbro, Amager North and north of Fælledparken, are located in zones with maximum pedestrian accessibility levels (DivAct = 1). Regarding travel distance, the results are also consistent with the spatial distribution of NM modal share: respondents living in central areas travel on average longer distances on weekdays than those who live in more peripheral zones.

In summary, the comparison between the results of SAL and the actual amount of travel by NM modes in the two case studies suggests that there is a clear influence of urban structure factors on travel behaviour. These results are in accordance with the results of EQQM, supporting the idea that the structure of centralities of a metropolitan area has a crucial influence both on the average length of walking and biking trips and on the number of such trips during weekdays. In Greater Oporto, people living in the city centre and near the main second-order centres tend to travel more by foot. In Greater Copenhagen the levels of NM modes use are higher near the main metropolitan centre. Areas with high levels of diversity of

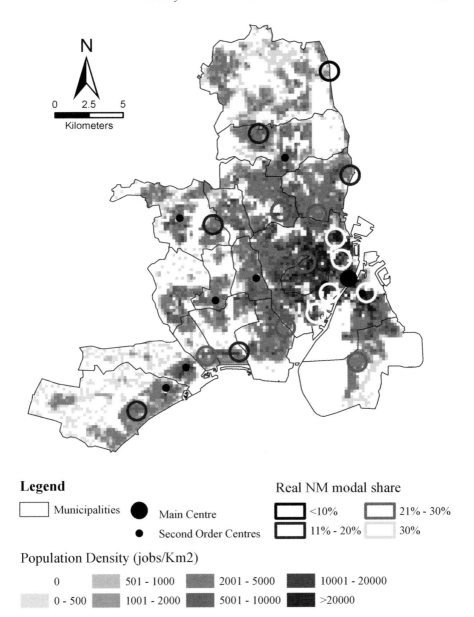

Legend

▭ Municipalities	● Main Centre	
	● Second Order Centres	

Real NM modal share

▭ <10%	▭ 21% - 30%
▭ 11% - 20%	▭ 30%

Population Density (jobs/Km2)

0	501 - 1000	2001 - 5000	10001 - 20000
0 - 500	1001 - 2000	5001 - 10000	>20000

Figure 9.1   Average share of non-motorized modes in Greater Copenhagen

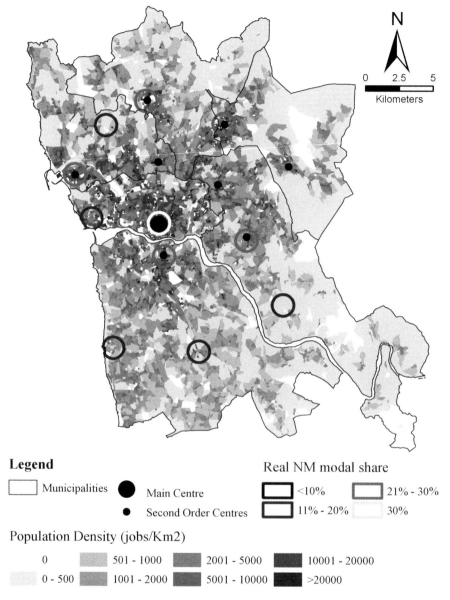

Figure 9.2   **Average share of non-motorized modes in Greater Oporto**

activities accessible by walking are generally located in both the main centre and the second-order centres of Oporto and Copenhagen.

The results concerning car use show also a significant consistency with the urban structure factors referred to above. In both case studies, the areas investigated with the lowest proportion of car use are generally located near the main metropolitan centre, namely Oporto centre (in GO) and Vesterbro, Amager North and Kongens Enghave (in GC), which present levels of car share below 30 per cent. In Greater Oporto, a tendency to lower car use in the proximity of second-order centres is also observed, although to a lesser extent. All these study areas are located in territories with a high diversity of activities, hence with high levels of accessibility by foot.

There are, however, some exceptions to this tendency: in both case studies there can be found specific study areas where car modal share does not seem to be related to any of the above mentioned structural characteristics. This finding illustrates the idea that there are other non-urban structure related factors influencing travel behaviour to a similar or even to a higher extent. Factors such as income levels, socioeconomic condition and car ownership, are believed to be particularly relevant.

In summary, the comparison of the results of the SAL in these two metropolitan areas and the actual travel behaviour of their residents found considerable evidence of the influence of the diversity of accessible activities on travel distance and on transport mode choice. In general, there is a tendency for people who live in areas with high activity diversity to travel more and more often by non-motorized modes and also to use the private car less. It is true that several other factors influence travel behaviour and that, in some cases, it is possible to find the low use of walking and cycling or high car use in areas where accessibility conditions are favourable. But we do not find high use of more energy efficient transport modes in areas where walking accessibility conditions are low. Providing favourable conditions for the use of these modes is therefore a necessary but not sufficient condition to achieve low carbon travel patterns.

Moreover, the analysis carried out in this section also confirms the importance of other urban structure factors, namely the proximity to the main central places. Comparing areas with similar SAL accessibility conditions, the research found considerable differences associated with the location of those areas in relation to the metropolitan structure of central places. In Copenhagen a central location relative to the whole urban area seems to be more relevant than in Oporto. This highlights the differences between these two cities, confirming our initial idea that Greater Copenhagen has a more monocentric performance when compared to Greater Oporto, which still is more polycentric.

Conclusions and Recommendations

Results from the application of the two methods, in both case studies, reveal a clear influence of urban structures on travel behaviour. In addition, our results clearly show that urban structure not only passively influences, but also actively constrains travel choices, enabling or limiting particular travel choices, with profound consequences on overall metropolitan sustainability. For instance, people living closer to urban centralities tend to travel less while using more soft modes (non-motorized) in comparison to residents living far from these urban centralities. On the one hand, the behaviour of the former group is influenced by the presence of a variety of activities, within walking distance. On the other hand, the absence of these conditions prevents residents of the latter group from similar behaviour. We should point out that the presence of a variety of activities at walking distance is not sufficient to constrain residents' travel choices to non-motorized modes but it clearly has an influence on more sustainable choices. Concluding, it can then be said that the presence of favourable urban structure conditions for low carbon travel has an influence on the actual behaviour of travellers, and that the absence of such conditions restrains people from making more environment friendly mobility choices. Clearly, the absence of these conditions has a stronger effect on behaviour than the presence, although both effects co-exist.

These findings were already visible through the separate applications of each method to each case study. However, this comparative study reinforced our previous conclusions. All results are consistent in confirming the influence or the constraint urban structure has on travel behaviour. The comparison of both case studies takes us further than these previous conclusions, showing the importance of the role of urban planning for low carbon mobility management.

The different planning traditions of the countries under analysis have developed different urban structures with different degrees of influence and constraint on travel behaviour. Copenhagen has a clearer influence of urban structure on travel distance and mode choice, namely the location relative to main and second-order centres, than Oporto, where such influence is more mixed. It is important to point out that on the one hand, Copenhagen has a longer tradition of planning than Oporto with a long-standing plan encouraging transit oriented development ('Finger Plan'); on the other hand, Oporto has suffered from a somewhat more liberal urban development tradition framed by a zoning system offering very large urban development areas, which, in combination with the high density of motorways and a weaker public transport service, have encouraged dispersion and urban sprawl based on car use. In this context, different results obtained by the EQQM confirm that more contained and consistent urban structures have more significant influence on travel behaviour while, in comparison, less well spatially defined urban structures have a less significant influence on travel behaviour. In addition, and in view of the more circumstantial results obtained, in this last case it is less clear how that influence does occur. As a corollary, we can say that, with the present conditions, it would be harder to influence travel behaviour changes on the basis of urban structure in Greater Oporto, rather than in Greater Copenhagen.

In this way, this research seems to confirm both main positions found in the literature concerning the influence of urban structure on travel behaviour. On the one hand, results support the argument that urban structure influences travel behaviour. However, the comparison of results carried out in this project suggests that less clearly shaped urban structures have a less significant influence on travel behaviour. Therefore, if we bear in mind the varying strength of urban structures, both sceptics and believers of the influence of urban structure on travel behaviour can seem to justify their position.

The comparison of the results of both methods reveals clear complementarities between them. First, at the conceptual level, since SAL assesses how urban structure constrains mobility choices, whereas EQQM assesses how particular urban structure variables influence real travel patterns. Second, at the operational level, revealing the importance of understanding both potential and real travel behaviours and their relationships, and revealing the importance of different urban structure variables on travel behaviour.

Results of both methods suggest the importance of centrality in travel behaviour and, particularly, in more sustainable travel choices. However each method uses a different operational form of the centrality concept. EQQM measures centrality with local density (combined population and job density) and resorts to a hierarchy of urban centres (from main to second-order centres, and centres with specific uses, such as rail or retail). SAL measures centrality resorting to accessibility measures considering the diversity of activities. When applied in combination, these methods assess the effect of urban structure variables found to be significant by most of the existing research reviewed in Chapter 3.

The influence of urban structure on travel behaviour as connected to centrality is manifold. There are various types and degrees of centralities considering the combination of density, diversity and types of centres. Results show that more sustainable travel can be influenced by several urban structure factors and that no particular combination is required as long as some type or level of centrality is provided.

It is important to recall that these methods, SAL and EQQM, assess two different roles of the urban structure on travel behaviour, constraint and influence, respectively. As referred to before, this by itself is already a complementary feature of these methods. Interestingly, comparison of results from both methods reveals more visible connections in Greater Oporto than in Greater Copenhagen. This happens because in Copenhagen, SAL does not reveal significant variability of results across the study area. In other words almost the entire study area offers very high and maximum walking accessibility levels and maximum accessibility levels by all other modes. In Oporto, the same can be found for car and public transport but more spatial variability can be found for walking accessibility. In the absence of this variability, comparisons between results of both methods are limited. This situation points towards two additional findings of this research.

First, when accessibility levels are high by all modes (and therefore all mode choices are available) the constraint role of urban structures is weak (unless there is political will to mobilize it to limit the use of the car). In this case, the effect of other variables on travel behaviour is more independent of the effect of diversity. Second, the constraint on using sustainable modes by urban structure acting simply to increase the accessibility by non-motorized modes is limited but, nonetheless, a first requirement. Differences between Copenhagen and Oporto show that Copenhagen offers more travel choices to people, consequently, people travel more but with increased mobility brought about mainly by sustainable modes (as discussed in Chapter 8). Oporto has still to provide these conditions while Copenhagen is at a point where urban structure is about to fulfil its potential as a 'carrot' for more environment friendly behaviour.

In conclusion, it is clear that urban planning has a role in mobility management. Urban planning can, on the one hand, constrain, and, on the other, influence travel choice. Whether consciously or not, urban planning has this power over travel behaviour. Centrality and how it is used to structure a particular city region or metropolis is clearly a key issue in taking full advantage of the urban structure effect. This conclusion provides additional scientific support to three urban planning principles, which although fairly well known for many years, have been frequently disregarded in contemporary planning practice, namely:

- densification of population around main centralities able to offer high local accessibility levels, avoiding the creation of new centralities that, often, disrupt the overall urban structure and are bound to weaken existing centralities;
- provision in all new urban developments of a high diversity of activities and fast and high capacity connections by public transport to and between existing centralities (these new urban developments, particularly of a large scale, are only justifiable in rare cases of population growth, an unusual situation in most cities in developed countries with stable or even shrinking populations); and
- diversification of urban functions in existing monofunctional areas, which are still present in many parts of our cities and metropolises.

If planning does not take advantage of its role in influencing travel behaviour, if no or a weak planning tradition exists, travel behaviour will become increasingly disconnected from urban form and less able to be constrained/influenced by it.

Some recommendations can also be made for each particular case study. It is clear that these two metropolitan areas are in different development stages and therefore require different actions. In other words, they are at different stages of the ability of an urban area to influence sustainable travel behaviour.

Copenhagen is at a stage were urban structure already provides high accessibility levels by all transport modes, offering to most of its population several alternative travel choices. In Oporto accessibility levels by walking are already high while public transport has yet to offer satisfactory levels of accessibility. In both case studies, accessibility levels by car are still higher than by walking or public transport. However, competitiveness of soft modes is higher in Copenhagen than in Oporto (considering that differences in accessibility levels are more significant in the latter case). The practical results of these differences are higher mobility rates in Copenhagen than Oporto. At the same time Copenhagen shows more sustainable travel patterns (lower average travel distance and mode share by car).

In this context, Copenhagen should be focussing on constraining car use (reducing the competitiveness of car use in comparison to public transport) considering the high level of accessibility offered by more sustainable modes. In parallel, urban dispersion policies should continue to be avoided, pressure will tend to rise among residents with strong preference for car use and car based environments.

On the other hand, Oporto has still to reinforce the competitiveness of the more environment-friendly transport modes – non motorized and public transport, through an effective coordination between transport policies and land use policies, for instance, shifting transport infrastructure provision from motorways to public transport, avoiding any new monofunctional dispersion while reinforcing the density of the centralities with high local accessibility. While in Oporto conditions are not yet ideal for car restraining measures, it is imperative to abandon car-dependent land use developments while taking consistent steps towards providing high levels of local accessibility.

Annex A
Case-Specific Applications

A.1 Activities Considered in Each Activity Type

The activities considered as the most important for travel generation were chosen from lists classifying all Portuguese and all Danish activities – the Portuguese Classifications of Economic Activities (Classificação Portuguesa de Actividades Económicas, CAE) and the Danish Industrial Classification (NACE/DB03), respectively. These lists provide a detailed overview of the activities present in Portuguese and Danish economies.

Employment, school, leisure, shopping and healthcare activities as well as public and private services were considered as the most relevant for travel generation. The detailed activities considered within these large groups were chosen from the referred lists. These activities (identified by its CAE in Table 5.3 and NACE/DB03 in Table 5.4) were then grouped into activity types (presented in the same tables). The classification and designation of each activity used for the SAL are presented in Table A.1 and Table A.2.

Besides of activities identified within the CAE and NACE/DB03 classifications, two further activities types were used. First, *parks, public gardens and squares* (activity type 4) were included, recognizing the importance of these urban elements for current leisure and free-time activities (although parks are not real economic activities, they are clearly travel generators). Second, *employment* was also included as an activity type, being aware of its importance for travel generation.

Information of availability of each activity type within each sub-region was defined based on statistical and geographical data. With regard to activity type 4 (parks) availability was defined geographically, giving those sub-regions including parks, public gardens or important squares the value of 1 for Act_4. With regard to activity type of employment, a sub-area was considered to have (enough) employment in case the employment available in that sub-area exceeded 50 per cent of its population (which is about the average rate of population in working age). For the remaining activity type, their availability by sub-area is evaluated based on statistical data of establishments by activity type by sub-area. If at least one establishment is found within the sub-area for a given activity type, that activity type will be considered available (therefore $Act_y = 1$).

Table A.1   CAE classification and designation used for Greater Oporto[1]

Division	Group	Designation
52	–	Retail Trade (except automobile) *Comércio por grosso e agentes do comércio, excepto de veículos automóveis e de motociclos*
	521	Retail trade in non-specialized shops *Comércio a retalho em estabelecimentos não especializados*
	522	Retail trade of food, drinks and tobacco in specialized shops *Comércio a retalho de produtos alimentares, bebidas e tabaco em estabelecimentos especializados*
	523	Retail trade of pharmaceutical, medical, cosmetic and hygiene products *Comércio a retalho de produtos farmacêuticos, médicos, cosméticos e de higiene*
	524	Retail trade of other products in specialized shops *Comércio a retalho de outros produtos novos em estabelecimentos especializados*
	525	Retail trade of second hand product *Comércio a retalho de artigos em segunda mão em estabelecimentos*
	526	Retail trade of outside regular shops *Comércio a retalho não efectuado em estabelecimentos*
	527	Reparation of personal and domestic goods *Reparação de bens pessoais e domésticos*
55	–	Accommodations and catering *Alojamento e restauração (restaurantes e similares)*
	553	Restaurants *Restaurantes*
	554	Bars *Estabelecimentos de bebidas*
	555	Canteens and catering *Cantinas e fornecimento de refeições ao domicilio (catering)*
64	–	Post office and telecommunication *Correios e telecomunicações*
	641	Post office activities *Actividades dos correios*
65	–	Financial support *Intermediação financeira, excepto seguros e fundos de pensões*

---

1   This table presents the CAE version 2.1 (revised in 2003) presenting only the general code until three digits (which according to this classification is the fourth level of classification or 'Group', the third level using only two digits is called the 'Division'). The table presents the third and fourth level of classification (Divisions and Groups) of the CAE classification as well as the designation of each activity class. The classification results of a free translation of the Portuguese designation (presented in italics).

Division	Group	Designation
66	–	Insurance, Funds and Pensions *Seguros, fundos de pensões e de outras actividades complementares de segurança social*
67	–	Auxiliary activities *Actividades auxiliares de intermediação financeira*
75	–	Public administration, defence and social security *Administração publica, defesa e segurança social obrigatória*
	751	General public administration *Administração publica em geral, económica e social*
	752	Foreign management, defence, justice, security, public order and civil guard *Negócios estrangeiros, defesa, justiça, segurança, ordem pública e protecção civil*
	753	Social security *Segurança social*
80	–	Education *Educação*
	801	Infant and elementary schools *Ensino Pré-escolar e básico (1° ciclo)*
	802	High schools *Ensino Básico (2° e 3° ciclos) e secundário*
	803	University *Ensino superior*
85	–	Healthcare *Actividades de saúde humana*
	851	Healthcare *Actividades de saúde humana*
	853	Social security activities *Actividades de acção social*
92	–	Recreational, cultural and sport activities *Actividades recreativas, culturais e desportivas*
	921	Cinematographic and video activities *Actividades cinematográficas e de vídeo*
	923	Other artistic and show business activities *Outras actividades artísticas e de espectáculo*
	925	Libraries, archives, museums and other cultural activities *Actividades das bibliotecas, arquivos, museus e outras actividades culturais*
	926	Sport activities *Actividades desportivas*
	927	Other recreational activities *Outras actividades recreativas*
93	–	Other service activities *Outras actividades de serviços*

Table A.2　　NACE/DB03 classification and designation used for Copenhagen Metropolitan Area (111-grouping)

Group	Designation
158120	Baker's shops
521100	Re. sale of food in non-specialized stores
522000	Re. sale of food in specialized stores
522909	Department stores
523000	Re. sale of pharmaceutical goods and cosmetic art
524109	Re. sale of clothing and footwear
524409	Re. sale of furniture and household appliances
553009	Restaurants
640000	Post and telecommunications
651000	Financial institutions
652000	Mortgage credit institutions
660000	Insurance
741100	Legal activities
742009	Consulting engineers and architects
751100	General public service activities
751209	Administration of public sectors
752000	Defence, police and administration of justice
801000	Primary education
802000	Secondary education
803000	Higher education
851100	Hospital activities
851209	Medical, dental and veterinary activities
920000	Recreational, cultural and sporting activities

Source: DST, 2007.

A.2 Distribution of Percentage of Trips by Travel Reason by Activity Types

For the development of the correction factor f_y considered for each activity type, in the measurement of the diversity of activity index, the percentages of trips by trip purpose were disaggregated by sub-types of trip purposes (as shown in Table 5.3). The trip purpose of employment required no special attention since no division of the value provided by INE (2000) and by DTU-Transport (2006) is needed. With regard to school activities, the 12 per cent of trips for this purpose were disaggregated by activity types 1, 2 and 3 according to the number of student within each activity.[2] For the remaining activities, the percentages of trips by trip purpose were disaggregated in proportion to the average frequency of use (days in a month).[3]

A.3 Independent Variables

Table A.3 provides an overview of the various independent variables, their assumed influences[4] on travel behaviour, and (for the control variables) the reasons why we have considered it appropriate to include the variable in the analysis.

------

2 Presenting the same average frequency of use (an average of 21 days per month) the division of trips by school level was made based on the number of students within each school level having to use this activity on a daily basis. In Oporto, the number of students in infant and elementary schools (around 91,000) and in high schools (around 125,000) was found within statistical data concerning the school year of 2006/2007 (GIASE, 2007). The number of student in universities (around 60,000) was estimated based on the information provided by the websites of the two main institutions of public graduate and postgraduate schools, the University of Oporto (www.up.pt [Accessed July 2007], revealing around 28,000 students) and the Polytechnic Institute of Oporto (www.ipp.pt, [Accessed July 2007], revealing around 15,000 students). Given the absence of aggregated data of graduate and postgraduate students in private institutions, this value was estimated to be similar to that of students within the Polytechnic Institute of Oporto. In the Copenhagen case study, the number of students enrolled in each level of studies was estimated based on data for Denmark in 2006, consisting of the following values: 253,000 (infant schools), 912,000 (high schools) and 229,000 (universities).

These data were published in Mejer and Gere (2008), retrieved from the Eurostat website in June 2009 (http://epp.eurostat.ec.europa.eu/cache/ITY_OFFPUB/KS-QA-08-042/EN/KS-QA-08-042-EN.PDF).

3 Only integer values were used for f_y requiring sporadic choices for the disaggregation of percentage of trip purpose when this was no straight forward. For instance, the 15 per cent of trips for healthcare and other activities were divided by six activities presenting a global value of frequency of use seven days. In this, to use integer values, activity type 16 (banks) was increased by 1 per cent, in comparison to remaining activities.

4 From theoretical or common-sense considerations, supplemented with information from the qualitative interviews.

Table A.3 The independent variables included in most of the multivariate analyses of the main survey

Independent variable used for Copenhagen	Independent variable used for Oporto	Assumed effects on travel behaviour	Arguments for including the variable in the analysis
Location of the residence relative to the main centre (non-linear transformation of the distance along the road network)		Longer travel distances in total, by car and by public transport, and shorter by non-motorized modes among outer-area residents. Higher proportion travelled by car and lower proportion by walk/bike. Yet reduced effects at long distances from downtown, and maybe somewhat lower amount of travel in the very most peripheral areas.	Urban structural variable of primary interest in this investigation. Not a control variable.
Logarithm of the distance from the residence to the closest second-order urban centre	Linear distance from the residence to the closest second-order urban centre	Longer travel distances in total, by car and by public transport, and shorter by non-motorized modes among those living far from a second-order centre. Higher proportion travelled by car and lower proportion by walk/bike.	Urban structural variable of primary interest in this investigation. Not a control variable.
Logarithm of the distance from the residence to the closest urban rail station	–[1]	Longer travel distances in total and by car, and shorter by public transport among those living far from an urban rail station. Higher proportion travelled by car. Maybe also more travel by non-motorized modes (in order to reach the station and the local service facilities located close to it).	Urban structural variable of primary interest in this investigation. Not a control variable.
Density of inhabitants and workplaces within the local area of the residence		Shorter travel distances on weekdays in total as well as by car among those living in high-density areas. Longer distances by walk/bike and higher proportions of these modes, lower proportion of car travel. Maybe a higher, compensatory amount of travel by motorized modes in the weekend. Ambiguous expectations regarding public transport on weekdays.	Urban structural variable of primary interest in this investigation. Not a control variable.

Independent variable used for Copenhagen	Independent variable used for Oporto	Assumed effects on travel behaviour	Arguments for including the variable in the analysis
$-^2$	Logarithm of the distance from the residence to the closest main regional retail centre	Longer travel distances in total, by car and by public transport, and shorter by non-motorized modes among those living far from a main regional retail centre. Higher proportion travelled by car and lower proportion by walk/bike.	Urban structural variable of primary interest in this investigation. Not a control variable.
Sex (female = 1, male = 0)		Shorter travel distances in total and by car among women than among men. Higher proportions of public transport and walk/bike.	The proportions of men and women among respondents varies somewhat between the areas. Besides, enables comparison of urban structural and demographic variables, and across population groups.
Age (deviation from being 'middle-age', logarithmically measured)	Age (real value)	Shorter travel distances in total and by car, and lower proportion of car travel among young and old people.	Age distribution varies between the residential areas, among others with a higher proportion of young people in the inner city. Besides, enables comparison of urban structural and demographic variables.
Number of household members below seven years of age		Shorter travel distances in total and by public transport, a higher proportion travelled by car and a lower proportion by public transport if there are small children in the household. Ambiguous expectations regarding travel by walk/bike.	Number of children varies between the areas, among others with fewer children in the inner city and large local variations in outer areas. Besides, enables comparison of urban structural and demographic variables, and across population groups.
Number of household members aged 7–17		Shorter travel distances by public transport, a higher proportion travelled by car and a lower proportion by public transport if there are schoolchildren in the household. Maybe also a lower proportion of walk/bike. Ambiguous expectations regarding the total travel distance.	Same as for the previous variable.

continued

Table A3 *continued*

Independent variable used for Copenhagen	Independent variable used for Oporto	Assumed effects on travel behaviour	Arguments for including the variable in the analysis
Workforce participation (yes = 1, no = 0)		Longer travel distances in total, by car and by public transport among workforce participants. Ambiguous expectations regarding the modal split and the distance travelled by walk/bike.	The proportion of workforce participants varies between the areas. Besides, enables comparison of urban structural and demographic variables, and across population groups.
Student/pupil (yes = 1, no = 0)		Shorter travel distances by car and longer by public transport and walk/bike among students/ pupils, with corresponding effects on the modal split. Ambiguous expectations regarding the total travel distance.	The proportion of students/pupils varies between the areas, with considerably higher shares in the inner city. Besides, enables comparison of urban structural and demographic variables, and across population groups.
Pensioner (yes = 1, no = 0)		Somewhat shorter total travel distance. Ambiguous expectations regarding the modal split and the distances travelled by the various modes.	The proportion of pensioners varies between the areas. Besides, enables comparison of urban structural and demographic variables, and across population groups.
Personal annual income (1000 DKK) in 17 classes	Personal annual income (8 classes: 1. < €5000; 2. €5,000–10,000; 3. €10,001–20,000; 4. €20,001–30,000; 5. €30,001–40,000; 6. €40,001–50,000; 7. €50,001–70,000; 8. > €70,000)	Longer travel distances in total and by car, and a higher proportion travelled by car, when income is high. Lower *proportions* of public and non-motorized transport.	Income levels vary considerably between the areas. Besides, enables comparison of urban structural and demographic variables, and across population groups.
Whether the respondent holds a driver's license (yes = 1, no = 0)		Longer travel distances in total and by car, and a higher proportion travelled by car among those who hold a driver' license. Shorter distance travelled by public transport and a lower proportion of this mode. Maybe somewhat more walk/bike travel, as these modes, alike with the car, are individual and provide some of the same flexibility.	The proportion holding a driver's license varies between the areas. Arguably though, the part of this variation which is not due to factors already included as variables in the analysis may to a high extent be a result of urban structural conditions, and should therefore perhaps not be controlled for.

Independent variable used for Copenhagen	Independent variable used for Oporto	Assumed effects on travel behaviour	Arguments for including the variable in the analysis
—[3]	Car ownership (measured as number of cars per adult household member)	Longer travel distances in total and by car, and a higher proportion travelled by car when car ownership is high. Shorter distance travelled by public transport and walk/bike, and lower proportions of these modes.	Car ownership varies considerably between the areas. Arguably though, the part of this variation which is not due to factors already included as variables in the analysis may to a high extent be a result of urban structural conditions, and should therefore perhaps not be controlled for.
Whether the respondent has a short or medium-long education as a tradesman or industrial worker[4] (yes = 1, no = 0)		Longer travel distances in total and by car, and shorter by public transport and walk/bike among those with a short or medium 'blue-collar' education. Also a higher proportion of car travel and lower proportions of public transport and non-motorized modes.	Same as for the previous variable.
Transport-related residential preferences (mentioning proximity to public transport, workplace and/or shopping opportunities important residential choice criteria = 1, otherwise 0)	—[5]	Shorter travel distances and less car driving among respondents emphasizing proximity to daily destinations and public transport stops as important residential choice criteria.	Residential preferences may vary between the areas, and this may imply self-selection of residents into neighbourhoods matching their travel preferences.
Regular transport of children to school or kindergarten (yes = 1, no = 0) Transport of children to school or kindergarten some days a week (yes = 1, no = 0)	Transport of children to school or kindergarten everyday (yes = 1, no = 0)	Longer travel distance by car, a higher proportion travelled by car and a lower proportion by public transport among those who bring children regularly. Maybe also somewhat longer total travel distance. Ambiguous expectations regarding the distance by walk/bike and the proportion of such travel.	The proportions with such responsibilities vary between the areas, maybe in a way different from the variation in the number of children in the households.

continued

Table A3 concluded

Independent variable used for Copenhagen	Independent variable used for Oporto	Assumed effects on travel behaviour	Arguments for including the variable in the analysis
Number of days at the workplace or school during the investigated week		Longer total travel distances the higher the number of days at workplace/school. Maybe also higher shares of public transport and walk/bike (due to the advantages of these modes in the rush hours, compared to car).	To the extent that the frequency of appearance varies due to commuting distances (e.g., because of more telework among outer-area residents), this is perhaps a factor which should not be controlled for. This variable is only included in the analyses of travel on weekdays and for the week as a whole.
Overnight stays away from home more than three nights during the investigated week (yes = 1, no = 0)	–[6]	Longer travel distances in total, by public transport, and a lower proportion of walk/bike among those who have many overnight stays away from home.	A sort of 'noise' which it might be desirable to eliminate in the estimation of the effects of the other variables (yet interesting – in other analyses – to see whether the frequency of overnight stays away from home varies with residential location in a 'compensatory' way).
Official trips during the investigated week (yes = 1, no = 0)	–[7]	Longer travel distances in total, by car and by public transport, and a lower proportion of walk/bike among those who have carried out official trips	A sort of 'noise' which it might be desirable to eliminate in the estimation of the effects of the other variables.
Has moved to the present dwelling less than five years ago (yes = 1, no = 0)		Longer total travel distance for all modes (in particular in weekends) among those who have moved. Also more travel by car and public transport, and less by non-motorized modes.	The proportion who has moved is likely to vary between the areas (some areas are more characterized by turnover than other areas).

[1] This variable did not show significant values in the analysis of the influence of structural variables on travel behaviour.

[2] New structural variable included in analysis with significant values of influence in travel behaviour and low multicollinearity

[3] Considering that car ownership may to a high extent be a result of urban structural conditions in Greater Copenhagen, this variable was excluded from the analysis for this research, although it has been used in previous applications of the EQQM to the same study area. In Greater Oporto this effect was not considered relevant.

[4] See previous footnote.

[5] The questions for this evaluation were not used in the Oporto survey.

[6] The number of responses to this question was too low in the Oporto case to consider valid for the analysis (eight respondents before excluding extreme total travel distances)

[7] The number of responses to this question was too low in the Oporto case to consider valid for the analysis (64 respondents before excluding extreme total travel distances)

Annex B
Average Travel Behaviour in the Study Areas

Table B.1   **Average actual travel behaviour in Greater Oporto's study areas**

Name	Total travel distance	Car travel distance	NM travel distance	Car share (%)	NM share (%)	NM DivAct (SAL)
Porto (Foz)	127.41	107.47	4.32	72.8	8.3	0.97
Porto (centre)	37.92	22.26	6.09	25.0	47.9	1.00
V.N. Gaia (centre)	101.07	84.28	3.63	58.3	17.4	1.00
Matosinhos (centre)	99.95	75.92	5.81	66.5	16.5	0.97
Carvalhos	138.98	118.77	2.31	76.6	4.1	0.96
Maia (centre)	136.68	117.96	3.30	72.4	12.5	0.97
Ermesinde	103.70	76.86	3.54	53.9	16.5	0.88
Gondomar (centre)	90.63	70.99	4.95	61.8	19.7	0.95
Esposade	103.03	76.80	2.83	59.0	08.9	0.75
Miramar	158.07	132.93	2.69	71.6	08.0	0.77
Foz de Sousa	130.08	115.04	1.49	72.0	10.2	0.33
Average	**112.74**	**91.99**	**3.72**	**63.4**	**15.1**	**0.95**

**Table B.2   Average actual travel behaviour in Greater Copenhagen's
study areas**

Name	Total travel distance	Car travel distance	NM travel distance	Car share (%)	NM share (%)	NM DivAct (SAL)
Vesterbro	101.31	28.93	30.42	21.5	56.2	1.00
Kartoffelrækkerne	142.22	77.23	23.26	46.6	35.8	1.00
North of Fælledparken	109.38	44.62	29.15	33.5	44.7	1.00
Frederiksberg North	160.82	110.82	18.57	60.2	25.6	0.92
Kongens Enghave	121.05	58.67	29.48	25.5	39.7	0.86
Amager North	94.05	38.82	30.86	22.7	57.6	1.00
Tårnby	157.82	112.30	26.78	60.0	25.4	0.95
Hvidovre	136.02	98.15	17.93	62.0	24.4	0.96
Vallensbæk Strand	153.40	97.71	18.29	48.6	28.7	0.97
Mosede	191.31	112.69	19.22	61.0	15.6	0.93
Skovlunde	145.55	95.92	11.89	55.5	15.7	0.96
Emdrup	138.33	108.58	18.98	68.1	25.9	0.99
Virum	143.77	93.15	11.95	53.0	16.4	0.99
Skovshoved	172.92	116.76	18.14	63.9	19.3	0.98
Vedbæk	221.75	192.56	6.42	83.7	6.3	0.87
Brøndby Strand	155.19	58.69	14.56	33.5	19.3	0.94
Høje Gladsaxe	84.09	48.98	13.31	36.6	29.6	0.95
Average	**142.35**	**87.58**	**20.51**	**49.2**	**29.6**	**0.97**

References

Aarts, H., Dijksterhuis, A., 2000, 'Habits as Knowledge Structures: Automaticity in goal-directed behavior'. *Journal of Personality and Social Psychology*, 78(1) 53–63.

AaU Spatial Data Library, 2009, *Calculations of the Growth in Urbanized Land Within Copenhagen Metropolitan Area. 1999–2008.* Aalborg: Aalborg University.

Acker, V., Witlox, F., 2010, 'Car ownership as a mediating variable in car travel behavior research using a structural equation modelling approach to identify its dual relationship'. *Journal of Transport Geography*, 18(1) 65–74.

Acker, V., Witlox, F., van Wee, B., 2007, 'The Effects of the Land Use System on Travel Behavior: A structural equation modeling approach'. *Transportation Planning and Technology*, 30(4) 331–53.

Aditjandra, P., Cao, X., Mulley, C., 2010, 'Understanding neighbourhood Design Impact on Travel Behaviour: An application of structural equations model to the British micro-analysis data'. Presented at the 12th World Congress on Transport Research in Lisbon, Portugal, 11–15 July, 2010.

Aguilera, A., Mignot, D., 2004, 'Urban Sprawl, Polycentrism and Commuting. A comparison of Seven French urban areas'. *Urban Public Economics Review*, 1.

Ajzen, I., 1991, 'The Theory of Planned Behavior'. *Organizational Behavior and Human Decision Processes*, 50, 179–211.

Ajzen, I., Fishbein, M., 1980, *Understanding attitudes and predicting social behavior*. Englewood-Cliffs, NJ: Prentice-Hall.

Albertsen N., 1999, 'Urbane Atmosfærer [Urban atmospheres]'. *Sosiologi i Dag*, 4, 5–29.

Alonso, W., 1964, *Location and Land Use* Cambridge, Mass.: Harvard University Press.

Anas, A., Arnott, R., Small, K., 1998, 'Urban Spatial Structure'. *Journal of Economic Literature*, 36(3), 1,426–64.

Antrop, M., 2004, 'Landscape change and the urbanization process in Europe' *Landscape and Urban Planning* 67(1–4) 9–26.

Ascher, F., 2003, 'Multi-Mobility, Multispeed Cities: A challenge for architects, town planners and politicians'. Paper for lecture at Rotterdam Architecture Biennial.

Augé M, 2000, *Non-Places: Introduction to an anthropology of supermodernity*. New York: Verso.

Aznar, G., 1993, *Lavorare meno, per lavorare tutti*. Torino: Bollati Boringhieri.

Balbo, L., 1991, *Tempi di vita. Studi e proposte per cambiarli*. Milano: Feltrinelli.

Bagley, M., Mokhtarian, P., 2002, 'The Impact of Residential Neighbourhood Type on Travel Behaviour: A structural equations modelling approach'. *Annals of Regional Science*, 62, 279–97.

Banister, D., 1994, 'Reducing the Need to Travel Through Planning'. *Town Planning Reviews*, 65(4), 349–54.

————, 2002, *Transport Planning*. London: Spon Press.

————, 2005, *Unsustainable Transport: City Transport in the New Century*. London: Routledge.

Bargh, J., 1997, 'The Automaticity of Everyday Life'. In: Wyer Jr, R. (ed.). *Advances in Social Cognition*. Mahwah, NJ: Erlbaum, 1–6.

Beauregard, R., 2009, 'Urban Population Loss in Historical Perspective: United States, 1820–2000'. *Environment and Planning A*, 41(3), 514–28.

Beckmann, J., 2001, *Risky Mobility. The filtering of automobility's unintended consequences*. PhD Thesis. Copenhagen: University of Copenhagen.

Bhaskar, R., 1993, *Dialectic: The pulse of freedom*. London: Routledge.

————, 1998, *The Possibility of Naturalism. A philosophical critique of the contemporary human sciences*. Third Edition. London and New York: Routledge.

————, 2008, *A Realist Theory of Science: With a new introduction*. First edition published in 1976. London and New York: Routledge.

Biermann, S., van Ryneveld, M., Venter, R., 2003, 'Costs of Peripheral Urban Development and Sustainable Urban Form'. In: CSIR. *SBE'03 Technology and Management for Sustainable Building*.

Blumenberg, E., Taylor, B.D., Smart, M., Ralph, K., Wander, M., Brumbaugh, S., 2012, *What's Youth Got to Do with It? Exploring the travel behavior of teens and young adults Los Angeles*. Los Angeles: University of California Transportation Center.

Boarnet, M., Crane, R., 2001a, 'The Influence of Land Use on Travel Behavior: Specification and estimation strategies'. *Transportation Research Part A: Policy and Practice*, 35(9), 823–45.

————, 2001b, *Travel by Design*. Oxford and New York: Oxford University Press.

Boarnet, M., Sarmiento, S., 1998, 'Can Land-Use Policy Really Affect Travel Behaviour? A study of the link between non-work travel and land-use characteristics'. *Urban Studies*, 35(7), 1,155–69.

Bransen, J., 2001, 'Verstehen and Erklären, Philosophy of'. In: Smelser, N.J, Baltes, P.B. (eds). *International Encyclopedia of the social and behavioral Sciences*. Oxford: Elsevier Science Ltd.

Breda-Vásquez, I., 1992, *O Processo de Suburbanização do Grande Porto*. Porto: Faculty of Engineering of the University of Porto, University of Porto.

Brotchie, J., 1984, 'Technological Change and Urban Form'. *Environment and Planning A*, 16, 583–96.

Brown, S., 2012, *Measures of Shape: Skewness and Kurtosis*. New York: Oak Road Systems.

Bruegmann, R., 2005, *Sprawl: A Compact History*. Chicago: Chicago University Press.

Bulmer, M.G., 1979, *Principles of Statistics*. New York: Dover Publications.

Calthrop, E., Proost, S., van Dender, K., 2000, 'Parking Policies and Road Pricing'. *Urban Studies*, 37(1), 63–76.

Cameron, I., Lyons, T., Kenworthy, J., 2004, 'Trends in Vehicle Kilometres of Travel in World Cities, 1960–1990: Underlying drivers and policy responses'. *Transport Policy*, 11, 287–98.

Caetano, M., Nunes, V., Nunes, A., 2009, 'Corine Land Cover 2006 for Continental Portugal'. Lisbon: Instituto Geográfico Português.

Cerasoli, M., 2005, *EUR: Traffico, Mobilità, Infrastrutture*. Eur2000.

Cervero, R., 1989, 'Jobs-Housing Balance and Regional Mobility'. *Journal of American Planning Association*, 55(2), 136–50.

———, 1995, 'Planned Communities, Self-containment and Commuting: A cross-national perspective'. *Urban Studies*, 32(7), 1,135–61.

———, 2002, 'Built Environments and Mode Choice: Toward a normative framework'. *Transportation Research Part D: Transport and Environment*, 7, 265–84.

———, 2003, 'Growing Smart by Linking Transportation and Land Use: Perspectives from California'. *Built Environment*, 29(1), 66–78.

Cervero, R., Kockleman, K., 1997, 'Travel Demand and the 3D's: Density, diversity and design'. *Transportation Research Part D*, 2(3).

Cervero, R., Wu, K-L., 1998, 'Sub-Centering and Commuting: Evidence from the San Francisco Bay area, 1980–90'. *Urban Studies*, 35(7).

Champion, T., 1995, 'Internal Migration, Counterurbanization and Changing Population Distribution'. In: Hall, R., White, P. (eds). *Europe's Population: Towards the next century*. London: UCL Press, 99–129.

Chatman, D., 2008, 'Deconstructing Development Density: Quality, quantity and price effects on household non-work travel'. *Transportation Research Part A: Policy and Practice*, 42(7), 1,008–30.

Chen, C., Gong, H., Paaswell, R., 2008, 'Role of the Built Environment on Mode Choice Decisions: Additional evidence on the impact of density'. *Transportation*, 35(3), 285–99.

Chen, C., McKnight, C., 2007, 'Does the Built Environment Make a Difference? Additional evidence from the daily activity and travel behavior of homemakers living in New York City and suburbs'. *Journal of Transport Geography*, 15(5), 380–95.

Cheshire, P., 1995, 'A New Phase of Urban-Development in Western-Europe: The evidence for the 1980s'. *Urban Studies*, 32(7), 1,045–63.

Cheshire, P., Hay, D., 1989, *Urban Problems in Western Europe: An economic analysis, London*. Boston: Unwin Hyman.

Chin, A., Smith, P., 1997, 'Automobile Ownership and Government Policy: The economics of Singapore's vehicle quota scheme'. *Transportation Research Part A: Policy and Practice*, 31(2), 129–40.

Christaller, W., 1966, *Central Places in Southern Germany*. Translated from German by Baskin, C.W. *Die Zentralen Orte in Süddeutschland*, 1933. Englewood Cliffs, NJ: Prentice-Hall.

Chu, S., 2002, 'Auctioning Rights to Vehicle Ownership: Singapore's experience with sealed-bid tenders'. *Transportation Research Part A: Policy and Practice*, 36(6), 555–61.

Clifton, K., Ewing, R., Knaap, G., Song, Y., 2008, 'Quantitative Analysis of Urban Form: A multidisciplinary review'. *Journal of Urbanism: International Research on Placemaking and Urban Sustainability*, 1(1), 17–45.

Coevering, P., Schwanen, T., 2006, 'Re-evaluating the impact of urban form on travel patterns in Europe and North-America'. *Transport Policy*, 13(4), 229–39.

Costanzo, M., Archer, D., Aronson, E., Pettigrew, T., 1986, 'Energy Conservation Behavior: The difficult path from information to action'. *American Psychologist*, 41, 521–8.

Crane, R., 1996, 'On Form versus Function: Will the New Urbanism reduce traffic, or increase it?' *Journal of Planning Education and Research*, 15.

Crane, R., Scweitzer, L., 2003, 'Transport and Sustainability: The role of the built environment'. *Built Environment*, 29(3).

Cullinane, S., 2003, 'Hong Kong's Low Car Dependence: Lessons and prospects'. *Transport Policy*, 11, 25–35.

Currie, G., Delbosc, A., 2009, 'Car Ownership and Low Income on the Urban Fringe – Benefit or Hindrance?' *Australasian Transport Research Forum*. Auckland, New Zealand.

Currie, G., Richardson, T., Smyth, P., Vella-Brodrick, D., Hine, J., Lucas, K., Stanley, J., Morris, J., Kinnear, R., Stanley, J., 2009, 'Investigating Links between Transport Disadvantage, Social Exclusion and Well-Being in Melbourne: Preliminary results'. *Transport Policy*, 16, 97–105.

Currie, G., Sendbergs, Z., 2007, 'Exploring Forced Car Ownership in Metropolitan Melbourne'. Social Research in Transport (SORT) Clearinghouse. Online database.

Curtis, C., Renne, J.L., Bertolini, L., 2009, *Transit Oriented Development: Making it happen*. Farnham: Ashgate Publishing.

Danermark, B., Ekström, M., Jacobsen, L., Karlsson, J.C., 2001, *Explaining Society. Critical realism in the social sciences*. London and New York: Routledge.

DANTE Consortium, 1998, 'DANTE. Designs to Avoid the Need to Travel in Europe'. Project Funded by the European Commission under the Transport RTD Programme of the Fourth Framework Programme.

Dargay. J., Goodwin, P., 2000, *Changing Prices: Dynamic Analysis of the Role of Pricing Travel Behaviour and Transport Policy*. London Landor Publishing Ltd.

Davison, L., Knowles, R., 2006, 'Bus Quality Partnerships, Modal Shift and Traffic Decongestion', *Journal of Transport Geography*, 14(2), 177–94.

Davoudi, S., 2003, 'Polycentricity in European Spatial Planning: From an analytical tool to a normative agenda'. *European Planning Studies*, 22(8).

De Masi, D., 1994, *Sviluppo senza lavoro*. Roma: Edizioni Lavoro.

Dieleman, F., Dijst, M., Burghouwt, G., 2002, 'Urban Form and Travel Behaviour: Micro-level household attributes and residential context'. *Urban Studies*, 39(3), 507–27.

Dodson, J., Sipe, N., 2008, 'Shocking the Suburbs: Urban location, homeownership and oil vulnerability in the australian city'. *Housing Studies*, 23(3), 377–401.

Donegan, K., Adamson, G., Donegan, H., 2007, 'Indexing the Contribution of household Travel Behaviour to Sustainability'. *Journal of Transport Geography*, 15, 245–61.

DST 2009, Population and Employment data by 250 × 250 meter grid cells for 2009 provided by the Danish Institute for Statistics.

DTU Transport, 2006, *Transportvaneundersøgelsen* (TU) [*Danish National Travel Survey*]. Distribution of trips per purpose in 2006. DTU Transport.

———, 2009, *Transportvaneundersøgelsen* (TU) [*Danish National Travel Survey*]. Number of trips per transport mode (2006–2009). DTU Transport.

Dziekan, K., Kottenhoff, K., 2007, 'Dynamic At-Stop Real-Time Information Displays for Public Transport: Effects on customers'. *Transportation Research Part A: Policy and Practice*, 41(6), 489–501.

Eagly, A., Chaiken, S., 1993, *The Psychology of Attitudes*. Orlando, FL: Harcourt Brace Jovanovich College Publishers.

Eck, J., Burghouwt, G., Dijst, M., 2005, 'Lifestyles, Spatial Configurations and Quality of Life in Daily Travel: An explorative simulation study'. *Journal of Transport Geography*, 13(2), 123–34.

European Environmental Agency, 2006, 'Urban Sprawl in Europe: The ignored challenge'. EEA report No. 10/2006. Copenhagen: European Environmental Agency.

———, 2007, 'Corine Land Cover 2000 (CLC2000) Seamless Vector Database'. Copenhagen: European Environmental Agency.

———, 2010, 'Corine Land Cover Seamless Vector Data'. Copenhagen: European Environmental Agency [Online]. Available at: http://www.eea.europa.eu/data-and-maps/data/clc-2006-vector-data-version#tab-metadata, accessed 16 February 2014.

Eurostat, 2008, 'Living Conditions in Europe'. Eurostat Pocketbooks. European Commission. ISSN 1725-5988 [Online]. Available at: http://ec.europa.eu/eurostat/documents/3930297/5962390/KS-DZ-08-001-EN.PDF/c9248f4b-57f8-4314-baad-021d0d87fbf4?version=1.0.

Ewing, R., 1997, 'Is Los Angeles-Style Sprawl Desirable?' *Journal of the American Planning Association*, 63(1).

Ewing, R., Cervero, R., 2001, 'Travel and the Built Environment'. *Transportation Research Record*, 1,780, 87–114.

———, 2010, 'Travel and the Built Environment'. *Journal of the American Planning Association*, 76, 1–30.

Filion, P., 2010, 'Growth and Decline in the Canadian Urban System: The impact of emerging economic, policy and demographic trends'. *GeoJournal*, 75(6), 517–38.

Fishbein, M., Ajzen, I., 1975, *Belief, Attitude, Intention, and Behaviour: An Introduction to theory and research*. Reading, MA: Addison-Wesley.

Fishman, R., 1996, 'Bourgeois Utopias: Visions of suburbia. In: Fainstein, S., Campbell, S. (eds). *Readings in Urban Theory*. Malden, MA, and Oxford, UK: Blackwell, 23–60.

Florida, R., 2002, *The Rise of the Creative Class*. New York: Basic Books.

Fosli, O., Lian, J., 1999, *Effekter av byspredning på bilhold og bilbruk* [*Effects of Urban Sprawl on Car Ownership and Car Usage*]. Oslo: Institute of Transport Economics.

Frank, L., Pivo, G., 1994, *Relationships between Land Use and Travel Behavior in the Puget Sound Region*. Seattle: Washington State Transportation Center.

Frenkel, A., Ashkenazi M, 2008, 'Measuring Urban Sprawl: How can we deal with it?' *Environment and Planning B-Planning & Design*. 35(1), 56–79.

Froud, J., Johal, S., Leaver, A., Williams, K., 2002, 'Not Enough Money: The Resources and choices of the motoring poor'. *Competition & Change*, 6(1), 95–111.

Fujii, S., Gärling, T., 2003, 'Development of Script-Based Travel Mode Choice after Forced Change'. *Transportation Research Part f – Traffic psychology and behaviour*, 6(2), 117–24.

Fujii, S., Gärling, T., Kitamura, R., 2001, 'Changes in Drivers' Perceptions and Use of Public Transport During a Freeway Closure'. *Environment and Behavior*, 33(6), 796–808.

Fujii, S., Kitamura, R., 2003, 'What Does a One-Month Free Bus Ticket do to Habitual Drivers? An experimental analysis of habit and attitude change'. *Transportation*, 30(1), 81–95.

Føllesdal, D., Walløe, L., Elster, J., 1996, *Argumentasjonsteori, språk og vitenskapsfilosofi* [*Argumentation Theory, Language and Philosophy of Science*]. Oslo: Oslo University Press.

Gärling, T., Axhausen, K.W., 2003, 'Introduction: Habitual travel choice'. *Transportation*, 30(1), 1–11.

Gärling, T., Eeka, D., Loukopoulosa, P., Fujii, S., Johansson-Stenmand, O., Kitamurac, R., Pendyalae, R., Vilhelmson, B., 2002, 'A Conceptual Analysis of the Impact of Travel Demand Management on Private Car Use'. *Transport Policy*, 9(1), 59–70.

Gärling, T., Gillholm, R., Gärling, A., 1998, 'Reintroducing Attitude Theory in travel Behaviour Research: The validity of an interactive interview procedure to predict car use'. *Transportation*, 25, 147–67.

Gärling, T., Rise, J., 2002, 'Understanding Attitude, Intention, and Behaviour: A common interest to economics and psychology'. In: Spash, C.L., Biel, A. (eds.). *Social Psychology and Economics in Environmental Research*. Cambridge: Cambridge University Press.

Garreau, J., 1991, *Edge City: Life on the new frontier*. New York: Anchor Books.

Garvill, J., 1999, 'Choice of Transportation Mode: Factors influencing drivers' willingness to reduce personal car use and support car regulations'. In:

Foddy, M., Smithson, M., Hogg, M., Schneider, S. (eds). *Resolving Social Dilemmas: Dynamics, structural, and intergroup aspects* Philadelphia, PA: Psychology Press.

GEP, 2007, *Quadros de Pessoal 2007*. Lisbon: Gabinete de Estratégia e Planeamento do Ministério do Trabalho e Solidariedade Social.

Geurs, K., Eck, J., 2001, *Accessibility Measures: Review and applications. Evaluation of accessibility impacts of land-use-transport scenarios, and related social and economic impacts*. Bilthoven: National Institute of Public Health and the Environment.

GIASE, 2007, *Recenseamento Escolar 06/07*. Gabinete de Avaliação e Informação do Sistema Educativo. Ministério da Educação.

Glaeser, E.L., Gottlieb, J.D., 2006, 'Urban Resurgence and the Consumer City'. *Urban Studies*, 43(8), 1,275–99.

Glaeser, E.L., Kolko, J., Saiz, A., 2001, 'Consumer City'. *Journal of Economic Geography*, 1(1), 27–50.

Guiliano, G., 1979, 'Public Transportation and the Travel Needs of Women'. *Traffic Quarterly*, 33, (4), 607–16.

———, 1989, 'Research Policy and Review 27. New directions for understanding transportation and land use', *Environment and Planning A*, 21, 145–159.

Giuliano, G., Dargay, J., 2006, 'Car ownership, Travel and Land Use: A comparison of the US and Great Britain'. *Transportation Research Part A: Policy and Practice*, 40(2), 106–24.

Giuliano, G., Narayan, D., 2003, 'Another Look at Travel Patterns and Urban Form: The US and Great Britain'. *Urban Studies*, 40(11), 2,295–2,312.

Giuliano, G., Small, K., 1993, 'Is the Journey to Work Explained by Urban Structure?' *Urban Studies* 30(9), 1,485–500.

Gleeson, B., Randolph, B., 2002, 'Social Disadvantage and Planning in the Sydney Context'. *Urban Policy and Research*, 20(1), 101–7.

Goffman, E., 1969, *Strategic Interaction*. Philadelphia: University of Pennsylvania Press.

Gollwitzer, P., 1993, 'Goal Achievement: The role of intentions'. *European Review of Social Psychology*, 4.

Golob, T., Kitamura, R., Long, L., 1997, *Panels for Transportation Planning: Methods and applications*. Boston: Kluwer Academic Publishers.

Gordon, I., Molho, I., 1985, 'Women in the Labour Markets of the London Region: A model of dependence and constraint'. *Urban Studies*, 22(5), 367–86.

Gordon, P., Kumar, A., Richardson, H.W., 1989, 'The Influence of Metropolitan Spatial Structure on Commuting Time'. *Journal of Urban Economics*, 26(2), 138.

Gordon, P., Richardson, H.W., 1996, 'Beyond Polycentricity'. *Journal of the American Planning Association*, 62(3).

Graham, S., 1998, 'The End of Geography or the Explosion of Place? Conceptualizing space, place and information technology'. *Progress in Human Geography*, 22(2), 165–85.

Guivert, J., 2007, 'Modal Talk: Discourse analysis of how people talk about bus and car travel'. *Transportation Research Part A*, 41, 233–48.

Haase, D., Lautenbach, S., Seppelt, R., 2010, 'Modeling and Simulating Residential Mobility in a Shrinking City using an Agent-Based Approach'. *Environmental Modelling & Software*, 25(10), 1,225–40.

Hägerstrand, T., 1970, 'What about People in Regional Science?' *Papers of the Regional Science Association*, 24(1), 7–21.

Hall, P., Hay, D., 1980, *Growth Centres in the European Urban System.* London: Heinemann.

Handy, S., 1996, 'Methodologies for Exploring the Link between Urban Form and Travel Behavior'. *Transportation Research Part D: Transport and Environment*, 1(2), 151–65.

Handy, S., Cao, X., Mohktarian, P., 2005, 'Correlation or Causality between the Built Environment and Travel Behavior? Evidence from Northern California'. *Transportation Research Part D*, 10, 427–44.

Handy, S., Clifton, K., 2001, 'Local Shopping as a Strategy for Reducing Automobile Travel'. *Transportation*, 28(4), 317–46.

Handy, S., Clifton, K., Fisher, J., 1998, *The Effectiveness of Land Use Policies as a Strategy for Reducing Automobile Dependence: A Study of Austin neighborhoods*. Research Report SWUTC/98/467501-1'. Austin: Southwest Region University Transportation Center, University of Texas.

Hanson, S., Pratt, G., 1995, *Gender, Work and Space*. London: Routledge.

Hartoft-Nielsen, P., 1997, 'Lokalisering, transportmiddel og bystruktur [Location, Conveyance and Urban Structure]'. *Byplan*, 6/97, 247–60.

———, 2001, *Arbejdspladslokalisering og transportadfærd [Workplace Location and Travel Behavior]*. Hørsholm: Forskningscenteret for skov og landskab.

Hartshorn, T.A., Muller, P.O., 1989, 'Suburban Downtowns and the Transformation of Metropolitan Atlanta Business Landscape', *Urban Geography*, 10(4), 375–95.

Harvey, A., Taylor, M., 2000, 'Activity Settings and Travel Behaviour: A social contact perspective'. *Transportation*, 27, 53–73.

Harvey, D., 1990, *The Condition of Postmodernity. An enquiry into the origins of cultural change*. Cambridge, MA: Blackwell.

Hjorthol, R., 1998, *Hverdagslivets reiser. En analyse av kvinners og menns daglige reiser i Oslo [The Travels of Everyday Life. An analysis of daily trips among women and men in Oslo]*. TØI report 391/1998. Oslo: Transportøkonomisk Institutt.

———, 2000, 'Same City – Different Options. An analysis of the work trips of married couples in the metropolitan area of Oslo'. *Journal of Transport Geography*, 8, 213–20.

———, 2008, 'Daily Mobility of Men and Women – A barometer of gender equality?' In: Uteng, T.P. and Cresswell, T. (eds). *Gendered Mobilities*. Aldershot: Ashgate Publishing, 193–210.

Iamtrakul, P., Hokao, K., 2012, 'The Study of Urbanization Patterns and Their Impacts on Road Safety'. *Lowland Technology International*, 14(2), 60–69.

INE, 2000, *Inquérito Geral à Mobilidade*. Lisbon: INE.

———, 2001, *Recenseamento Geral da População 2001*. Lisbon: INE.

———, 2013, Base de Dados [Online]. Available at: www.ine.pt, accessed on 19 July 2013.

———, 2014, Base de Dados [Online]. Available at: www.ine.pt, accessed on 16 February 2014.

Infrastructure Commission (Infrastrukturkommissionen), 2008, *Danmarks transportinfrastruktur 2030* [*The Danish Transport Infrastructure 2030*]. Copenhagen: The Infrastructure Commission.

Ingram, G., 1998, 'Patterns of Metropolitan Development: What have we learned?' *Urban Studies*, 35(7), 1,019–35.

Johansson, I., 1984, 'Är Newtons mekanik ännu inte filosofiskt förstådd?' In: Wellin, S. (ed.). *Att förstå världen. Vetenskapsteoretiska essäer*. Bodafors: Doxa.

Jones, P., 1978, 'Destination Choice and Travel Attributes'. In: Hensher, D., Dalvi, Q. (eds). *Determinants of Travel Choice*. England: Saxon House, 266–311.

Jørgensen, G., 1992, *Erhverv i boligkvarteret – en vej til bedre bymiljø?* [*Workplaces in the Residential Area – A strategy for a better urban environment?*]' Hørsholm: Statens Byggeforskningsinstitut.

Kabisch, Haase D, 2011, 'Diversifying European Agglomerations: Evidence of Urban population trends for the 21st century'. *Population Space and Place*, 17(3), 236–53.

Kaiser, F., 1993, *Mobilität als Wohnproblem – Ortsbindung im Licht der emotionalen Regulation*. Bern: Peter Lang Publishing Group.

Kasanko, M., Barredo, J.I., Carlo, L., Mccormick, N., Demicheli, L., Sagris, V., Brezger, A., 2006, 'Are European Cities Becoming Dispersed? A comparative analysis of 15 European urban areas'. *Landscape and Urban Planning*, 77, 111–30.

Kenworthy, J.R., Laube, F.B., 1999, 'Patterns of Automobile Dependence in Cities: An international overview of key physical and economic dimensions with some implications for urban policy'. *Transportation Research Part A*, 33, 691–723.

Kenyon, S., Lyons, G., 2003, 'The Value of Integrated Multimodal Traveller Information and Its Potential Contribution to Modal Change'. *Transportation Research Part F – Traffic psychology and behaviour*, 6(1), 1–21.

Kim, C., 2008, 'Commuting Time Stability: A test of a co-location hypothesis'. *Transportation Research Part A*, 42.

Kitamura, R., Fujii, S., Pas, E., 1997, 'Time-Use Data, Analysis and Modeling: Toward the next generation of transportation planning methodologies'. *Transport Policy*, 4(4), 225–35.

Kloosterman, R.C., Lambregts, B., 2007, 'Between Accumulation and Concentration of Capital: Toward a framework for comparing long-term trajectories of urban systems'. *Urban Geography*, 28(1), 54–73.

Kloosterman, R.C., Musterd, S., 2001, 'The Polycentric Urban Region: Towards a research agenda'. *Urban Studies*, 38(4), 623–63.

Knowles, R.D., 2012, 'Transit Oriented Development in Copenhagen, Denmark: From the Finger Plan to Ørestad'. *Journal of Transport Geography*, 22, 251–61.

Kockelman, K., 1997, 'Travel Behavior as Function of Accessibility, Land Use Mixing, and Land Use Balance: Evidence from San Francisco Bay Area'. *Transportation Research Record*, 1,607, 116–25.

Krizek, K.J., 2003, 'Neighborhood Services, Trip Purpose, and Tour-Based Travel'. *Transportation*, 30(4), 387–410.

Kubisch, A.C., Anspos, P., Brown, P., Chaskin, R., Fulbright-Anderson, K., Hamilton, R., 2002, *Voices from the Field II: Reflections on comprehensive community change*. Washington, DC: The Aspen Institute.

Lahti, P., 1995, 'Ecology, Economy, Energy and other E-lements in Urban Future'. In: Lehtonen, H., Johansson, M. (eds). *Att omringa ekologi.* Report no. C36. Esbo: YTK/VTT.

Lanzendorf, M., 2000, 'Social Change and Leisure Mobility'. *World Transport Policy and Practice*, 6(3).

Lanzieri, G., 2011, 'The Greying of the Baby Boomers. A century-long view of ageing in European populations'. *Statisticsinfocus*, 23 [Online]. Available at: http://epp.eurostat.ec.europa.eu/cache/ITY_OFFPUB/KS-SF-11–023/EN/KS-SF-11–023-EN.PDF, accessed 12 July, 2013.

Larsen, J., Urry, J., Axhausen, K., 2006, *Mobilities, Networks, Geographies.* Aldershot: Ashgate Publishing.

Lesthaeghe, R., 1995, 'The Second Demographic Transition in Western Countries: An interpretation'. In: Mason, K., Jensen, A. (eds). *Gender and Family Changes in Industrialised Countries*. Oxford: Clarendon Press.

Lee, B., McDonald, J., 2003, 'Determinants of Commuting Time and Distance for Seoul Residents: The impact of family status on the commuting of women'. *Urban Studies*, 40(7), 1,283–302.

Lefévre, B., 2010, 'Urban Transport Energy Consumption: Determinants and Strategies for Its Reduction'. *Sapiens*, 2: 1–17.

Levinson, D.M., Kumar, A., 1994, 'The Rational Locator: Why travel times have remained stable'. *Journal of the American Planning Association*, Summer.

Limtanakool, N., Dijst, M., Schwanen, T., 2006, 'The Influence of Socioeconomic Characteristics, Land Use and Travel Time Considerations on Mode Choice For Medium- and Longer-Distance Trips'. *Journal of Transport Geography*, 14(5), 327–41.

Lindlof, T.R., 2008, 'Verstehen vs Erklären'. In: Donsbach, W. (ed.). *The International Encyclopedia of Communication* [Online]. Available at: http://dx.doi.org/10.1111/b.9781405131995.2008.x.

Linneman, P., Summers, A., 1993, 'Patterns and Processes of Employment and Population: Decentralization in the US'. In: Summers, A., Cheshire, P., Senn, L. (eds). *Urban Change in the United States and Western Europe: Comparative analysis and policy*. Washington, DC: Urban Institute Press.

Lloyd, P.E., Dicken, P., 1977, *Location in Space: A theoretical approach to economic geography*. London Harper & Row.

Lyons, G., Chatterjee, K., Beecroft, M., Marsden, G., 2002, 'Determinants of Travel Demand – Exploring the future of society and lifestyles in the UK'. *Transport Policy*, 9(1), 17–27.

Maat, K., van Wee, B., Stead, D., 2005, 'Land Use and Travel Behaviour: Expected effects from the perspective of utility theory and activity-based theories'. *Environment and Planning B: Planning and Design*, 32, 33–46.

Maddison, D., Pearce, D., Johansson, O., Calthrop, E., 1996, *The True Costs of Road Transport*. London: Earthscan Publications.

Mageean, J., Nelson, J., 2003, 'The Evaluation of Demand Responsive Transport Services in Europe'. *Journal of Transport Geography*, 11(4), 255–70.

Marshall, S., 2003, *Barriers, Solutions and Transferability*. Deliverable report D4 of the European project TRANSPLUS (Transport Planning, Land Use and Sustainability). Brussels: European Commission.

Marshall, S., Banister, D., 1997, 'A Strategic Assessment of Travel Trends and Travel Reduction Strategies'. *Innovation: The European Journal of Social Sciences*, 10(3).

———, 2000, 'Travel Reduction Strategies: Intentions and outcomes'. *Transportation Research Part A: Policy and Practice*, 34(5), 321–38.

Martens, M., 2006, *Adaptive Cities in Europe: Interrelationships between urban structure, mobility and regional planning strategies*. Amsterdam: University of Amsterdam.

Mejer, L., Gere, E., 2008, *Education in Europe: Key statistics 2006*. Eurostat, Data in Focus.

Meyer, M., 1999, 'Demand Management as an Element of Transportation Policy: Using carrots and sticks to influence travel behavior'. *Transportation Research Part A: Policy and Practice*, 33(7–8), 575–99.

Milakis, D., Vlastos, T., Barbopoulos, N., 2008, 'Relationships between Urban Form and Travel Behaviour in Athens, Greece. A comparison with Western European and North American results'. *European Journal of Transport and Infrastructure Research*, 8(3), 201–15.

Moland Project, 2010, *Growth of Area Categories Copenhagen*. Ispra, European Commission, Joint Research Centre, Institute for Environment and Sustainability.

Monsen, G., 1983, *Bedriftsytting – endring i arbeidsreise og energifo rbruk [Relocation of Businesses – Changes in journeys to work and energy use]*. Oslo: University of Oslo.

Municipality of Copenhagen, 2011, 'Fra god til verdens bedste. Københavns cykelstrategi 2011–2025 [From Good to Best in the World. Copenhagen's biking strategy 2011–2025]'. Published draft plan. Copenhagen: Municipality of Copenhagen.

Næss, P., 1993, 'Transportation Energy in Swedish Towns and Regions'. *Scandinavian Housing & Planning Research*, 10(4), 187–206.

————, 2004 'Prediction, Regressions and Critical Realism'. *Journal of Critical Realism*, 3, 133–64.

————, 2005, 'Residential Location Affects Travel Behaviour – But how and why? The case of Copenhagen metropolitan area'. *Progress in Planning*, 63, 167–257.

————, 2006a, *Urban Structure Matters: Residential location, car dependence and travel behaviour*. London: Routledge.

————, 2006b, 'Accessibility, Activity Participation and Location of Activities. Exploring the links between residential location and travel behavior'. *Urban Studies*, 43, 627–52.

————, 2006c, 'Are Short Daily Trips Compensated by Higher Leisure Mobility?' *Environment & Planning B*, 33, 197–220.

————, 2007a, 'The Impacts of Job and Household Decentralization on Commuting Distances and Travel Modes: Experiences from the Copenhagen region and other Nordic urban areas'. *Informationen zur Raumentwicklung*, 2/3, 149–68.

————, 2007b, *Residential Location and Travel in Hangzhou Metropolitan Area*. NIBR report 2007:1. Oslo: Norwegian Institute for Urban and Regional Research.

————, 2008, 'Gender Differences in the Influences of Urban Structure on Daily-Life Travel'. In: Priya, T., Cresswell, T. (eds). *Gendered Mobilities*. Aldershot: Ashgate Publishing, 173–92.

————, 2009a, 'Residential Self-Selection and Appropriate Control Variables in Land Use – Travel studies', *Transport Reviews*, 29, 293–324.

————, 2009b, 'Residential Location, Travel Behavior, and Energy Use: Hangzhou Metropolitan Area compared to Copenhagen'. *Indoor and Built Environment*, 18, 382–95.

————, 2010a, 'Journey to Work'. In: Hutchinson, R. (ed.). *Encyclopedia of Urban Studies*. Thousand Oaks, London and New Delhi: Sage Publications.

————, 2010b, 'Residential Location, Travel and Energy Use: The case of Hangzhou Metropolitan Area'. *Journal of Transport and Land Use*, 3(3), 27–59.

————, 2011, '"New Urbanism" or Metropolitan-Level Centralization? A comparison of the influences of metropolitan-level and neighborhood-level urban form characteristics on travel behavior'. *Journal of Transport and Land Use*, 4(1), 25–44.

————, 2013, 'Residential Location, Transport Rationales and Daily-Life Travel Behavior: The case of Hangzhou Metropolitan Area, China'. *Progress in Planning*, 79(1), 1–50.

Næss, P., Jensen, O.B., 2002, 'Urban Land Use, Mobility and Theory of Science – Exploring the potential for Critical Realism in empirical research'. *Journal of Environmental Policy and Planning*, 4, 295–311.

————, 2004, 'Urban Structure Matters, Even in a Small Town'. *Journal of Environmental Planning and Management*, 47, 35–56.

―――, 2005, *Bilringene og cykelnavet* [*The Car Tires and the Bike Node*]. Aalborg: Aalborg Universitetsforlag.

Næss, P., Næss, T., Nicolaisen, M., Clemens, E., 2009, *The Challenge of Sustainable Mobility in Urban Planning and Development in Copenhagen Metropolitan Area*. Second Edition. Department of Development and Planning Publication series.

Næss, P., Næss, T., Strand, A., 2010, 'Oslo's Farewell to Urban Sprawl'. *European Planning Studies*, 19(1), 113–39.

Næss, P., Røe, P., Larsen, S., 1995, 'Travelling Distances, Modal Split and Transportation Energy in Thirty Residential Areas in Oslo'. *Journal of Environmental Planning and Management*, 38(3), 349–70.

Næss, P., Sandberg, S., 1996, 'Workplace Location, Modal Split and Energy Use for Commuting Trips', *Urban Studies*, 33(3), 557–80.

Næss, P., Sandberg, S., Røe, P., 1996, 'Energy Use for Transportation in 22 Nordic Towns'. *Scandinavian Housing & Planning Research*, 1, 79–97.

Næss, P., Strand, A., Næss, T., Nicolaisen, M., 2011, 'On Their Road to Sustainability? The challenge of sustainable mobility in urban planning and development in two Scandinavian capital regions'. *Town Planning Review*, 82 287–317.

Nechyba, T., Walsh, R., 2004, 'Urban sprawl'. *Journal of Economic Perspectives*, 18(4), 177–200.

Negroponte, N., 1995, *Being Digital*. New York: Knopf.

Newman, P., Kenworthy, J.R., 1989, 'Gasoline Consumption and Cities. A comparison of US cities in a global survey'. *Journal of the American Planning Association*, 55.

―――, 1991, 'Transport and Urban Form in 32 of the World's Principal Cities'. *Transport Reviews*, 11, 249–72.

―――, 1999, *Sustainability and Cities. Overcoming automobile dependence*. Washington, DC, and Covelo, CA: Island Press.

―――, 2000, 'Sustainable Urban Form: The big picture'. In: Burton, E., Jenks, M., Willaims, K. (eds). *Achieving Sustainable Urban Form*. London and New York: Routledge, 109–20.

Nielsen, T., 2002, *Boliglokalisering og transport i Aalborg* [*Residential Location and Transport in Aalborg*]. PhD thesis. Aalborg: Aalborg University.

Nowlan, D.M., Stewart, G., 1991, 'Downtown Population Growth and Commuting Trips: Recent experience in Toronto'. *Journal of the American Planning Association*, 57, 165–82.

Ouelette, J., Wood, W., 1998, 'Habit and Intention in Everyday Life: The multiple processes by which past behavior predicts future behavior'. *Psychological Bulletin*, 124, 54–74.

Pacione, M., 2009, *Urban Geography: A global perspective*. Abingdon: Routledge.

Parkhurst, G., 2000, 'Influence of Bus-Based Park and Ride Facilities on Users' Car Traffic'. *Transport Policy*, 7, 159–72.

Parr, J., 1993, 'The metropolitan area in its wider setting'. In: Summers, A., Cheshire, P., Senn, L. (eds). *Urban Change in the United States and Western Europe: Comparative analysis and policy*. Washington, DC: Urban Institute Press.

Parthasarathi, P., Levinson, M., Karamalaputi, R., 2003, 'Induced Demand: A microscopic perspective'. *Urban Studies*, 40(7), 1,335–51.

Patton, M., 1987, *How to Use Qualitative Methods in Evaluation*. Newbury Park, CA: Sage.

Paulley, N., 2002, 'Recent Studies on Key Issues in Road Pricing'. *Transport Policy*, 9(3), 175–7.

Pinho, P., Vilares, M. (eds), 2009, *Avaliação do impacto global da 1ª Fase do projecto do Metro do Porto*. Porto: FEUP Edições.

Power, A., 2001, 'Social Exclusion and Urban Sprawl: Is the rescue of cities possible?' *Regional Studies*, 35(8), 731–42.

Pratt, A., 1996, 'Coordinating Employment, Transport and Housing in Cities: An institutional perspective'. *Urban Studies*, 33, 1,357–75.

Punpuing, S., 1993, 'Correlates of Commuting Patterns: A case study of Bankok, Thailand'. *Urban Studies*, 30(3), 527–46.

Quastel, N., 2009, 'Political Ecologies of Gentrification'. *Urban Geography*, 30(7), 694–725.

Raux, C., Souche, S., 2004, 'The Acceptability of Urban Road Pricing: A theoretical analysis applied to experience in Lyon'. *Journal of Transport Economics and Policy*, 38, 191–215.

Reis, J., 2009, *Urban Structures and Mobility – A case study in Copenhagen*. Master's thesis. Porto: Faculty of Engineering of the University of Porto, University of Porto.

Rieniets, T., 2005, *Shrinking Cities – Growing domain for urban planning?* [Omline]. Available at: http://aarch.dk/fileadmin/grupper/institut_ii/PDF/paper_presentation_EURA2005.pdf, accessed 10 December 2011.

Root, A., 2001, 'Can Travel Vouchers Encourage More Sustainable Travel?' *Transport Policy*, 8(2), 107–14.

Rose, G., Marfurtb, H., 2007, 'Travel Behaviour Change Impacts of a Major Ride to Work Day Event'. *Transportation Research Part A: Policy and Practice*, 41(4), 351–64.

Rye, T., 2002, 'Travel plans: do they work?' *Transport Policy*, 9(4), 287–98.

Ryley, T., 2006, 'Use of Non-Motorised Modes and Life Stage: Evidence from Edinburgh'. *Journal of Transport Geography*, 14(50), 367–75.

Sayer, A., 1992, *Method in Social Science. A realist approach*. London: Routledge.

———, 2000, *Realism and Social Science*. London, Thousand Oaks and New Delhi: Sage Publications.

Scheiner, J., 2005, 'Daily Mobility in Berlin: On 'Inner Unity' and the explanation of travel behaviour'. *European Journal of Transport and Infrastructure Research*, 5(3), 159–86.

Scheiner, J., Holz-Rau, C., 2007, 'Travel Mode Choice: Affected by objective or subjective determinants?' *Transportation*, 34, 487–511.

Scheiner, J., Kasper, B., 2002, 'Lifestyles, Choice of Housing Location and Daily Mobility: The lifestyle approach in the context of spatial mobility and planning'. In: *42nd congress of the European Regional Science Association (ERSA)*. 27–31 August 2002. Dortmund: Department of Transport Planning, University of Dortmund.

Schipper, L., Deakin, E., Spearling, D., 1994, 'Sustainable Transportation. The future of the automobile in an environmentally constrained world'. Paper presented at seminar organized by Transportforskningsberedningen, Stockholm, 23 September 1994. Berkeley: University of California Transportation Center, University of California.

Schlich, R., Schonfelder, S., Hanson, S., Axhausen, K., 2004, 'Structures in Leisure Time: Temporal and spatial variability'. *Transport Reviews*, 24(2), 219–38.

Schwanen, T., 2002, 'Urban Form and Commuting Behaviour: A cross-European perspective'. *Tijdschrift voor Economische en Sociale Geografie*, 93.

Schwanen, T., Dieleman, F.M., Dijst, M., 2001, 'Travel Behaviour in Dutch Monocentric and Policentric Urban Systems'. *Journal of Transport Geography*, 9(3), 173–86.

———, 2002 'A microlevel analysis of residential context and travel time'. *Environment and Planning A*, 34, 1,487–507.

———, 2004a, 'Policies for Urban Form and their Impact on Travel: The Netherlands experience'. *Urban Studies*, 41(3), 579–603.

———, 2004b, 'The Impact of Metropolitan Structure on Commute Behaviour in the Netherlands: A multilevel approach'. *Growth and Change*, 35(3), Summer, 304–33.

Schwanen, T., Mokhtarian, P., 2005, 'What if you Live in the Wrong Neighborhood? The impact of residential neighborhood type dissonance on distance traveled'. *Transportation Research Part D: Transport and Environment*, 20(2), 127–51.

Scott, A.J., 2011, 'Emerging cities of the third wave'. *City*, 15(3–4), 289–321.

———, 2013, 'Retrospect', *City*, 17(3), 384–6.

Shepherd, S., 2003, 'Towards Marginal Cost Pricing: A comparison of alternative pricing systems'. *Transportation*, 30(4), 411–33.

Silva, C., 2004, *Interchange in Urban Public Transport: A necessary or misjudged problem? A case study in Porto*. Porto: Faculty of Engineering of the University of Porto, University of Porto.

———, 2008, *Comparative Accessibility for Mobility Management. The Structural accessibility layer*. Porto: Faculty of Engineering of the University of Porto, University of Porto.

———, 2013, 'Structural Accessibility for Mobility Management'. *Progress in Planning*, 81, 1–49.

Silva, C., Pinho, P., 2010, 'The Structural Accessibility Layer (SAL): Revealing how urban structure constraints travel choice'. *Environment and Planning A*, 42, 2,735–52.

Silva, C., Reis, J., Pinho, P., 2014, 'How Urban Structure Constraints Sustainable Mobility Choices: Comparison of Copenhagen and Oporto'. *Environment and Planning B*, 41, 211–28.

Simmonds, D., Coombe, D., 2000, 'The Transport Implications of Alternative Urban Forms'. In: Williams, K., Burton, E., Jenks, M. (eds). *Achieving Sustainable Urban Form*. London and New York: Routledge, 121–30.

Siren, A., Haustein, S., 2013, 'Baby Boomers' Mobility Patterns and Preferences: What are the implications for future transport?' *Transport Policy*, 29, 136–44.

Social Exclusion Unit, 2003, 'Making the Connections: Final Report on transport and social exclusion'. London: Social Exclusion Unit.

Srinivasan, S., 2008, 'A Spatial Exploration of the Accessibility of Low-Income Women: Chengdu, China and Chennai, India'. In: Uteng, T., Cresswell, T. (eds). *Gendered Mobilities*. Aldershot: Ashgate Publishing, 143–58.

Statistics Denmark, 2008, *Hovedstad mm 1901–2008*. Copenhagen: Statistics Denmark.

Statistics Denmark, 2010a, 'Hovedkonti (faste priser, mio. kr.) efter prisenhed, konto og tid. B.1*g Bruttonationalprodukt, BNP'. Copenhagen: Statistics Denmark [Online]. Available at: http://www.statistikbanken.dk/statbank5a/default.asp?w=1280, accessed 17 October 2010.

Statistics Denmark, 2010b, 'Motorkøretøjer pr. døgn efter vejstrækning og tid'. Copenhagen: Statistics Denmark [Online]. Available at: http://www.statistikbanken.dk/statbank5a/default.asp?w=1280, accessed 20 July 2010.

———, 2010c, 'BNP samt BNP pr. indbygger efter prisenhed, type, landsdel og tid'. Copenhagen: Statistics Denmark [Online]. Available at: http://www.statistikbanken.dk/statbank5a/default.asp?w=1280, accessed 3 March 2010.

———, 2014, 'Statistikbanken' [Online]. Available at: http://www.statistikbanken.dk/statbank5a/default.asp?w=1366, accessed 16 February 2014.

Stead, D., 2001, 'Relationships between Land Use, Socioeconomic Factors, and Travel Patterns in Britain'. *Environment and Planning B: Planning and Design*, 28, 499–528.

Stead, D., Williams, J., Titheridge, H., 2000, 'Land Use, Transport and People: Identifying the Connections'. In: Williams, K., Burton, E., Jenks, M. (eds). *Achieving Sustainable Urban Form*. London and New York: Routledge, 174–86.

Steg, L., Geurs, K., Ras, M., 2001, 'The Effects of Motivational Factors on Car Use: A multidisciplinary modelling approach'. *Transportation Research Part A: Policy and Practice*, 35(9), 789–806.

Steg, L., Vlek, C., Slotegraaf, G., 2001, 'Instrumental-Reasoned and Symbolic-Affective Motives for Using a Motor Car'. *Transportation Research Part F – Traffic psychology and behaviour*, 4(3), 151–69.

Storper, M., Manville, M., 2006, 'Behaviour, preferences and cities: Urban theory and urban resurgence'. *Urban Studies*, 43(8), 1,247–74.

Storper, M., Scott, A.J., 2008, 'Rethinking Human Capital, Creativity and Urban Growth'. *Journal of Economic Geography*, 9(2), 147–67.

Storper, M., van Marrewijk, C., van Oort, F.G., 2012, 'Introduction: Processes of change in urban systems'. *Journal of Regional Science*, 52(1), 1–9.

Strømmen, K., 2001, *Rett virksomhet på rett sted – om virksomheters transportskapende egenskaper. [Right workplace at the right location – on the transport-generating properties of workplaces]*. PhD dissertation. Trondheim: Norwegian University of Technology and Science.

Taylor, M., Ampt, E., 2003, 'Travelling Smarter Down Under: pOlicies for voluntary travel behaviour change in Australia'. *Transport Policy*, 10(3), 165–77.

Thøgersen, J., Møller, B., 2008, 'Breaking Car use Habits: The effectiveness of a free one-month travelcard'. *Transportation*, 35(3), 329–45.

Thorpe, N., Hillsa, P., Jaensirisak, S., 2000, 'Public Attitudes to TDM Measures: A comparative study'. *Transport Policy*, 7(4), 243–57.

Torrens, P., 2008, 'A Toolkit for Measuring Sprawl'. *Applied Spatial Analysis and Policy*, 1(1), 5–36.

Triandis, H., 1977, *Interpersonal Behavior*. Monterey, CA: Brooks/Cole.

Turok, I., Mykhnenko, V., 2007, 'The Trajectories of European Cities, 1960–2005'. *Cities*, 24(3), 165–82.

Urry, J., 1995, *Consuming Places*. London and New York: Routledge.

Van, U., Senior, M., 2000, 'The Contribution of Mixed Land Use to Sustainable Travel in Cities'. In: Williams, K., Burton, E., Jenks, M. (eds). *Achieving Sustainable Urban Form*. London and New York: Routledge, 139–48.

van Acker, V., Witlox, F., 2010, 'Car Ownership as a Mediating Variable in Car Travel Behavior Research Using a Structural Equation Modelling Approach to Identify its Dual Relationship'. *Journal of Transport Geography*, 18(1), 65–74.

van den Berg, L., Drewett, R., Klaassen, L., Rossi, A., Vijverberg, C., 1982, *Urban Europe: A study of growth and decline*. Oxford: Pergamon Press.

van der Laan, L., 1998, 'Changing Urban Systems: An empirical analysis at two spatial levels'. *Regional Studies*, 32(3).

van Wee, B., 2002, 'Land Use and Transport: Research and policy challenges'. *Journal of Transport Geography*, 10(4), 259–71.

Vance, C., Hedel, R., 2008, 'On the Link between Urban Form and Automobile Use: Evidence from German survey data'. *Land Economics*, 84, 51–65.

Verplanken, B., Aarts, H., 1999, 'Habit, Attitude and Planned Behaviour: Is habit an empty construct or an interesting case of goal-directed automatic?' *European Review of Social Psychology*, 10, 101–34.

Verplanken, B., Aarts, H., Van Knippenberg, A., 1997, 'Habit, Information Acquisition, and the Process of Making Travel Mode Choices'. *European Journal of Social Psychology*, 27, 539–60.

Verplanken, B., Aarts, H., Van Knippenberg, A., Van Knippenberg, C., 1994, 'Attitude versus General Habit: Antecedents of travel mode choice'. *Journal of Applied Social Psychology*, 24, 285–300.

Viegas, J., 2001, 'Making Urban Road Pricing Acceptable and Effective: Searching for quality and equity in urban mobility'. *Transport Policy*, 8(4), 289–94.

Vuk, G., 2005, 'Transport Impacts of the Copenhagen Metro'. *Journal of Transport Geography*, 13(3), 223–33.

Wachs, M., 1992, 'Men, Women, and Urban Travel. The persistence of separate spheres'. In: Wachs, M., Crawford, M. (eds). *The Car and the City. The automobile, the built environment and daily urban life*. Ann Arbor, MI: University of Michigan Press.

Wen, C., Koppelman F., 2000, 'A Conceptual and Methdological Framework for the Generation of Activity-Travel Patterns'. *Transportation*, 27(1), 5–23.

Wilczyński, W., Wilczyński, P., 2011, 'Population of American Cities: 1950–2009'. *Bulletin of Geography*, 16, 153–72.

Williams, K., Burton, E., Jenks, M. (eds), 2000, *Achieving Sustainable Urban Form*. London and New York: Routledge.

Yin, R., 1994, *Case Study Research: Design and methods*. Thousand Oaks, London and New Delhi: Sage Publications.

Zegras, C., 2010, 'The Built Environment and Motor Vehicle Ownership and Use: Evidence from Santiago de Chile'. *Urban Studies*, 47(8), 1,793–817.

Zegras, C., Shrinivasan, S., 2006, *Household Income, Travel Behavior, Location and Accessibility: Sketches from two different developing contexts*. Transportation Research Record 238, 128–38.

Index